ON RACE
AND PHILOSOPHY

ON RACE
AND PHILOSOPHY

Lucius T. Outlaw (Jr.)

Routledge
New York and London

Published in 1996 by
Routledge
29 West 35th Street
New York, NY 10001

Routledge
11 New Fetter Lane
London EC4P 4EE

Copyright © 1996 by Routledge

Printed in the United States of America.

Library of Congress Cataloging-in-Publication Data

Outlaw, Lucius, 1944–
    On race and philosophy / Lucius Outlaw.
        p.   cm.
Includes bibliographical references and index.
ISBN 0-415-91534-1. (cl)   —   ISBN 0-415-91535-X (pb)

    1. United States—Race relations—Philosophy. 2. Afro-American
philosophy. 3. Race relations—Philosophy. 4. Ethnicity—
Philosophy. I. Title.

E185.615.O9   1996   96-25170
305.8'00973—dc20   CIP

DEDICATION

With special thanks, to: Lillie Mae Brooks Outlaw, 1921–1990, who would have been so very proud; Lucious Turner Outlaw Sr., who will be very proud; Lucius Turner Outlaw III, "Buster," who is my heart; Kofi Atiba Brooks-Bobbitt Outlaw, who is "my dude!" and renews my love; Chike Hasani Hopkins Outlaw, who is the smile of love that brings joy to my life; Freida Diane Hopkins Outlaw, without whom there is no place in this life or the next I wish to be; Emma Bobbitt Hopkins Smith, the Byrds, Stacie, Caryn, the Thanksgiving group, the rest of our family. Without you all, your love and support, I would not amount to much. And to Howie Winant, now lying in a coma. Awake, Howie, rejoin your family, and then continue helping us in our struggle for justice.

CONTENTS

ACKNOWLEDGMENTS

Thanks to Maureen MacGrogan, my editor at Routledge, for her vote of confidence and guiding encouragement throughout this publishing project; and to Karen Deaver, who oversaw the book's production, and the other folks who assisted the production, especially Norma McLemore, a most competent and thoughtful copyeditor, who took care in respecting the author. And to the folks at Haverford College, an especially fine (even unique) place to live and work, where the labor of preparing the book was completed during a college-supported sabbatical made possible, in significant part, by a fellowship from the American Council for Learned Societies. Special thanks to the ACLS. Finally, heartfelt thanks to the good friends of RTG (the Racial Theory Group, a.k.a. Rho Tau Gamma) — Raphael Allen, Kimberly Benston, Eddie Glaude, William Hart, Paul Jefferson, Wahneema Lubiano, Fasaha Traylor, and Howard Winant — for challenging discussions that more than once required me to "subject myself to serious self-criticism" and provided me several years of much needed food for thought along with nourishing congeniality.

PREFACE

The essays in this collection have been selected from writings produced over a period of more than twenty-five years. While several considerations have served as criteria for selecting which essays to include, the most obvious of these is suggested by the title of the collection, *On Race and Philosophy*. In writing each essay I was concerned, in various ways, with matters that involve raciality and the collection of endeavors and traditions of thought that in Western academic institutions, in particular, are called "philosophy." The persistence of these concerns across the essays provides the thematic focus for the collection.

The concerns motivating the writings have been with me far more than my years of efforts and involvements as a teacher and scholar in American higher education within the professionalized discipline of philosophy while working and living in several different college and university communities (private and public; historically and predominantly black, historically and predominantly white). Indeed, they have been with me as constant, influential companions all of my life beyond the age of innocence. And for a male child of African descent — a "Negro" — born (1944) and raised within the hard and fast, sometimes brutal life-orienting strictures of the racial apartheid of segregation in Starkville, Mississippi, the period of innocence had to be short, as those of us of the Emmett Till generation came to know only too well. (This has been true for Negro females as well as for males, and for every generation of descendants of Africans brought to this nation as slaves.)

These social-historical and autobiographical contexts have provided the sources of the concerns that impelled me to write the essays. Simply put (but, I assure you, much more complicated in the living): while growing up, racial segregation did not *make sense* to me. I could not *make* it make sense. The pictures of America and its promises, as well as those of Mississippi, that were presented to me in classes in civics and history *made no sense* when compared to my experiences of the sharply drawn, tightly structured, and forcefully maintained race-focused realities of daily life and the scripted limitations on the futures of colored folk. The disparities and contradictions between the two — the pictures and the realities; the high principles and rhetoric of grand promises, and the arrogant, indignant, legalized inhumanity intended to thwart colored folks' sharing the dreams of opportunity, let alone working to realize them — were painfully obvious, as was intended.

And I got it. Couldn't miss it. My father, Lucious T. Outlaw Sr., a combination janitor, facilities manager, and grounds-keeper, spent seven days a week, fifty-two weeks a year, insuring the smooth, efficient, manicured functioning of Starkville's large, prominent, and segregated First Baptist Church for its white members (who filled the place to capacity almost every Sunday, while countless others listened in through the broadcast of the services over WSSO, the local radio station), while my mother and I joined other black folks worshipping . . . the *same* God? . . . at colored Second Baptist Church (not as large or as prominent, except among black folks, perhaps: we had more school teachers and principals, businessmen and businesswomen, funeral-home operators, high-class clubs of working-class women, high-achieving pretty girls and handsome guys, plus the town's only black doctor among our members compared to colored Griffin Methodist, our only serious competitor). Christian white folks required segregation because Negroes, it was claimed, were incompatibly different from, and in important ways inferior to, them. Made no sense to me.

As I would *think* about segregation more and more while growing up, and discuss it with my friends, the whole situation made less sense. And for all the time I was spending in Second Baptist, God wasn't much help. How could He explain and justify the indignities, inhumanity, and injustice that were part and parcel of racial segregation? Maybe He listened to the prayers of white folks with His white ear, and those of colored folks with His colored ear? (Don't get me wrong, though: I did believe in God. At least until I was in college and deeply ensconced in and influenced by my studies of Western philosophers, several rationalists among them especially. But that's another part of the story. There wasn't much choice growing up in the house of Lillie Mae Brooks Outlaw: I was her only child. She and God had cut a deal over me even before I was conceived: after none of the six babies she had given birth to had survived, she promised God that if He gave her a child, she'd give the child back to Him. [No she-God or gender-neutral language in use back then. There were no "post-Modern" Negroes in Starkville in the '40s, white folks either, quiet as kept.] I was born and survived. So, until I went off to college I saw the insides of enough churches around Mississippi and other states to last my soul a lifetime."

Schooling made the situation even worse for me and thus had an effect quite contrary to what was intended by those white folks who would have us colored folk educated to stay in the places to which they would assign us. (Let the truth be told: not all white folks felt this way at the time, in Starkville and elsewhere.) As many slave masters and mistresses and those who, after enslavement was abolished, assumed similar positions in the social hierarchy understood all too well, serious learning made Negroes unfit for a life restricted by the arrangements of racial segregation, arrangements clothed in rationalizations and valorizations and mixed into pre-fabricated conceptions of self that we were to be educated to imbibe. The agenda was to insure that in living through the conceptions in playing out our lives in their most quotidian routines we would internalize and accept as the natural order of things, thus legitimate and help to sustain and reproduce, the complementary and mutually reinforcing hierarchical arrangements and value systems of white supremacy and Negro inferiority.

Not hardly. Almost all of my teachers in the colored Oktibbeha County Training School (later renamed the W. C. Henderson Elementary School and the W. C. Henderson High School when new buildings were constructed) — Mrs. (Sena) Hardy, Miss (Annie M.) Strong, Miss (Viola R.) Johnson, Miss (Ella) Reeves, Miss (Bernice A.) Eiland, Mrs. (Ella) Nash, Miss (Rosa) Stewart, Mrs. (Willie) Leonard, Mrs. (Eva) Sherrod, Mr. (George) Manning, Mr. (Robert) Norwood, Mr. (Willie James) Perry, Mr. (Hal) Purnell, Mr. (Robert) Banks, and others (especially the younger ones who came on the scene), a number of whom also coached us, directed the band, and guided us in other extra-curricular activities; Scout Masters Charles and Maurice Evans and their wives; teachers of Sunday School and Vacation Bible School; older guys who taught me and other boys how to play football, basketball, and baseball, how to ride our bikes and make model airplanes — all of these folks, through their confirming belief in me and others and their loving, motivating expectations for us, combined with the nurturing and learning I and others were receiving in our homes, from our extended families, and in neighborhoods in which almost any adult could, and would, correct you if they thought you were out of line — would even whip your butt and then tell your mama and daddy, either of whom would likely promptly whip your butt again, especially if you had been fool enough to sass that adult ("You ain't *my* mama!" You only made that mistake once if you were serious about trying to be good aided by a healthy, respect-encouraging fear of death your mama or daddy had helped you to develop . . .) — these colored folks worked their Negro magic in concert and with studied deliberation, guided by the steely wisdom of survival that had been gained over centuries of tempering experiences of the searing fires of oppression and passed on to prepare subsequent generations to move on up a bit higher: that is, not just to survive, but to overcome and *flourish.* These loving people, working as individuals as well as through various institutions and organizations, touched many of our young lives — in spite of our brash, youthful stupidity — and insured that the very last thing that I and others would ever develop was an inferiority complex that had anything to do with our being Negro.

No, indeed. Many of the folk of W. C. Henderson Elementary and High School, Second Baptist Church, Griffin Methodist Church, and other segments of colored Starkville thought *quite* highly of ourselves. In the words of one of my best friends, Jerry Jones: we weren't conceited, just convinced. And if you watched my good friends and classmates Jerry, Richard (Holmes), L.T. (Williams) and a number of others on the football field, watched the whole team, Willie James Perry's team, you would be convinced, too. For his team was the embodiment and indisputable example of an orientation that infused and guided many of us in school, at work, at church, and elsewhere around Starkville: that of being *good*, *very* good, at what we did.

Many of us young folks were *groomed* to be good. Willie James Perry, for one (and he was far from being the only one), would have it no other way. You couldn't be on his football or baseball teams if you didn't — or couldn't — work almost to exhaustion (if you were not in top physical condition) at being the best. Or on his girl's basketball team. (They were so good during our last years in high school that watching them became boring: with one or two exceptions, no other teams were enough of a match to make the games interesting.) And Mr. (Fenton) Peters, another of our teachers who coached the boy's basketball team, didn't play either, in the gym or in his classes. Consequently, I and many of my schoolmates, particularly those I hung with, never thought our Negro selves inferior to white folks. We knew better.

You had only to witness my mother, Lillie Mae — an ardent church-going woman, who worked as a maid for certain white folks (only those of her own choosing), and who was also a very accomplished seamstress who made dresses and suits from McCalls and other patterns, or custom-designed then made the clothing, for herself and other women — getting dressed up and "putting on the dog," whether in organizing and directing local, regional, and national church programs for young folks, or when hosting and participating in "teas" and meetings of her various clubs and organizations with other women (with their purses matching or complementing high-heel shoes that called attention to their fine legs, gloves in hand, hats [some with veils] perched *just so* on freshly done hair atop the heads of girdle-shaped bodies poured into some of the prettiest and most fashionable dresses worn by colored women, and by most white women) to understand clearly that this was not a woman with an inferiority complex about being Negro. That's sizing things up with the wrong end of the measuring stick. Lillie Mae was much closer to the other end. And she made darn sure I measured up along with her. Then she did her level best to push me farther than she had been able to reach at the time. Afterwards, she kept working at improving herself: taking correspondence courses in high school subjects while I was growing up; completing high school at a church institution in nearby West Point and receiving her diploma, as did her younger sister, Pearlie Ann (we still call her "Cookie"), during commencement exercises one summer when I was home from college; taking courses in church work during regional and national Baptist meetings; working for years in the area of student support as a counselor and dormitory director at Rust, Tougaloo, and Mary Holmes colleges; initiating and participating in cooking, sewing, and other crafts-focused organizations and activities, in addition to her church work, until she died of cancer.

And my father was the *consummate*, confident student of life under racial segregation and an especially gifted strategist, but one firmly girded by principles of honesty, decency, and integrity. He was (is) masterful! He tutored me incessantly about the structuring intersectings of race, class, gender, religion, and economics in the accumulation, exercise, and distrib- ution of power: in other words, he taught me that white folks with money and education, particular men among them especially, had most of the power and exercised it in every way they could to control things to their ben- efit; colored folks had to get more of this power, principally through becom- ing educated, *the* means to economic viability and independence, in order to get where and what they wanted in the world. But, he instructed, colored folks had to learn how to deal with white folks in power, how to "handle them with kid gloves," he would say, in order to get what we wanted since there was no way for us to bypass them.

Pop (as I now address him) was a masterful, disciplined conservator (I used to think him just "conservative") who found ways to make a way for his family and did so with principled dignity. I'll never forget the day he and I were walking along the sidewalk of Main Street when we met a white man walking in the opposite direction who confronted him and demanded "Get out of the way, boy, and let a white man pass." My daddy, never raising his voice, looked that white man squarely in his eyes and said, in a firm, deter- mined voice that left me cold (truth is, I was already scared as hell about the situation): "I'm not a boy." Pointing to me, he continued: "And, this is my son. You will not disrespect me in front of him. I will be respected." Without another word, that white man lowered his eyes, stepped aside, walked around us, and went on his way. Daddy and I continued along our way with- out his saying another word. He needn't have. He had demonstrated in the most forceful way imaginable — in a white man to black man face-off in broad-open daylight, on Main Street, in Starkville, Mississippi — that he had fashioned for himself a strategy by which to live in dignity and self-respect, and to require white men and women to recognize and respect him as he did so. I have not always agreed with Pop about his strategies, but the lessons of dignity and self-respect he provided me are among the most treasured and important legacies that have helped to shape me. No chance, then, that I would grow up with a poor self-concept, a sense of inferiority, because I was colored, a Negro.

Thus, the invidious characterizations of colored folks conveyed in the boisterous, threatening rhetoric of racial segregation didn't make sense to me, didn't coincide with my sense of myself. Within the context of my racial- ly constricted, yet nurturing, social world, one that, in many ways, served me particularly well, when I *thought* about the arrangements of that world and of the larger colored-white world of America as I experienced and knew it — and I had to think about and know those arrangements in order to keep from violating the rules of segregation, as the penalties for doing so became harsher the older one got — neither the rules of arrangement nor the racist rationalizations of them made sense in ways that I found acceptable.

This was especially the case after I mulled over — mostly fumed over —

any one of the many discussions-bordering-on-arguments my daddy and I had about the unfairness of it all. (Well, they were not really discussions: he did most of the talking while I was supposed to listen. But I always had a hard time keeping my mouth shut when I thought I had a point that simply *had* to be made.) During these sessions he frequently pointed out to me the virtues of white folks going to church in large numbers while he insisted that colored folks would do well to emulate this behavior. Didn't make sense to me since I was in church on Sundays worshipping the same God(?) as the white folks raising the roof off their church in song and prayer yet many of them (though not all) wouldn't hesitate to call me "nigger" on Monday, and every other day of the week, as well, Sundays included. Didn't make sense: those same praying and singing white folks, no matter how decent they were otherwise nor what their ages, from the very youngest to the oldest, would all call daddy himself, my mother, or any colored adult by their first name no matter what the colored person's age, achievements, contributions, or social position, while I was not allowed to call any adult by their first name and expect to keep on living (at best struggle to live, with a very sore butt), especially not one who was white. In the latter case this was true for colored adults, as well. Didn't make sense, since my mother was walking through the back door of the homes of prominent, Christian white folks to clean their house, prepare meals, and care for their children in some cases all for fifty cents an hour while Cookie (who lived with us for some years and, just three years older than me, was more an older sister to me than my aunt) and I were home cleaning our home and often cooking for ourselves. I wasn't about to be persuaded by my daddy's arguments. He didn't have a chance, 'cause *it didn't make sense.*

As the years of high school drew toward a close, it was time to plan for the next phase of my life, which I was determined would to be devoted to making sense of things and plotting a course for myself that would involve becoming increasingly independent of the controlling strictures of racial segregation. For me and a number of others in my high school class that meant heading off to college, not an unusual course of action for young colored folks in Starkville. In fact, one of the strong incentives was the presence on the east side of town of Mississippi State University (formerly known as Mississippi State Agricultural and Mechanical College, but around town was just "the College" or "State," sometimes "Miss'ippi State"): colored folks could work at the University in low-level positions (I washed windows and cleaned buildings on the campus to earn money during the summer before my first year of college), but, because of racial segregation, could not attend to get an education. (My classmate and close friend, Richard Holmes, would be the first Negro knowingly admitted to State — in 1965.) That was another part of the whole segregation business that didn't make sense to me and epitomized the absurdity and injustice of it all: I loved to read books, but State's library as well as Starkville's public library were off-limits to colored folks for reading purposes. Mississippi State's library was about the tallest building in Starkville. I used to look at it in utter amazement and anger: that tall, pretty building, filled with all kinds of books that I couldn't get to and read, and they called that college an "institution of *higher* learning." That's about when I decided that racially prejudiced white folks were pretty damn stupid, no matter how tall and well-stocked their libraries. That was a big influence on my deciding that I was not going to college in Mississippi.

Of course, I could have followed any number of other young colored folks from Starkville and attended one of the Negro colleges in the state: Jackson State, Alcorn State, Mississippi Valley, among others. Instead, I wanted out of Mississippi. Pop claims that he proposed Morehouse College but that I refused on the grounds that "I'm not going to any college that doesn't have girls." (I don't remember saying that, but I've never argued that I didn't since it would have been the kind of thing I'd say about a setup that didn't make sense to me after I had spent my life up to that point surrounded by the kind of fine, smart girls I socialized with in and around Starkville and other towns and communities. No way.) Instead, following up a suggestion from a young itinerant preacher who made rounds in Starkville's colored Baptist churches after he had been trained at the colored National Baptist Theological Seminary in Nashville, I wrote for information and an application from Fisk University. Fisk, you see, offered a major in Philosophy and Religion, studies I wanted to pursue. (Well, that's a bit misleading: it was the study of religion that interested me since I wanted to prepare myself further for the ministry. But that's a part of my story I shall skip over, for . . . reasons . . . .) I applied to Fisk and to the shock and consternation of a number of colored folks (and some white folks, too, I was later to learn), and the joy and pride of more, my family and I included, I was admitted. Not only was I going to college, and one not in Mississippi (not unique to young Negroes from Starkville, for others had gone away to colored schools in Texas [Wiley College], Tennessee [Tennessee State University], and elsewhere), but I was going to what a significant number of folks, colored and white, regarded as one of the premier — perhaps *the* premier — Negro colleges in America.

In doing so I embarked on what, with much hindsight, can only be regarded as one of the most momentous journeys of my life, one that requires a fuller telling in its own right than can be given here. What is pertinent to this telling, first of all, is that I entered an institution unabashedly dedicated to the cultivation of character and to the education of a Negro leadership elite. Though not all persons within the institution (or without) were in agreement about this agenda, I was not among them. Each member of the faculty with whom I studied, as well as Blanche Cowan, the Dean of Women, Reginald Hughes, the Dean of Men, and Benjamin Pugh, director of Bennet Hall, my freshman dorm, and other members of the University's staff, were adamantly unapologetic about the strenuous demands they made of me and other students. As we students used to say with the respect of recognition and more than a bit of trepidation: if you didn't measure up in getting your work done the University would provide you with a banana, a comic book, and a one-way bus ticket home. When the second semester of my freshman year began with the release of grades from the first and a classmate who had attended boarding school in New England before coming to Fisk, and whose millionaire father was member of Fisk's Board of Trustees, was dismissed from the University for poor academic performance, it was crystal clear to me that the only way the son of a maid and a janitor would be able to continue at Fisk would be by doing his work and doing it well. So, I hunkered down.

The second pertinent point about the Fisk experience is my venturing onto the path of majoring in philosophy and religion. During my sophomore year, however, as I was getting settled into the major, there was a fateful night of intense discussions with my roommate and close and influential friend, Eddie Island, from Hot Springs, Arkansas, that involved some of the most penetrating, painful, scary, and ultimately liberating explorations of my beliefs and commitments and the agenda I had for my life that I had ever experienced. I faced up to the realization that the agenda was not one *I* had set for myself of my own free choosing, and was one that I had thought I could not relinquish. With Eddie's assistance I came to the realization that I could, and found the courage to act on that realization. One near-immediate result was my plotting a new course in my major: studying philosophy and, as best I could, avoiding the study of religion. The ministry was out as an option: I had become convinced that the broad and crooked was a lot more fun and interesting than the straight and narrow.

You can imagine, I trust, the impact this decision had back home, especially when Lillie Mae heard of my change of course. This was the woman, remember, who had made a deal with God about my life. You see, an earlier "decision" on my part to become a minister had satisfied her that after having made sure I saw the insides of all those churches and participated actively in them, she had indeed kept her part of the bargain. Within days of telling her and Pop that I had decided not to be a minister, I received a letter from her, virtually still damp from her tears, in which she agonized over somehow having gone wrong in raising me in allowing me to go off to Fisk to be misled by atheists. My being a minister would have been, for her, not only a joyful fulfillment of her end of the deal with God, but would have been sufficient to virtually assure her a front-row seat in heaven. (Lillie Mae didn't believe in being anywhere near the back where God was involved, and wouldn't allow me to sit in back during church — much to my chagrin, since that's where many of my friends were, thus where all of the surreptitious fun was happening during services.) My decision put a lot of things in jeopardy, especially her pride-of-place with God.

But you could not take a young colored man from Mississippi who was somewhat bright (a quarter of an inch to the right of average and valedictorian of my class), motivated by life under racial segregation to be aggressively inquisitive and dogged in the quest to *make sense* of life, a voracious reader (during the last years of high school I kept a list on the back of the door to my room of books I had finished reading — books borrowed from the school library or in some cases given to me, through my father, by white folks — while in a quiet race to out-read Cleveland Cross, a close friend and classmate with whom I was always in friendly competition to see who would get the highest grades); and who, in order to find respite from boredom and loneliness during long periods alone as an only child, had learned that my mind was one of my greatest assets (running my mouth a close second), my imagination especially; put him with very bright, curious, independently minded, and articulate students from across America and from other nations in courses and seminars led by teachers who constantly took you to the limits of your capacity and, believing you could do much more, expected — and required — you to; require him to read, think about, discuss engagingly and intensely, and write about challenging ideas from the likes of Sartre, Kierkegaard, Plato, C. P. Snow, Karl Marx, Joseph Conrad, Aristotle, Einstein, Thomas Aquinas, and many, many others (during my sophomore year, for example, I acquired nearly forty books that I had been required to read in whole or in part in regular classes, Honors classes, and Honors Colloquia. I was *exhausted* when the school year was over, but, intellectually, *invigorated*) — you can't do all of that and not expect the person to be profoundly affected by the experiences.

I was. I became an ardent, convinced humanist and individualist passionately committed to not fully worked-out notions of freedom and autonomy that I took to be somehow connected, in a fundamental way, to human reasoning and free choice. During those fateful college years I began to refashion a conception of myself that was centered on my ability to reason well, which I took to be the defining human capacity to make sense of the world, and on the freedom to live by one's own choosing. With these new assets I went off in search of making sense of the world and of my life and in the process declared God to be mostly irrelevant, to me at any rate.

(Well . . . , let me not get carried away here. For all my new found, mildly radical humanism, all those previous years in church didn't amount to nothing: I was not enough of a fool to dismiss God directly. I was not yet an atheist, even, just a developing agnostic. Since I was already venturing far along the downhill side of a slippery slope into hell, I wasn't about to be a complete fool: I hedged my bet just a touch and eased in and out of church some Sundays in case it turned out later that I had to accept that there was a God who required my allegiance in determining whether I ended up in a very real heaven with golden streets and gorgeous angels, most of whom would be strangers to me, or in an equally real, but much less than pleasing, hell populated by a lot of people in great pain and suffering, many of whom I would know from back home. Truth is, the better way of putting it is I declared my mama's deal with God null and void since it had resulted in an agenda being set for my life without my being consulted and without my consent. So, I proposed a new deal for God: "You don't mess with me, I certainly won't mess with You." Besides, I had the perfect out: if God, in creating me, made me free and rational, and required of me that I "come to Him *freely*" in order to repent, then *I* must decide the course of my life in this regard. I had already lived enough of my life under false freedom, coerced to do so by certain white folks who would have colored folks worship them, literally. Since I was determined to be free of such situations, I wasn't going to be coerced any longer by either God or my mama. So, I struck off down the road of life determined to "dance on the knife's edge," as I characterized the venture for myself. It was exhilarating! But it was damn near hell for a while there trying to live in the same house with Lillie Mae when home from Fisk during breaks. I'll forgo telling you about the time I was home and she sicced the pastor of our church on me to have him persuade me back to the straight and narrow. Preacher lost that battle.

God hasn't messed with me yet, as far as I can tell. Pop accounts for all the good fortune in my life up to this point as *only* being due to the grace of God. These days if I respond at all when he talks in this way it's only to say "Yep. Know what you mean, Pop." Years ago I overcame the overeducated, misguided, arrogant stupidity of thinking that I could and should try and persuade my father otherwise about his God. A better approach is suggested by one of my wife Freida's favorite proverbs: "Whatever floats your boat." My daddy, aided immensely by Lillie Mae, had a hell of a time keeping enough water under our family's boat and keeping it headed in the right direction without running aground or smashing up on the rocks of Mississippi's and America's racial segregation. With their help I have been able to launch and sail a boat with Freida that, for now at least, is riding our family along quite well.)

So, I immersed myself in studying philosophy and other subjects (. . . and in a few other activities as well; what W.E.B. Du Bois said about beautiful women at Fisk was as true when I stepped on the yard in 1963 as when he did in 1885), determined to make sense of the world and to find a place of freedom and well-being for myself. In particular, I became intrigued by what I was encountering in my readings in courses in philosophy: it seemed the persons I was studying had devoted themselves to making sense of things, had figured out what it meant to make sense of things, and knew how to go about doing so. Finally I had found the help I needed and longed for. Now, perhaps, I would be aided in developing the understandings with which I could help with ending racial segregation and all of its associated and consequent injustices and contribute to the work of transforming America into a racially just nation.

I was pushed and carried along in my pursuit by the currents of the Civil Rights movement swirling around me from my first year in college

(1963). And I went exploring new territories. The fall semester of my junior year I spent as an exchange student at Dartmouth College and lived in a fraternity house. (Believe me, my time at Dartmouth was quite a learning experience and was pleasant overall, except when I needed to go into town to get my hair cut. Sometimes, though, it was just plain weird, as when I was talking with one of my philosophy professors in his office one evening when the Great Power Failure of '65 hit the East Coast. The professor, who was white, interrupted what he was saying only to note "Oh, the lights went off . . ." and went on talking. I thought it more than a bit strange: since I could no longer see him, I knew damn well he couldn't see me. So, for a young man from Mississippi, sitting in the dark talking to a white man I couldn't see and didn't know very well was not easy. I was glad to finally get out of his office.) The summer between junior and senior years, three other students from Fisk and I traveled to Europe on a chartered ship, along with several thousand other students and adults, on our way to six weeks of living in folk high schools in Denmark, Norway, and Sweden — as participants with persons from Scandinavia, Europe, Africa, and the Caribbean — in a program promoting international peace and cooperation through understanding gained from intimate discussions, meals, and travels.

That turned out to be a momentous summer, some of the influence of which, much farther down the road of time, would be manifested in this collection of essays. For that was the summer that Stokely Carmichel (today a.k.a. Kwame Touré), then head of "Snick" (for SNCC: Student Non-violent Coordinating Committee), having joined the March Against Fear across Mississippi initiated and led by James Meredith (a colored Mississippian who was able to enroll in the University of Mississippi only with the protection of the local National Guard, which had been placed under federal authority by the President of the United States, John F. Kennedy), at the rally at the conclusion of the march had uttered the fateful call for colored folks to pursue "Black Power!"

From thousands of miles away in Denmark, where we were at the time, it seemed as though America had gone berserk in response. Even the Danes wanted to know what it all meant. But so did I and the other Fisk students; so did many of the perplexed Americans in our international group in search of international understanding and peaceful relations. (To the benefit of many of us, among the students from the U.S. participating in the summer program was Howard, a reserved but tenacious young black Mississippian from Tougaloo College who was a member of SNCC with substantial field experience. Howard was interviewed on television to help the Danes understand the call for Black Power!) And for those of us, myself included, who were deeply and passionately committed to pursuing the quest for freedom from racial segregation by redeeming the promises of racial integration — Negroes and whites overcoming together without regard for race — the call from a young Negro civil rights worker for political effort focused on gaining power organized and exercised racially for Black Power!—was a most difficult notion for some of us to wrap our minds around, let alone our hearts.

And there was another major complication: the war in Vietnam. This war had been the focus of intense discussions and political actions during my time at Dartmouth, but less so at Fisk; during the briefings we students were given at the State Department before departing for Europe and Scandinavia; during teach-ins on the ship to Europe; and in discussions with folks in Scandinavia. (I was astounded one night when a young Danish woman I had gotten to know said to me in response to my question to her about whether she agreed with the critics of America's involvement in the war we were then listening to on radio: "Oh, Lou, everyone knows you Americans are wrong for being involved in the war the way you are.") You should know: America's involvement in the war was not then a major issue for me. Racial injustice was my primary concern, integration its solution, rational understanding the means by which to achieve it. Because of my passionate hatred for the injustice of our nation's legalized racial segregation, I was becoming something of a disaffected Negro American just on the cusp of being so radicalized as not to stand when the national anthem was played. Yet, there I was in Europe being regarded, first off, as an *American*, though a *colored* or *Negro* American, and often finding myself in the position of having to *defend* America! And just at those existentially challenging personal and historical moments Stokely Carmichel (drawing off the intellectual resources and practical efforts of SNCC folks and others working in Lowdnes County, Alabama, who had determined that, given the greater number of black folks in the county compared to white folks, though the whites held institutional power, through organized voting black folks could come to have political power, and perhaps more) uttered the fateful words "Black Power!" that were captured in bold headlines in the international edition of the *New York Times* that we Fisk students read hungrily each day in Scandinavia whenever we could find a copy. In doing so Stokely threw into the civil rights fray the exploding bombshell of a color-coded agenda and scheme of values in terms of which I would now have to struggle at recomposing my identity, the meaning of my life, my life's agenda. The first encounters with a powerful, frightening unknown that is unleashed at home and lands in the midst of your psyche when you're thousands of miles away is *very* hard to deal with.

But deal with it I did, throughout my senior year at Fisk. Doing so was complicated by my being president of the Student Government Association, which meant I was in the very thick of things when students who wanted to form a campus chapter of SNCC had to petition Student Government to become a chartered organization. The president of Fisk at the time, and a number of influential members of the Board of Trustees, did not want a campus chapter of an organization whose national leader was that firebrand Stokely Carmichel. They "offered" to provide Student Government (me, really) with criteria for chartering new student organizations. I was fighting to keep the matter in the hands of Student Government. (I had been elected president by campaigning for increased student rights, independence, and involvement in decision making wherever the issues concerned students, and had been branded a radical by one of my opponents.) But, on the other side were the petitioning students, among them Nikki Giovanni, who, with the energizing forcefulness of their newly forged *black* consciousness, proceeded to press us Joe College and Susie College student government types hard against the walls of our Negro self-conceptions and our Negro-focused politics, challenging us to dare to refashion both, guided by a conception of blackness that, though factored out through the prism of race, was to be understood through legacies stretching back to Africa that were being recovered, studied, and enlisted in The Struggle. During these intense struggles the SNCC folks tap-danced on my brain, painfully stretching my sense of self in new directions well beyond America into Africa and the Third World. For much of senior year I had one hell of a headache. (I was also engaged in a senior independent study project in philosophy exploring some of the phenomenological work of Maurice Merleau-Ponty. I completed it, but Merleau-Ponty came awfully close to getting the short end of the stick. Understanding written phenomenological accounts of consciousness is real hard when you're living through the maelstrom of being pressed to change your own consciousness from Negro to *Black* while the ground of meanings of your self-identity, self-understanding, and your understanding of the world is moving beneath your feet.)

Not exactly what you wish for when you're trying to complete all your work, get admitted to graduate school, and keep up life with your girlfriend while making frequent trips to the president's office — at his request, mind you — to discuss pressing campus political matters. I was having a hard time making sense of things once again. But this time my studies in philosophy were not of much help. (In fact, they were something of a decided liability in the midst of raging campus and national debates about the virtues of undergoing a conversion from being Negro to thinking and acting Black while letting your hair grow long and starting to fashion it into an "Afro" to symbolize a newly constituted identity anchored in legacies that bypassed Europe and all things European and American that were "white.") For in not one of my classes in philosophy at Fisk (nor in graduate school, it would turn out) did I *ever* read a text written by a Negro, a Black person, an African. And since the quest for Black Power! required, first, the transformation of Negro minds as a necessary condition for Black liberation, what was I to do? I had made my stand-off with God and Lillie Mae with unshakable conviction. But this situation was even more serious: the core foundation of my strength of conviction, my sense of self, was now under *radical* challenge.

By the defining terms of the challenge, I could not turn to the Keepers of Rationality, philosophers, for immediate help in making sense of things, since all of those known to me were now suddenly seen as being white descendants of various peoples of Europe. Actually, at the time it didn't really occur to me to look to them. There were other, much more relevant resources available to me at Fisk, primarily in courses. There was Dr. (Leslie) Collins's famous Negro Literature course. (Though "Doc Collins," as he was often spoken to and spoken of affectionately and respectfully by students, was steadfast in using "Negro" to identify the literature and writers in his course, those of us who were on the way to becoming Black understood matters differently. However, we tended not to challenge Doc Collins on this.) And there was the course on Africa taught by the legendary Nigerian anthropologist Chike Onwachi. I took both courses that turbulent and fateful senior year.

But another resource had equally profound effects, in many ways: Fisk's annual Spring Arts Festival. Spanning a week or more, the Festival focused on creative achievements by black folks in music, art, literature and poetry, dance, and other areas (such as historiography) and showcased the most accomplished persons in these fields who could be persuaded to come to the campus. Many were persuaded. And during my final semester at Fisk I cut a number of classes (actually, it was expected that we would attend Festival events) and other activities to sit in seminars, open readings, and discussions with Gwendolyn Brooks, Lerone Bennett, Ron Melborn, Don L. Lee (now Haki R. Madhubuti), Leroi Jones-become-Amiri Baraka, Visiting Writer John Oliver Killens, and many others in addition to the giants on the faculty such as Arna Bontemps and Robert Hayden and the influences of the living legacies of the likes of musicologist John W. Work. During an evening gathering near the end of the Festival, Baraka gave a powerful reading and speech that "took house," as we used to say, and left me stunned but clearly with one foot firmly on the other side of that all but imperceptible and fluid line between Negro and Black self-consciousness. After his presentation I approached him, shook his hand, and thanked him, saying "I may have entered Fisk as a Negro, but I'll leave a Black man." I wasn't trying to impress Baraka. No, I spoke with firm conviction, for I had committed myself to a new course in life. Having already decided that I would become a college teacher, a teacher of philosophy, after being moved by Baraka, my SNCC peers, and many other folks to a place where much else that was giving me such a challenging headache was beginning to make sense, I made an irrevocable decision that I would prepare myself to contribute to the Black Revolution that was underway through my teaching, of philosophy, and, if at all possible, do so in a black institution. I now had a mission and motivation for graduate school.

For a number of reasons, that graduate school turned out to be Boston College, a Jesuit university in Boston's very well-to-do suburban community of Chestnut Hill. My first day on campus I thought I had made a terrible mistake and shown up at the wrong school. For all around me were a lot of clean-cut, preppy, mostly Catholic white boys in coats and ties moving briskly about and I in my short-sleeve shirt with my camera hanging from my shoulder and not another black face in sight (a situation I was to endure in the philosophy department all my years at BC, but happily not in the university as a whole, thank goodness: my second year at BC Freida entered the university as a graduate student in the School of Nursing). Luckily, a number of the graduate students, in particular several guys in my entering group in philosophy with whom I would become good friends and hang out, were for the most part of a different breed. That first day I hooked up with newcomers bearded, long-haired Tom Scally and on-his-way-to-balding Ed Goff. These two quite soon became my best friends at BC. Ed, from Arkansas, had just graduated from Vanderbilt University where he had been one of the founding members of Vandy's chapter of SDS (Students for a Democratic Society), was a fervent opponent of racial segregation and participant in the Civil Rights movement, and head-over-hills in love with a real fine woman from Fisk (whom I knew and had asked out but she turned me down because she was going out with someone else that I learned later was Ed) to whom he is still married. (Ed has been a member of the faculty of Villanova University since we left graduate school. He and Florence — Flossie, we call her — a librarian at Bryn Mawr College, live five minutes away from us and remain treasured members of our extended family.)

The three of us, along with the wild, long-haired, Berea College graduate, social radical tending toward anarchism Raymond Howard, were something of an odd crew in BC's fermenting philosophy department. Each of us entered the program motivated by pressing social concerns: racial injustice, the war in Vietnam, the injustices of capitalism. In addition to reinforcing each other's commitments while challenging the thoughts embodying, and the expressions of, those commitments in our heated discussions during seminars; our sometimes substance-assisted discussions after seminars, over poker, and with faculty-members; with each passing year we pressed our concerns on professors and the curriculum as we turned more and more to philosophers and other engaged intellectuals and thinking activists who had been concerned with social and political issues. Often we found these resources on our own rather than through course work and mostly without aid from the faculty in the philosophy department, though there were a number of persons on the faculty in the department and throughout the university, Jesuits among them, who were deeply and actively committed to the Civil Rights and Anti-War movements.

In those days we had much to draw on in the greater Boston area to fuel our energies, what with thousands of students attending over twenty colleges and universities within a twenty-five radius of the city, many of them passionately involved in the swirling currents of political and cultural revolution-making rushing across the nation. Ed, Tom, and I worked hard in our studies in philosophy to find resources we could bring to bear on the concerns we shared, on our private and personal concerns, and on our efforts with other persons and organizations. I was involved with an interracial religious organization that was devoting its energies to enhancing interracial understanding and cooperation by focusing its efforts on white churches, struggling to bring them into working and social relations with black churches around Boston. Among other tasks, I edited the organization's journal, which focused on social issues, while I struggled mightily to avoid being compelled to reveal that, by then, I was all but a convinced atheist. (Nothing like having some good white Christians suddenly discovering that the young Negro-Black man with whom they were holding hands and singing "We Shall Overcome" had cut loose from God.) Moreover, I was deeply involved in a number of networks of black undergraduate, graduate, and professional-school students at Harvard, Boston University, Wheelock, MIT, Wellesley, Brandeis, Northeastern, Simmons, as well as Boston College; and with black folks (and some white folks) in organizations in Roxbury (black Boston) and working in area businesses. (One of the most sustaining of these networks was made up of folks who had graduated from Fisk. For a year or more my apartment became something of a place for holding frequent weekend Fisk reunions during which we certainly didn't sit around "talking philosophy" as a number of my really devoted philosophy graduate colleagues liked to do.)

These involvements were fueled, to a large extent, by the debates and practical struggles raging throughout America: the Black Panther Party was flourishing; so was the quest for Black Power, now being pursued by countless organizations, including the likes of the Republic of New Africa; the Anti-War Movement was at its zenith, having helped to force then–President Lyndon Johnson to decide that he would not run for a second term; the Democratic Party was otherwise shaken by young folk disrupting its National Convention in Chicago; cities all across the nation were in the flames of summer riots; Martin Luther King Jr. and his leadership of a movement for nonviolent change were under severe pressure from angry and all too Black young folks impatient with his tactics of moral persuasion and seeming gradualism as a way of gaining social justice. "What time is it? *Revolution* time!!" was for many the rallying cry. With King's death by assassination that fateful April of '68, the Movement was at a momentous crossroads. And many of us found ourselves standing at the same junction struggling against our painful rage as we pondered with the old folks "How long, oh Lord?" "Will white America *ever* do right by black folks?"

When word of King's death reached me I was participating in a philosophy department seminar in which graduate students presented papers for discussion. Amy, a good friend in the class ahead of me, walked up to me and said, "Lou, haven't you heard? Dr. King has been killed." The only black person around, I had to get out of there. Without a word I walked out of the seminar, off the campus of Boston College, took the trolley away from well-to-do Chestnut Hill back into Boston to my apartment on the edge of an increasingly black community in which the fires of pain and anger were already starting to burn brightly. I had to give vent to my pain and think straight. I walked along Columbus Avenue toward Roxbury, watching and listening as folks struggled to make sense of what had happened. Fiery, radical, uncompromising Malcolm X was gone; now so was the non-violent Christian. For days after I pondered hard: what was I to do that would make a difference? With all those people moving in the streets, what was the point of my sitting at my desk reading and trying to make sense of Sartre's *Being and Nothingness*? What was the relevance of any of my studies to the life-and-death struggles raging all around me? Not one black life, or death, showed up on any of the pages I was struggling to keep in focus through my pain and frustration as I labored to learn how to make sense of things from the philosophers I was required to read.

I was able to stabilize myself and maintain my focus by renewing the commitment I had made at Fisk to prepare myself to contribute through teaching. I began in earnest to do what some of my black contemporaries called "double duty": that is, in addition to reading texts and completing the work assigned in courses and seminars, I began to turn more of my attention out of class to numerous texts on the informal curricula of the Black Power and Anti-War movements, still in search of resources to help me make sense of things. Frantz Fanon, Karl Marx, Herbert Marcuse, W.E.B. Du Bois, and Harold Cruse, among many others, were the focus of my efforts. Intense debates with various folks in the various networks helped, as well. So, too, attending all those meetings and lectures on various campuses, in public places, and organizations' meeting places. In addition, I began to take every opportunity I could to integrate these efforts into my studies in philosophy at Boston College.

It was another head-wrenching period, but one in which I had found and started mining a definite lode of resources in social and political philosophy. I reached a major turning point in my efforts when one evening I attended a standing-room-only lecture at Boston University given by Herbert Marcuse (he had been a major influence on Angela Davis when she was a student studying philosophy at Brandeis University). Inspired by what he had to say, I began to read his work and through him found my way into the Frankfurt School of Critical Social Theory and on to an entire generation of humanistic, Marxist, democratic socialists throughout Eastern and Western Europe. About the same time I began to tap into traditions of stringent Black Nationalist critiques of white supremacy along with my studies of Marx-inspired critiques of capitalism. But the integration of the results of my efforts into a coherent perspective would take a while still.

My partners at BC, Tom, Ed, and Raymond, were traveling similar roads. We made known our interests more forcefully to philosophy department faculty, who were increasingly open to our pressures. By our third year the department began to give serious thought to how it might organize and offer a program of studies in social and political philosophy. A major compliment to our efforts was bestowed on me when the chairman of the department called me to his office during the spring of that year, when my partners and I were preparing to move on to teaching jobs (we hoped), and informed me that though the department had a policy against "in-breeding" by hiring its own graduates, he was offering me a full-time faculty position in the department to help them develop a program in social and political philosophy. To say I was stunned is an understatement . . .

I was honored and more than a little tempted. But I had received another call to come and talk about a teaching position, this one from Fisk. After my visit to Fisk and conversations with various folk there (the president of Fisk, James Lawson, when I met with him to discuss, I thought, the prospects of my returning to Fisk to join the faculty, began by saying "Lucius, there's no question but you're coming back to Fisk to teach. That's settled. Now let's talk about something else. I hear you're married. What's your wife's name and how is she doing?"), and remembering the commitment I had made to myself during my senior year, one reconfirmed many times during the trying, growing, and even wonderfully fun years in Boston, which road I would take was very clear to me. Without hesitation, but after careful consideration, I expressed my deep appreciation to the folks in philosophy at BC for their offer and I made ready to "go South to join The Struggle." I worked ten to twelve hours a day, seven days a week, from sometime in March or April through August of 1970 writing a complete draft of my dissertation before heading off to Nashville. (I would complete the work of revising, submit, and successfully defend the dissertation, *Language and the Transformation of Consciousness: Foundations for a Hermeneutic of Black Culture*, and be awarded the Ph.D. in 1972.)

In leaving BC for Fisk I noted to myself that my formal studies in philosophy were over and my real learning was about to begin, the learning that would allow me to fulfill my commitment to teach, black students primarily; teach them how to think critically about, to analyze and understand, the institutional forces, and the people involved, operating to structure black lives in oppressive unfreedom. What was clear to me, however, as a result of the transformation and heightening of my self-consciousness from my last year at Fisk as an undergraduate through my years as a graduate student, was that I was inadequately prepared to do so in terms of my knowledge of the work of generations of black scholars and activists before me who had devoted much of their lives to such matters. Over the next ten years I would work intensively at correcting this deficiency, to a significant extent by delving deeply into traditions of Black Nationalist and other currents of African American social and political thought (Martin Delany, Frantz Fanon, Frederick Douglass, Booker T. Washington, Du Bois, Marcus Garvey, Julius Nyerre, and others). Still, I also read more of and taught many of the canonical figures and traditions in Western Philosophy, among them Plato, Aristotle, Kant, Hegel, Descartes, and Marx; Phenomenology and Existentialism (Sartre, Merleau-Ponty, Alfred Schutz), Critical Social Theory (Horkheimer, Adorno, Marcuse, Habermas, and Albrecht Wellmer), humanistic Marxism of Eastern Europe, of Yugoslavia in particular (Marković and Stajanović), and many other subjects and figures.

During those years I joined forces with a handful of other black philosophers — Howard McGary Jr., Leonard Harris, Bernard Boxill, William Jones, Robert C. Williams (deceased), Joyce Mitchell Cook (at first, the only female among us), Ifeanyi Menkiti, Robert Chemooke, Albert Mosley, John Murungi, Tom Slaughter, Laurence Thomas, Cornel West, Bill Lawson, George Garrison, Blanche Radford-Curry, Johnny Washington — working to define a place for ourselves within the philosophy profession, socially and intellectually, on terms that took into account and expressed our consciousness of being *black*. "Black Philosophy" was the name we gave to our quest to revise the philosophical canon to include articulations by African and African-descended thinkers, and to set the normative parameters for the work we did that focused on the concerns and interests of black people. (The first essay in this collection, "Black Folk and the Struggle in 'Philosophy'," was written as a contribution to those efforts.) We pursued our concerns through a number of historic conferences devoted to philosophical explorations of the experiences of black people that, for the most part, were held at black institutions (Tuskegee Institute, now Tuskegee University; Morgan State University), during divisional meetings of the American Philosophical Association, and, on one rare occasion, at Wingspread, the headquarters of the Johnson Foundation, to which a few of us were invited to spend several days working out our notions of "Black Philosophy" and the curricular and professional implications.

As the 1970s gave way to the 1980s, however, it became increasingly clear to me that the effort to make room for black folks in the enterprise of philosophy required more than was part of my initial efforts. There was the question of Africa in the overall scheme of things, a question that had been nagging at me since I first confronted it seriously and enrolled in Onwachi's anthropology course my senior year at Fisk. And while at BC I had worked on a grant-writing project with a philosophy professor who wanted funds to explore the question of whether Africans thought philosophically using some combination of Aristotelian and medieval categorical schemes as his measuring sticks. Knowing of my interest in the philosophical exploration of experiences of black folks, he asked me to join him in the project. When I did, my first task was to revise the proposal he had drafted and develop it to meet the guidelines — and the deadline — of the funding source. When I read his draft I was appalled and troubled by his approach to what he regarded as African thought. Since he was one of the most accomplished among the faculty in philosophy and otherwise a genuinely nice person, I swallowed hard and labored mightily to rework the proposal narrative into what I was satisfied was much more credible and respectful of African people. Mercifully, the proposal was not funded. The spirits of the Ancestors are to be thanked with appropriate libations.

But in joining the professor in the effort I was in deep water, particularly since there were no precedents known to me for what we were proposing to do. Be reminded that I had never had a philosophy course in which African and/or African-descended people, articulations by any such person, had even been a matter of discussion. And there were very few bibliographic references to guide me. However, among those the professor had listed (or I found while doing library research for the project — I honestly can't remember which), one did catch my attention, which I acquired and added to my personal library: Placide Tempels's *Bantu Philosophy*. It would be a decade, though, before I would give the book serious attention. (In part because early on when I was back teaching at Fisk I loaned my copy to a student in one of my seminars who was especially interested in the subject of philosophizing in Africa. He didn't return it and left the University before I could persuade him to do so. Only after I began teaching a course on African philosophy in the early 1980s would I get several new copies that I now steadfastly refuse to loan.) Long on passion and commitment, I was short on knowledge. From the early 1980s on I have worked to correct this, in part by participating in philosophy conferences in Africa (Kenya, Egypt), by hosting a conference (1982) that brought together African and African-American philosophers and other scholars to discuss the "state of the fields" of African and African-American philosophy, by forging personal and professional relations with a number of African philosophers, and by continuing study and discussion.

These efforts grew out of my realization that making room in philosophy for black folks required more than finding, demanding, or clearing the needed space in which to situate reclaimed, refashioned, or newly created philosophical ventures. Consequently, in recent years I have turned my attention to critical explorations of the enterprise of philosophy itself, and not just of its obvious canonical racial exclusiveness but of the insidious yet constitutive ways in which valorizations of raciality have been at work, mostly silently but quite effectively, to bring about and maintain over centuries a complex intellectual and cultural hegemony with particular racial and ethnic profiles. A long time and a good way down a long road from Starkville, Mississippi, my quest to make sense of a social world ordered by norms of raciality has led me to investigate the racialization and coloring of reason, the resource I had hoped would be the key to realizing a world of justice.

I am still hopeful, even optimistic. Primarily because I am now convinced that the human ability to consider and judge in making committed choices about how and why to live is the only real resource we have by which to work in concert to survive, evolve, and, if all goes well, to flourish. In order to do so, we will, then, have to continue to develop and exercise this complex ability — we will, in other words, have to *philosophize,* but in ways and to ends quite different from those to which we professionals have generally been socialized to devote ourselves. And philosophize about raciality if we are to make sense of it in ways that will help us to flourish.

I have tried to do so and share some of my efforts as a modest contribution encouraged, to no small degree, by the changes I see whenever I am back in Starkville. Several years ago during one of those returns to visit my parents, I went to a grocery store one night to pick up a few things. When I entered the store I was stopped dead in my tracks by something that grabbed my attention immediately: two young store employees standing together in public having a casual conversation, one a white female, the other a black male. Now, when I was their age in Starkville what they were doing would likely have gotten me killed. The two of them, however, went about their conversation with no apparent sense that there was anything unusual about what they were doing. By then, compared to centuries of previous Mississippi history, it was not so unusual. But I was dumbfounded, and stood looking at the two of them with my mouth open. Soon they concluded their conversation and walked in opposite directions to return to their work assignments. After several steps, the young woman called out to the young man saying something I was in too much shock to catch. He, in turn, responded by saying something like "Yeah, well, I'll see you later at . . . [your place?]." I didn't hallucinate and envision a crowd of angry, gun-toting, rope-swinging Klansmen with a burning cross stopping by *his* place later, but I was very, very moved by how very ordinary the exchange between the two young people seemed to have been. They worked together and apparently were after-work acquaintances to whatever extent; they may even have been friends. And as far as I could tell, no one else in the store besides me seemed to have taken much notice of their public, face-to-face conversation.

After the two of them had gone about their business, I was still standing in the same spot just inside the door to the store, astounded, remarking to myself how much things had changed in Starkville compared to the years when I was growing up, when any social intimacies involving a black male and a white female were a mixture that would set some of the most virulently racist white men off on a hunt for "nigger" blood. Things had changed. I thought, once again, of Emmett Till and noted just how significant the change. And the change made sense. My hope was reconfirmed.

I offer these essays as testimonials of hope and modest effort and as invitations to you, kind reader, to join me — and untold others past and present — in the effort to think carefully and clearly about how we might resolve America's most persistent dilemma. There are already signs of what is possible in Starkville.

🌿

INTRODUCTION

On Race and Philosophy

I

Raciality and ethnicity are two of the most pervasive aspects of life in America. That there are different races and ethnic groups (or "ethnies," as I'll refer to them in this collection), that each person is a member of one or more races and ethnies, is taken for granted by most people. And difficulties of various kinds involving considerations of raciality (considerations, that is, of various characteristics that, all together, are thought to define a particular race) and ethnicity (characteristics that, taken together, are thought to distinguish an ethnie as a subgroup of one or more races) are abundant. Yet, what determines a race or an ethnie, and whether it is ever appropriate to take raciality or ethnicity into account when making moral judgments about persons, are hardly settled matters, including whether it is correct to say that races, in particular, even exist.[1] This too is an important aspect of prevailing difficulties. Raciality, especially, continues to be the focus of intense political struggle, and thus is presently a topic of equally intense and wide-ranging discussion. I wish to contribute to the discussion by showing why I find it important to consider raciality and ethnicity as real, constitutive aspects of determinate populations of human beings.

As a philosopher I come at this by way of my participation in certain professionalized practices and tradition-mediations of "philosophizing" that, over the centuries, have themselves been affected by racial and ethnic concerns in important ways, and have made their pernicious contributions, not always acknowledged, to invidious racializations (that is, identifying characterizations of a group of people as a distinct race). This aspect of the history of philosophizing—in the West in general, in America in particular—must be considered before any leading role can be assigned to philosophers in addressing the serious and challenging problems confronting this nation and others that involve valorizations of raciality and ethnicity. Some of these problems will be discussed in the essays that follow.

🌿

In this Introduction I want to sketch out a consideration of race and ethnicity as the results of ongoing projects that are definitive of human sociality, which must be recognized as such. Let me make clear at the outset, however, that it is my very firm belief that we must continue to identify and to condemn all actions, beliefs, attitudes, and evaluations that make use of invidious considerations of raciality and ethnicity. But I also believe that it is very important that we continue to make use of the concepts *race* and *ethnie* (or *ethnic groups*) and their derivatives (*raciality, ethnicity*) as important resources for continuing efforts to critically (re-)construct and maintain social realities. For in complex societies in which race and ethnicity continue to be factors at the heart of social conflict, it is as urgent as ever that we engage in such projects with careful mindfulness of biologically and culturally constituted social groupings of races and ethnies, though sometimes it will also be important to have little or no regard for a person's or people's raciality and/or ethnicity. The delicate, complicated, but crucial task is to find ways of having appropriate regard for raciality and ethnicity while being guided by norms that we hope — and our best judgments lead us to believe — will help us to achieve stable, well-ordered, and just societies, norms bolstered by the combined best understandings available in all fields of knowledge that have to do with human beings and that are secured by democratically achieved consensus.

In this collection I will share considerations I have developed over a number of years in my explorations of raciality. Here I shall work to give greater cogency to my arguments that we must find enhanced and reasonable ways of understanding raciality and ethnicity and of referring to social collectivities as races and ethnic groups. This greater understanding will enhance social relations and praxes in the continuous struggle to achieve stable and just societies in which humans might flourish. I take it to be the case that at least some professional philosophers, myself included, along with thoughtful persons in other walks of life, can contribute to the clarifying work of developing social and political philosophies and policies that might help us to fashion communities in which racism and invidious ethnocentrism have been minimized and curtailed (I do not expect either ever to be eliminated completely and for good), even while races and ethnies are both conserved and nurtured, without chauvinism, to the enrichment of us all.

II

First, two extended quotes offering thoughts about human racial groupings. Each prompts provocative, highly charged questions that have to be addressed as we work our way through the problematics of raciality and ethnicity.

Once a race has become established as the principal population of a region, it has a tendency to stay there and to resist the genetic influences swept in by later invasions.... When two races come into contact and mixture occurs, one race tends to dominate the other. The local advantage that the genetically superior group (superior for its time and place) possess may be primarily cultural or primarily physiological, or a combination of both.... There is, however, a third kind of dominance, expressed by the resistance of a population to the intrusion of large numbers of outsiders into its social and genetic structures. Call it xenophobia, prejudice, or whatever, people do not ordinarily welcome masses of strangers in their midst, particularly if the strangers come with women and children and settle down to stay. Social mechanisms arise automatically to isolate the newcomers as much as possible and to keep them genetically separate. . . . [This] is the behavioral aspect of race relations. The genetic aspect operates in a comparable way. Genes that form part of a cell nucleus possess an internal equilibrium as a group, just as do the members of social institutions. Genes in a population are in equilibrium if the population is living a healthy life as a corporate entity. Racial intermixture can upset the genetic as well as the social equilibrium of a group, and so, newly introduced genes tend to disappear or be reduced to a minimum percentage unless they possess a selective advantage over their local counterparts . . . were it not for [these] mechanisms . . . , men would be not black, white, yellow, or brown. We would all be light khaki, for there has been enough gene flow over the clinal regions of the world during the last half million years to have homogenized us all had that been the evolutionary scheme of things, and had it not been advantageous to each of the geographical races for it to retain, for the most part, the adaptive elements in its genetic *status quo*. [Carleton S. Coon, *The Origin of Races* [2]]

The American Negro has always felt an intense personal interest in discussions as to the origins and destinies of races: primarily because back of most discussions of race with which he is familiar have lurked certain assumptions as to his natural abilities, as to his political, intellectual and moral status, which he felt were wrong. He has, consequently, been led to deprecate and minimize race distinctions, to believe intensely that out of one blood God created all nations, and to speak of human brotherhood as though it were the possibility of an already dawning to-morrow.

Nevertheless, in our calmer moments we must acknowledge that human beings are divided into races; that in this country the two most extreme types of the world's races have met, and the resulting problem as to the future relations of these types is not only of intense and living interest to us, but forms an epoch in the history of mankind.

It is necessary, therefore, in planning our movements, in guiding our future development, that at times we rise above the pressing, but smaller questions of separate schools and cars, wage discrimination and lynch law, to survey the whole question of race in human philosophy and to lay, on a basis of broad knowledge and careful insight, those large lines of policy and higher ideals which may form our guiding lines and boundaries in the practical difficulties of every day. For it is certain that all human striving must recognize the hard limits of natural law, and that any striving, no matter how intense and earnest, which is against the constitution of the world, is vain. The question, then, which we must seriously consider is this: What is the real meaning of Race; what has, in the past, been the law of race development, and what lessons has the past history of race development to teach the rising Negro people? [W. E. B. Du Bois, "The Conservation of Races"[3]]

For several hundred years now, most instances of concern in intellectual and social life with *race* and racial groups, as well as with *ethnicity* and ethnie, have been dominated by two concerns: either the identification and rank-ordering of populations of people for purposes of exploitation of and/or invidious discrimination against those said to be lower in rank by those who think themselves members of a race and/or ethnie of higher rank; or, by denunciations of and struggles against "racism" and invidious "ethnocentrism," as we have come to designate such practices, and against rationalizations of both. Between these two types of endeavors a third is barely able to sustain itself free of suspicion or involuntary conscription by racists or the inappropriately ethnocentric as support for their invidious projects. This third endeavor is the studied consideration of the varieties of human collectivities referred to as "races" and "ethnies" with no concern for rank-ordering, exploitation, or invidious discrimination, a consideration that, instead, adds to the storehouses of credible and morally appropriate knowledge of human beings as we have been and have come to be in all ways: physically, biologically, and culturally; visibly as well as beneath the outer configurations that first meet our culturally socialized senses.

It is an endeavor of this third kind that I shall undertake, one that is not focused on either racism or anti-racism. Rather, I want to inquire into the hows and whys of humans forming themselves into bonding, self-reproducing social collectivities that are distinguished by biological and socio-cultural characteristics that are shared by the members of each collectivity. These groupings frequently grow larger and form into subgroupings, and all the groups together form a relatively distinct, self-reproducing breeding population constituted as such by shared socio-cultural systems. As these populations and their subgroups survive and reproduce themselves, and thereby persist in and across times and spaces, significant efforts are devoted to perpetuating the cultural meaning-systems and institutionalized practices, in either preserved or altered forms, in and through which both cultural and physical characteristics become valorized elements of the social and personal identities definitive of group members. The conflicts involved in these efforts are increased when there is contact with persons from physiologically and culturally "different" populations.

The complicated processes (biological, socio-cultural, historical) by which such populations and population subgroups are formed and maintained are what I refer to as *raciation* and *ethnicization*. I will argue that raciation and ethnicization are facts of human evolutionary histories. I mean by this that they are important aspects of the socially contingent, but anthropologically necessary, ways in which we humans, as social animals, organize meaningfully, give order to, and thus define and construct the worlds in which we live, our *life-worlds*, and do so in the process of surviving while subject to the evolutionary forces of social and natural histories.

I assume that these social collectivities and the processes of their formation and maintenance are better known to evolutionary and social biologists, paleontologists, and physical and cultural anthropologists than they are to people in the humanities. Many contemporary philosophers, myself included, have been seriously miseducated when it comes to our knowledge of humans as beings of complexly interrelated socially conditioned, natural-biological, and socio-cultural histories. In seeking to understand raciation and ethnicization, relations involving racial populations and their ethnic subgroups, as well as understanding the variability and historicities of these populations and subgroups, I hope to partially but significantly re-educate myself as a philosopher.

In doing so, once again I take inspiration and guidance from W. E. B. Du Bois, who recounts in his third autobiography that he "conceived the idea of applying philosophy to an historical interpretation of race relations." However, Du Bois distinguished what he regarded as "the lovely but sterile land of philosophic speculation" from the objects (and objectives) of the fields of history and the newly developing social sciences that were constituted by the realities of social life. For Du Bois, historiography and empirical sociology would provide the means by which he would gather and interpret "that body of fact which would apply to my program for the Negro." And in this gathering and interpreting it would be philosophy in the form of what he termed the "keen analysis" of his Harvard philosophy teachers William James, Josiah Royce, and George Santayana—James's pragmatism especially—combined with the historically informed empirical research methods that he learned from Harvard historian and teacher Albert Bushnell Hart, that Du Bois would continue to develop and apply to the study of race relations.[4]

After completing his graduate studies, Du Bois, in "The Conservation of Races," put his plan to work as he posed and set out to answer the questions, quoted earlier, that he thought must be seriously considered: "What is the real meaning of Race; what has, in the past, been the law of race development, and what lessons has the past history of race development to teach the rising Negro people?" For Du Bois, in order to achieve a proper understanding of raciality one must "survey the whole question of race in human philosophy" to be able to form the guiding higher ideals and policies for dealing with "the practical difficulties of every day."[5]

It is this Du Boisian approach to races and raciality that I wish to take up and extend, as well, to considerations of ethnicity and ethnies. In the process I hope to persuade others who are concerned with racial and ethnic matters in their philosophizing, especially philosophers, to give Du Bois's work the kind of careful consideration that is cultivated in attending to the works of canonical figures in philosophy. For Du Bois's approach is especially promising for working out conceptions of raciality and ethnicity that could help articulate a political philosophy appropriate to a modern, liberal-democratic society in which diversities of philosophical doctrines as well as of valued social collectivities, including races and ethnies, are normal and important features.[6]

Note, for example, that Du Bois, in his effort to characterize a race, took particular care to observe that while physical differences "play a great part" in distinguishing each race, "no mere physical distinctions would really define or explain the deeper differences—the cohesiveness and continuity of these groups. The deeper differences are spiritual, psychical, differences—undoubtedly based on the physical, but infinitely transcending them." Du Bois thought there were "forces" that "bind together" members of a race, and he took these to be: first, a racial identity and "common blood" (by which Du Bois means, as I read him, biological descent from common ancestor[s]); "secondly, *and more important*, a common history, common laws and religion, similar habits of thought and a conscious striving together for certain ideals of life" (emphasis added). A race, then, for Du Bois, is a collection of persons of common biological descent who are bound together by the meaning-systems and agendas constitutive of shared cultural life-worlds. And the development of different races, understood thus, he saw as having involved processes of "growth" characterized by "the differentiation of spiritual and mental differences" even as processes involving "the integration of physical differences" (i.e., cross-racial breeding) were also having their effect.[7]

Du Bois has frequently been misunderstood as a typical late nineteenth-century thinker who regarded raciality as being determined by a fixed set of heritable biological characteristics. However, he was hardly a "typical" thinker, either for the late nineteenth or the early to mid-twentieth centuries. What remains instructive for me is the nuanced way in which Du Bois struggled to conceptualize socio-cultural groups called "races" or "nations." Though these groups tend to be distinct from one another in terms of physical features shared by their members, they cannot be distinguished precisely by such distinctions. For significant variations exist in the distribution of the characteristics thought to define a race among persons identified as members of the same racial group. In addition, the physical characteristics that are thought to distinguish a particular race are, as Du Bois noted, "most exasperatingly intermingled" among those of other races. For Du Bois, no definitive set of heritable physical characteristics suffices to characterize a race. This reality defeats the classificatory efforts typical of natural philosophers concerned with identifying the invariant, determining, essential natures of natural kinds, races included.

Du Bois was decidedly atypical in his cutting against the grain of prevailing natural philosophy as he contributed to the development of modern social sciences. Mindful of the work of Charles Darwin, he understood the variability of heritable traits. He understood, as well, the permeability of the social and political boundaries established to mark and maintain racial groups. For he repeatedly drew from his own family history to note how frequently these boundaries were transgressed (he counted among his ancestors persons both white ["of Dutch descent"] and Negro [Africans "descended from Tom, who was born in West Africa"] with the result that Du Bois himself was often described as a "mulatto"), which resulted in the intermingling of physical characteristics and thus wide variations in the phenotypes of members of a given race.[8] This, in significant part, is why Du Bois turned to the realms of history and sociology to identify the characteristics shared by members of culturally — as well as sexually — constituted self-reproducing groups that, when given significance by members of the group, act as "forces" to bind them together *as a group* and become part of the members' personal and social identities.

Understanding such groups requires a philosophical anthropology and social ontology that include an understanding and appreciation of senses of *belonging* and of a shared *destiny* by which individuals are intimately connected to other individuals in ways that make for the constitution of particular kinds of social collectivities, what I term *social-natural kinds*. Races and ethnies are such "kinds" of collectivities; raciation and ethnicization the processes by which they are formed and maintained; raciality and ethnicity the interrelated sets of historically contingent and conditioned, socially defined, always varying and contestable physical and socio-cultural features relatively definitive of a race or ethnie.

I want to think seriously about the natural history — the evolution — of social-natural kinds: that is to say, the ways and consequences of the intersectings of natural and social evolutionary processes through which humans form and maintain bio-cultural social groupings. In addition, I wish to argue against those who regard raciality and ethnicity (and gender) as nothing more than arbitrary, fluid, socially contestable "fictive," "imagined," or "ideological" "social constructions," that, according to some persons, are not even *real* even though real enough in what are regarded as their social or "material" effects. Such approaches to the "socially constructed" involve conceptions of the *real* that are much too simple in that they generally regard only material kinds as real while allowing that the fictive or imagined can and do have real effects when played out through social practices. Approaches of this sort fail to appreciate more fully varieties of kinds of *reals* and the full range of social realities. As a result, they help to impoverish social ontologies and thereby to impair the development of a social and political philosophy appropriate to a society that is diverse ethnically, racially, and culturally. As I have noted already, a major concern for me is the articulation of just such a philosophy supported by a combined social ontology and philosophical anthropology different in important ways from those that have been at the heart of modern liberal individualism: that is, revised to take seriously racial and ethnic groups in order to be a resource for praxes that might help us to realize social peace and harmony with justice.

To these ends, my concern, as was Du Bois's, is to work out an understanding of raciality and ethnicity, the processes of their formation and maintenance, that is focused on the ordering world-making of evolving humans. For, I think, it is in and through this world-making, driven by survival needs and competition for resources, that raciation and ethnicization develop as responses to the need for life-sustaining and meaningfully acceptable *order* of various kinds (conceptual, social, political). Understanding these aspects of our species-being (to re-invoke a central notion from the early Karl Marx) will enable us, I think, to understand better how racial and ethnic groups come to be and go about defining and identifying themselves. With this understanding it will be possible to better appreciate some of what goes on when racial and ethnic groups meet under various conditions, in the past and present, and why these particular forms of intergroup relations sometimes come to have such importance that they lead to bloodshed.

The processes of ordering world-making certainly provide the context within which we can properly understand what are termed "racialism" and "ethnocentrism": the belief that races and ethnies, particularly one's own, are both real and valued. But I am convinced that neither of these is necessarily, certainly not always practically, pernicious and to be opposed automatically. Racialism neither is nor need become racism; nor must ethnocentrism become invidious. In neither case should the one be conflated with the other: that is, racialism with racism, ethnocentrism with invidious ethnocentrism. Racism and invidious ethnocentrism are best understood as sets of beliefs, images, and practices that are "imbued with negative valuation" and employed as modes of exclusion, inferiorization, subordination, and exploitation in order to deny targeted racial or ethnic groups full participation in the social, political, economic, and cultural life of a political community.[9] Such beliefs and practices are contingent, never necessary, no matter how frequent.

INTRODUCTION

❧

Among engaged contemporary thinkers who have turned their attention to racial and ethnic matters are those who argue in favor of discarding the term "race" because, they reason, it is now loaded with centuries of pernicious valorizations accumulated from dehumanizing mobilizations of sentiments and practices ranging from the merely impolite to the genocidal. Further, the term has no "scientific" validity, some claim (frequently without giving an account of what they mean by either "science" or "scientific"). Additionally, in racially and ethnically complex nation-states such as the United States there are no "pure" races, if there ever were any, nor persons who do not have genes from one or more of the old, now increasingly intermixed racial groups. Consequently, it is claimed, identifying persons and groups as races cannot be accomplished with precision and is at best arbitrary, and doing so often results in more harm than good. As with some "social constructionists," some persons who appeal to the authority of undifferentiated "science" even go so far as to claim that there is no such thing as a race. However, in continuing to side with W. E. B. Du Bois's position in 1897, I share his concern for the "conservation" of races (and, I would add, of ethnic groups). Thus, I think it important that serious philosophical attention be devoted to an appreciative but critical re-thinking of ethnicity and raciality.

But why bring such a dangerous and seemingly discredited notion as "race" into philosophy to be legitimized, even if not "properly" justified, in support of a possibly misguided quest to "conserve" racial and ethnic groups? For should not philosophizing, as has been claimed for centuries, be devoted to setting out principles and norms of reason to guide human beings in fashioning lives through which they can become fully, flourishingly *human*? Various philosophers have long argued that if such principles and norms—of truthfulness and justice, for example—are to be binding on all, they must not rest on the valorization and privileging of the norms and life-agendas of any particular groups, races, or ethnies. Principles and norms for ordering social and individual life that grow out of and are dedicated to serving the life interests of a particular people are always conditioned by and relative to those interests. The abundant evidence of anthropological diversity makes clear that human groups do not, simply by virtue of being human, share the same interests and agendas except in the most general of terms (as, for example, "to live and live well," "to see offspring live and prosper," "to not be treated unfairly by others"). Conflict emerges when, in contexts of intergroup life (and even within groups), different meanings and weights are given by members of different groups to those things about which they care and compete, and for which they are sometimes prepared to die. It seems, then, that the only way to avoid having such conflicts become socially destructive is to have principles to guide practices and efforts to resolve disputes which owe their source and validity, their truth-

fulness and reasonableness, to the life-worlds and life agendas of no particular people, perhaps, but which can be binding on *all* persons and peoples
by being grounded on, say, the principles and normativity provided by reason alone. For only then can the norms and principles ensure mutual well-
being in a shared world.

Why not, then, join the quest for such norms and principles and work
with others to help stave off what many regard as the resurgence of destructive racialism and ethnocentrism, or "tribalism," around the world? Why
seem to provide honorific philosophical justification to balkanizing dehumanization by valorizing talk of "race" and "ethnicity" and thus contribute
to the dangerous politics of identity and difference recognition?[10] Why not
work to save the political and economic revolutions of liberal democracy and
free-market capitalism by redeeming the modern Enlightenments' expecta-
tion that the resources of critical reason embodied in and exercised by the
mature, autonomous individual are our best and last hope for realizing the
good life of peace with justice for all?

These are, indeed, serious questions, as problems having to do with
raciality and ethnicity continue to plague social and political life throughout
the world. Why, then, endow raciality and ethnicity with highly honorific
philosophical significance? The answer, simply put: *because we must.* The
increasing frequency of conflicts tied to valorizations of differences among
peoples that we characterize as "races" and/or "ethnic groups" ought to be
sobering, for contemporary philosophers especially. For many of us have
shared the expectations that

> the kinds of features that divide one group from another would
> inevitably lose their weight and sharpness in modern and modernizing
> societies, that there would be increasing emphasis on achievement
> rather than ascription, that common systems of education and com-
> munication would level differences, that nationally uniform economic
> and political systems would have the same effect. . . . The 'liberal
> expectancy' flows into the 'radical expectancy'—that class circum-
> stances would become the main line of division between people, eras-
> ing the earlier lines of tribe, language, religion, national origin, and
> that thereafter these *class* divisions would themselves, after revolution,
> disappear.[11]

These expectations were born in the philosophical anthropologies and
political philosophies of modern European and American Enlightenments
and nurtured in the centuries-old liberal-democratic, capitalist, and even
socialist-communist revolutionary experiments with forming decidedly
modern societies and nation-states. These legacies continue to serve as
reservoirs of hope for many who would complete the realization of the
promises of modernity.

But it has not come to pass that physical and cultural differences among groups of peoples in terms of which they continue to be identified, and to identify themselves, as races and ethnies have either ceased to exist or ceased to be taken as highly important in the organization of society, especially in situations where there is competition for resources thought vital to lives organized, to significant extents, through racial and/or ethnic identities. Of course, some protest that such identities are inappropriate, in part because the notions of the racial or ethnic group involved in them lack science-certified empirical confirmation or philosophically certified logical precision. However, it strikes me that these protesters, while well-intended, are nonetheless misguided, for they have forgotten a very important injunction from Aristotle that for any given science or systematic attempt to achieve certified knowledge one should seek no more precision than the subject matter allows. Since races and ethnies are *populations* identified as such on the basis of the degree to which persons share *more or less* particular sets of varied and varying physical and cultural characteristics, care must be taken to specify what empirical criteria would be appropriate for determining when references to any particular race or ethnie are valid. These will be those criteria by which, conventionally, statistical frequencies are set as definitive over some population range. A combined social ontology and philosophical anthropology informed by the best empirical and interpretive work of this kind (provided by physical, cultural, and paleoanthropologists; evolutionary biologists and geneticists; and others), as well as by attention to everyday social life, will no longer support expectations that racial and ethnic differences and concerns will disappear—nor justify efforts to ensure that they do disappear—as societies modernize.

On the basis of a revised philosophical anthropology that draws on an enhanced social ontology mindful of social collectivities, then, perhaps those who philosophize would not mislead themselves in thinking that the elimination of antagonisms tied to invidious valorizations of raciality and ethnicity can be facilitated by "lexical surgery" that removes "race" from usage and replaces it, instead, with references to, say, "communities of meaning" as offered by Kwame Anthony Appiah[12] or, as he has proposed more recently, to "ethnic identities," since he claims there is no such thing as a race. It is as though "something awkward or troublesome can be got rid of by the mere process of calling it by another name."[13] I worry that efforts of this kind may well come to have unintended effects that are too much of a kind with racial and ethnic cleansing in terms of their impacts on raciality and ethnicity as important means through which we construct and validate ourselves.

Of course, centuries of wrongdoing as a function of racism and invidious ethnocentrism have cost millions their lives and many millions more unjust curtailment of their lives and possible futures. And the wrongdoing continues, assisted now by wider distribution of ever more efficient weapons of human destruction and less ostensive but still very potent new strategies and means, including coded talk and practices that mobilize persons of various racial and ethnic groups into projects of defensive and offensive racism and invidious ethnocentrism. It is, indeed, the very reality of injustices and atrocities motivated by racial and ethnic concerns that highlights for me the need for venturing into these difficult waters. Appeals to "reason" have not been either an effective vaccine against the ravaging viruses of racism and invidious ethnocentrism or an antidote to the social ills they produce. In fact, both racism and invidious ethnocentrism are generally highly rationalized ventures. As was noted long before now, reason can be a whore who sleeps with anyone.

I remain convinced that what success can be achieved in reducing racism and invidious ethnocentrism and their effects will not come as a result of declarations of the "illusory," "superstitious," or "misguided" nature of talk of raciality (or ethnicity) on the assumption that "race" has no proven or possible *real* referent, or that the living referents are actually constituted such that the demarcations intended by "race" are at best arbitrary social conventions that inscribe physical characteristics with meanings that cannot be anchored in any abiding biological and/or anthropological fashion. I agree: there are no "pure" races; nor are there unique characteristics — physical and cultural — that would be included in any definition of a given race or ethnie in contrast to the statistical frequencies of appearance of the various combinations of biological and visible physical and cultural characteristics of socially defined raciality; nor is raciality the function of an invariant, trans-historical, trans-geographical, biological essence that makes races natural, unchanging kinds. Again, human populations and their sub-groupings are better understood as *social-natural kinds*: that is, groupings of humans that are formed and named under contingent socio-historical, cultural conditions, according to social conventions (often under conditions of conflict in which there are disparities of power possessed by those naming and named), groupings of biologically and socially evolving living beings who are also part of socially conditioned natural histories. For important reasons we should understand races and ethnies as *natural*: that is, as particular types of bio-social collectivities that develop or evolve, as do all things in the natural world, but in ways that are characteristically human.

Humans are biological beings, however we make sense of our biological aspects: that is to say, our biological makeup, in providing species-specific biological boundary conditions, is foundational to our very being even though this makeup does not determine how we are to give meaning to its various aspects. Certainly, in thinking of a population of individuals as a distinct race we can be freed of the mistaken notions that race-defining biological characteristics are shared equally by all members of a population; that the characteristics are unique to and thereby definitive of the race; and that biological characteristics completely determine the cultural productions, individual capacities and achievements, and moral significance of any group of people. However, it does not follow from this that we are required to give up all use of "race" as a group-identifying or group-characterizing term. We need only remember that it is not biology, certainly not in the *last* instance, that determines the cultural productivity characteristic of any group, or that determines the moral significance of racial groups: that is to say, determines the regard we should have for racial and ethnic groups and their members, in themselves and in relation to one another.

Humans are also social animals: that is, we require associations of various kinds, associations secured by affections, loyalties, and attachments that are contingent and variable, yet are necessary for any person to become fully human. I am especially interested in exploring conceptions of raciality and ethnicity that include appropriate considerations of shared, heritable biological characteristics and shared socio-cultural elements. Together these are important constitutive aspects of the meaningful orderings of a life-world, the base of which is a determinate social collectivity. Still, it must be remembered that the boundaries of all such collectivities, except for those that are completely isolated from other, different groups, shade off into those of other collectivities. As has been noted, races, as large populations of persons identified by the statistical frequencies with which certain characteristics are shared, "are always fuzzy around the margins."[14]

I propose, then, an inquiry into raciality and ethnicity via a treacherous "third path" between racism and invidious ethnocentrism, on the one side, and anti-racism and anti-invidious ethnocentrism, on the other. What I propose can help us to recognize and nurture races and ethnies as we reconsider raciation and ethnicization as processes by which we humans produce and reproduce ourselves as crucial aspects of our "social construction of realities."[15] In pursuing this path I wish to think carefully about Carleton Coon's question (knowing that for some anthropologists and others Coon was a racist whose work was thus suspect): Why is it, after thousands of years, that human beings are not all "light khaki" instead of exhibiting the variety of skin tones (and other features) more or less characteristic of various populations called races? Are these developments only to be accounted for as resulting from boundary-setting projects motivated by racism and invidious ethnocentrism? Might these populations not be the result of bio-cultural group attachments and practices that are conducive to human survival and well-being, and hence must be understood, appreciated, and provided for in the principles and practices of, say, a liberal, democratic society? If bio-diversity is thought good for other species and for the global ecosystem, why not for the human species and its bio-cultural ecosystems? Might we find in Du Bois, then, a possible model of how we might work at understanding raciality and ethnicity, and at developing an appropriate philosophy by which, in his words, "to lay, on a basis of broad knowledge and careful insight, those large lines of policy and higher ideals which may form our guiding lines and boundaries in [meeting] the practical difficulties of every day"?[16]

Facing up to these questions in pursuit of understandings of raciality and ethnicity, in light of past and present histories, is treacherous, indeed. But face them we must if we would not have these matters in their pernicious forms so dominate our personal and shared lives that they become the fires that consume us all. We are compelled, then, to philosophize: to pursue understandings to guide our praxis. And we must develop, as well, an understanding of the collections of practices, discourses, traditions, organizations, media, etc., which constitute philosophizing, an understanding that is appropriate to the task of coping with problems involving raciality and ethnicity if the resources of the enterprise of philosophy are to be of assistance. For social and political philosophies suitable for and contributing to the realization of a stable, well-ordered, and just multi-racial, multi-ethnic society must provide appropriate accounts and appreciative provisions for the racialities and ethnicities of the members of such a society, but do so without either endorsing or degenerating into chauvinism.

"Philosophizing" — that is, various ways of thinking and discoursing about various things and matters — is a decidedly varied venture engaged in by various persons variously situated, is thus inherently contingent and conditioned socially and historically, thereby epistemologically and normatively. Consequently, any tradition or genre of philosophizing is characterized by diversity. And there are many such traditions. As A. J. Mandt has noted, contemporary professionalized, academic philosophy in America, for example, is a structured "web" of communities of discourse, "partly overlapping and partly discontinuous with one another":

> The totality forms a "great community" that is highly organized even though its constituent parts are largely autonomous. The great community has norms that define its limits, but these norms are equivocal and conventional. They are interpreted differently in various subcommunities. . . . Although in each locality norms operate productively as conventions that shape philosophical activity, their extension to the larger community makes them the basis for *merely* conventional justifications.[17]

But in addressing matters of raciality and ethnicity, I think it important to shift consideration from philosophizing as manifested in various prevailing forms, agendas, and reconstructed histories to a consideration of philosophizing generally: that is, as intellectual activities engaged in by some individuals in virtually all human societies that are devoted to figuring out the means and rules for surviving, stabilizing living, and perpetuating the biological and cultural reproduction of the society through successive generations, in certain spaces (both natural and built), in and through time. Such activities are to be found wherever and whenever self-reproducing groups of human beings worry about such matters. It is in considering the processes

multiple communities within philosophy (handwritten marginal note)

philosophy (handwritten note)

phil = making sense (of) life worlds
considering how people phil in diff l-ws
will lead to context for discussing race

by which associated humans construct meaningfully ordered life-worlds that we find the appropriate context for understanding raciation and ethnicization. And it is also here that we find the context for understanding the collection of practices and discourses that constitute philosophizing, or what I term the authoritative "figuring out" of the various means by which life-world ordering and maintenance are to be accomplished. What follows is my own brief sketch of an account of the hows and whys of life-world ordering in and through which raciation, ethnicization, and philosophizing take place.[18]

III

Projects of "figuring out" of a kind that have come to be called philosophizing (other kinds include the various human, natural, and social sciences; arts, religions and theologies; mythical systems; etc.) will *always* be found among the activities of human populations and their subgroups that survive across time. For in surviving, humans are always faced with and must resolve the problem of the *recurrent need for order* in and through which they *secure* living, and living well, in the face of constant change, especially in the form of entropy and the challenges of the unfamiliar. Simply put: meaningfully ordered shared life is essential for human survival and well-being.

With challenges to ordered life come anxiety, particularly when the challenges raise concerns regarding the survival of the social unit, or key aspects of a group's way of life—for example, practices and legitimations ordering relationships through which biological reproduction is achieved and a population and its sub-groups replenish themselves with new members and thus continue their history into the future, and the preservation of meaning-endowed naturally and socially constituted environs thought vital to social (and individual) well-being. Challenges of these kinds can be especially threatening because humans are not "hard wired" with the necessary means for meeting all challenges successfully: that is, such resources are not part of our gene-based neuro-physiological makeup. Rather, it is *only* out of trial and error that successful, life-ordering, and stabilizing strategies become knowledge-certified by some among those who survive the trials and are able to determine the whys and hows of failure and success. The results of these efforts, under certain conditions, get organized into order-producing and -maintaining strategies and forms of explicit knowledge, which are further institutionalized as economies of stockpiles of knowledge and practices further associated with typified social roles. Together these provide the means, utterly necessary, for humans to control expectations and behavior in a social collectivity. Through the socialization of members into the collectivity, and the socialization of non-members, as well, about the collectivity, expectations and behavior are channeled into predefined patterns of rule-structured ordering that secure the social group against entropy and the unfamiliar.

"Culture" is the term we speakers of English use to refer to these meaning-endowed and -endowing, socially and personally identity-forming and socializing, socially binding, historicizing, time-and-space configuring, order-forming and order-maintaining and -reproducing belief systems, practices, institutions, and structures that provide the historically contingent and dependent beings that we are — who, as individuals, are thoroughly inept at birth and unable, for more than a decade, to provide for our own survival and well-being — with the means of constructing necessarily meaningfully ordered life-worlds. This constructing work is accomplished within the boundary conditions of our evolving species- and sub-species-specific biological and anthropological compositions while in continuous interactions with socially conditioned natural and built environments and socio-cultural worlds constructed, in part, by predecessors. These worlds must be maintained, even refined, by persons in the present and those coming after if life is to continue as before, or better: that is, with increased chances of survival and without at least some members of the collectivity having to start over from scratch, if they survive at all.

Group life, social life in general, and thereby individual lives, depend on the socio-cultural repertoires as accumulations of tried and proven knowledges and practices and as a context for innovation. These repertoires are not just means for securing food, clothing, and shelter, but are the cultural resources that provide the defining practices and fabrics of meanings vital for the formation and maintenance of anthropologically crucial personal and social identities and histories (i.e., biographies and traditions) that socialize individuals and tie them together in the making and re-making of social wholes. And when we inquire into the social-natural histories of humans, we find that the subgroup or the population, not the individual, is the unit of survival and the bearer of group-defining cultural, as well as physical, traits.

Utterly decisive in this regard are the normed ways in which, first, a self-reproducing collectivity (and its subgroups, if any) has developed in its environments over time; and, second, how members of the natal collectivity and subgroups identify themselves, physically and culturally (physically through their culture[s]), how they order life within their social spaces, especially if the collectivity and/or any of its subgroups live in proximity with "foreigners" who are decidedly "different" in ways that are important to how native individual and social life is ordered. Obvious examples include differences in dress, language, and other cultural practices. But of particular importance are norms of somatic aesthetics that help to regulate the preferences and practices in terms of which partners are chosen for the intimacies that frequently (must) result in the birth of new members and in terms of which the offspring are bonded with, nurtured, and socialized into the collectivity. In this area, especially to those who have the responsibilities of ensuring the collectivity's persistence across time, significantly different and objectionable strangers are likely to be seen as posing serious challenges to the preservation of the home group's embodied identity and thus to the collectivity's bio-cultural future as would be realized through its descendants.

This is hardly a trivial matter. Embodied identities are vital aspects of "the order of things" in terms of which a bio-social collectivity's life-world is defined. So, too, are norms that define and regulate the relationships that determine descent. For the socio-culturally conditioned choosing of partners (importantly, among other reasons) for the biological production of descendants is, to paraphrase Aristotle, the principal means by which a great many of us humans satisfy our desire to achieve relative immortality by leaving others behind after our death who look and carry on somewhat like ourselves. Thus there are self-reproducing populations that share distinguishing physical and cultural features that set the demographic boundaries of a life-world, features that become part of the reservoir of normed resources drawn on in the construction and maintenance of personal and social identities. Thus also our identities become more or less tightly woven to our bodies and secured with webs of legitimations drawn from these cultural reservoirs and their sacred canopies of rationalizing, justifying "explanations." Consequently, neither the reservoirs, the legitimations, nor the identities can be trifled with if an established form of meaningful ordering is to be preserved in and across social times and spaces.

This is the historically contingent, yet anthropologically necessary, socio-cultural matrix that must be appreciated in endeavoring to understand how physical and cultural factors are taken up and given social meanings so as to become mutually reinforcing in the processes through which social collectivities are "constructed": that is, the processes in and through which geographically determinant populations and subgroups of sexually reproducing individuals become adaptively differentiated biologically and culturally, groupings we have come to call "races" and "ethnies" (though there have been other designations for such groupings, in various languages, throughout human history). Such groupings are both social and natural (*social-natural kinds*). That is, humans are part of the natural world and subject to its laws as well as to species-specific limits and possibilities as set by evolving, culturally influenced biological and anthropological boundary conditions. Sociality — organized associations among humans — is a crucial aspect of these natural conditions of human existence: they are necessary for survival. Still, humans are without a fixed, pre-established "nature" that determines the historical particularities of existence and telos. Within the boundary conditions is an enormous (though not infinite) range of plasticity that must — can only — be developed and nurtured under social and cultural conditions guided by agendas whose particular goals and objectives cannot transcend, but are not preset in their particularity by, these same boundary conditions.

As with other species of living organisms, so too with humans in the long run: only those populations and/or their subgroups survive across generations and in various environments who are successful in building up, storing, refining, and mediating to contemporaries and successors life-sustaining, order-producing collections of knowledges and practices of particular kinds. These must be distributed to and placed under the guardianship of particular persons who have the responsibilities of storing, refining, and mediating these knowledges while protecting them from loss or corruption. Among these resources are conceptions of the collectivity devised to define the members in ways that bind them together so that, through sanctioned cooperation, chances for survival are increased. Thus comes the valorizing of descent associations with members of the natal subgroup and its extended population, and of the defining ways of life of members as well as of the ways of life of others "significantly" different by descent — hence, in particular circumstances, by physical appearance and/or by culture. This is the basis of the normativity of social life that we call "ethnocentrism." Extended to an entire (geographic) racial population, we might call it "racialism." However, this is the same matrix from which is produced, under the pressures of challenges and competitions threatening "the order of things," those defensive mobilizations that take the form of invidious ethnocentrism and racism.

Now, as situations of living change, so must the knowledges undergirding social life be revised — otherwise they become inadequate to meet new challenges. Still, as knowledges are "software," that is, not part of our biological makeup or "hardware," they are especially vulnerable to corruption, entropy, or to becoming inadequate to changing circumstances, which is why knowledges must be protected, if not revised, and maintained. So, too, must "the order of things" be protected. Hence, the necessary creation of a canopy (often sacred) of cognitive and normative interpretations that rationalize and justify — that is to say, "legitimate" — the knowledges that determine the constructed "order(ing) of things," including the determination of such crucial matters as what is spoken of as the "real" and the "right," the "true" and the "good," and each of their opposites.

The production of protective, legitimating canopies requires, of course, particular folk, namely, those who "figure out" such matters. But their functions are socially vital, which is why their positions and roles must be valorized in ways to give them "authority" and, thereby, power: the power to *define the real, the true, and the good*, including the characterizing and identifying definitions of members of the group and of "others," as well as of the overall "order of things." Such persons direct the institutionalization of legitimated and thereby valorized knowledges and provide for their transmission by developing, over time and varying according to socio-cultural groupings, various "conceptual machineries"—systems of myths, theologies, cosmologies, philosophies, sciences, therapies, etc.—through which to rationalize and justify "the order of things."

This, in general, is what I take to be the social location of those who have come to be called "philosophers." Their self-assigned responsibilities have been to identify, codify, and stand guard over the rules for producing and certifying the knowledges needed to produce order and to sustain life against changes and variations thought to be inimical to "the order of things." Hence the fetishization by philosophers of various traditions (but by no means all) of univocal, universal, change-impervious Truth and Goodness, Right or Justice, and of the tools (e.g., systematized and formalized logic) and strategies (e.g., certain forms of "justification") by which these are supposedly acquired. Here, too, is the source of the efforts to achieve legitimization (as in Plato's Myth of Metals) that would give to philosophizing in certain forms and practiced by certain certified persons its authority and honorific status. Today, however, in contemporary, decidedly "modern" and complex societies in particular, philosophers are generally all but ignored outside of classrooms and gatherings mostly of other philosophers except in certain academic (and a few other) institutions when they lecture to crowds of varying sizes more or less respectfully eager to hear the curious, perhaps interesting, and only very rarely famous, speaker. The likes of Cornel West—a philosopher become public intellectual and international celebrity—are rare, indeed.

The legitimation of "the order of things" is crucial, especially for members of succeeding generations who, not having been present at the purported "beginning," are unusually naive and skeptical with regard to various aspects of "the order of things." This will be the case especially if present orderings and productive arrangements (economic and political, for example) have, over time, made life less challenging and anxiety producing: in part by not only having routinized the securing of what is necessary for survival, but by routinely providing, in relative abundance, both the needed and the desired; in part by the society having become more complex, porous, and accommodating of the once "strange," thereby freeing up energies from defensive mobilizations and productive labor that can then be re-deployed in various forms of learning-recreation, sometimes in avid pursuit of pleasures found in partaking of the "exotic" and "strange" or the just plain "new" and "different" (such as watching television programs from various countries and/or with characters played by persons of various races or ethnies, or just hanging out at the mall with the multi-culti posse). Under such conditions it is more difficult to convince the young (or the mature and "liberated" cosmopolites) that the "old" ordering of things should remain more or less "the same." All the more pressing, then, is the need for convincing legitimations of "the order of things" to keep enough members of the group "at home" to ensure the viability and reproduction of the life-world and its members. And for those groupings in whose behalf certain members have fashioned and deployed various concrete and rationalizing practices by which to colonize for their exploitation larger and extended spaces and peoples in pursuit of their ordered lives, and have justified doing so, in part, by claims regarding the superiority of the race and its ethnies — in such instances racialism or ethnocentrism, in the words of Anthony Appiah, has "gone imperial."

Unless legitimated order replaces anxiety with calm and comfort, if threats to order are not met and neutralized, anxiety can and will become terror as the loss of familiar and comforting ordering proceeds to such an extent that it threatens the configuration and stability of the life-world as a whole. By endangering the life-world's key structures and/or processes, these threats, whether real or imagined and responded to as though real, arouse the prospect of serious decline, chaos, or complete loss of the order that gives meaning to unifying personal and social identities. For without such identities persons come to feel that there is no meaningful present explained, justified, and made endurable by biographies, histories, and traditions that situate the present in connections to reconstructed pasts and hoped-for futures. And without connections of this kind there is but personal and social chaos leading to more and more desperate reactions to remove the threat and to restore order before the onset of psychic and physical death, arriving slowly over periods of decline (best visible in retrospect, though this view is unavailable to the dead), quickly over relatively short periods, or abruptly.

Whether disorder and decline lead to death is a complex matter involving the anticipation and apprehension of the threat(s), of what is (or is thought to be) threatened, of the nature of the threat(s), and how they are responded to: in what ways, by whom, when, and for how long. Among the means used, regardless of the nature of the threat, must be forms of social organization and conceptual machineries that are devised to define while ordering the known and the real. The unfamiliar and strange, the undesirable, if they cannot be accommodated into prevailing universes of meaning on acceptable terms, will have to be placed in restricted zones — whether conceptual, physical, or social — and kept there in quarantine, or eliminated entirely (as in genocidal projects of racial or ethnic "cleansing"), to prevent the biological and/or social influences that might presage undesirable and threatening changes to "our" traditions and "way of life." The appropriate keepers of the social orderings and conceptual machineries for maintaining "the order of things," appropriate, that is, to the threat and area threatened, must mobilize arsenals of weapons from knowledge stockpiles with which to meet and resolve the challenges to order. And they must do so by providing defining accounts in terms of which policies are formulated to direct actions and behaviors that neutralize the threats and maintain or restore order.[19]

Raciality and ethnicity, then, are indeed "social constructions." But we humans *must* construct ourselves. And in doing so we form social collectivities requisite to which personal and social identities are also formed. Along with other aspects of life-world cultural repertoires, these identities include valorizations of our bodies (of the shared features that distinguish members of the natal group and the collectivity). These identities are set in various ways, and they work—and are worked on—dialectically in the ongoing processes of regulating the reproduction and maintenance of shared bio-cultural life. In their particular configurations and valorizations, such identities are not biologically determined; hence they are not, in this sense, necessary. However, social as well as personal identities are necessary, but are historically and socially contingent in their configurations and valorizations. Part of the regulatory work such identities perform is played out in mate selections leading to the birth of offspring. Depending on the "program" directing the processes of socialization of offspring and social life generally, these identities contribute, more or less, to the reproduction of the bio-cultural collectivity, that is, to the race and/or ethnie.

So it is that we are not all khaki, as Carleton Coon observed (though, again, there are times when, for quite good and important reasons, we should and do act as though we are), and why, generally (hardly universally), so much resistance exists to our *becoming* all khaki. Should this resistance be facilitated? Or, to put this important question differently: how might we work to conserve "colored" populations and subgroupings (and white is a color, as well), races and ethnies, without making it easier for racialism and ethnocentrism to "go imperial"? I have sketched a case in terms of which such groupings can be seen as social-natural kinds whose valorizing legitimations are initially internal to the groupings. Though this makes these legitimations and valorizings historically and socially relative and, because humanly based, certainly contingent, in multi-racial and multi-ethnic societies we can still orient ourselves to live in important ways beyond the various socially constructed borders that give order and definition to our respective race and/or ethnie-based life-worlds. In this way we can share a larger, more encompassing life-world, perhaps by agreeing to public political principles that have sufficient overlap with the various life-world orienting doctrines to which we may be committed to provide a basis for a shared life, one which leaves each race and ethnie almost—though not quite—as they were and wish to be. (This is, of course, the old but recurrent problem of trying to achieve unity while preserving diversity, and a particularly vexing problem for liberal democracies.)[20]

Is the realization of such a shared life a practical possibility? Yes. Is doing so possible practically, all things considered? A definitive answer to this question cannot come from philosophizing alone, only from pursuing it, in practice, in everyday life.

he seems to view challenges to "the order of things" coming from a bored & pampered younger generation rather than an angry or rebellious oppressed group. How does this jive w/ his own life from preface?

he assumes difference precedes racism/ethnocentrism (invidious) and that these are reactions (gone haywire, but springing from natural or good reactions) come from the encounter w/difference. I think difference/racism are co-constructed. Look at Smedly

he says in fn 19 that he will say more about the racist/ethnocentric nature of the ∅ elite in future essays in this text

Does he see each end world as having a nec. ∅ elite that is only a problem when it tries to foist itself on other worlds? Does he see each life-world as discrete & not over-lapping w/others?

❦

1

BLACK FOLK AND THE STRUGGLE IN "PHILOSOPHY"

I

Since the early 1970s, a new generation of young black philosophers has been pressing the case for the articulation and recognition of "black philosophy" and in doing so have sparked heated debates. It is no accident that questions have been raised regarding accomplishments by black folks in the area of intellectual endeavors called "philosophy." Nor has the form in which the questions have been posed fortuitous—"Is there a 'Black' philosophy?" "Can there be a 'Black' philosophy?"—or the responses to them. Both the questioning and the responses owe their origins to a discernible complex of historical factors that have come together in a particular way to condition their emergence. For what is revealed in the struggle to confront the issue of "Black philosophy" is the expansion of the continuing history-making struggles of African and African-descended peoples in this country (and elsewhere) to achieve progressively liberated existence as conceived in various ways. Even more concretely, this questioning is one of the impacts of the increased number of black folks entering the ranks of academics with training in the discipline of philosophy on the downturn of yet another wave of resurgent black nationalist consciousness, as many characterize the historical situation.[1]

This timing is an important factor to be taken into account in understanding the debates regarding black folks and philosophy. Generally, particular historical tendencies and developments do not appear or unfold in all sectors (social, political, economic) of complex societies in the same way and at the same time—in other words, there is often a lag in the rates of change among the different sectors and even within sectors that are internally diverse (for example, professionalized disciplines in higher education). Further, there are specific historical reasons why the absolute number of black folks in academic philosophy has shown a recent marked increase. Both sets of factors have conditioned the emergence of the questioning and

❦

the forms of responses. Yet, another factor has more importance: the self-conceptions of those of us involved in "academic" philosophy. That the debate itself has so far (though hopefully not in the future) remained for the most part academic (and meekly so, at that) is revealing with respect to both academic philosophy and black folks who in increasing numbers (though not necessarily with an increase in critical insight of sufficient radicality) are moving into this field of knowledge production and mediation in this country at this time in its historical development. It is with some of the aspects of this complex, yet extremely important historical situation that I wish to deal.

II

Philosophy itself, both as a notion and as various forms of praxis, remains seriously problematic today, again for historical reasons. It has become almost wholly "academic": the activity of trained "professionals" whose primary function has been reduced to being overseers in museums of the history of ideas. In itself this is a valuable function, for it ensures the preservation of valuable insights and strivings and their perpetuation via the practice of the mediation of tradition. Still, it does not represent a fulfillment of the larger historical and social function of philosophy understood as a dynamic enterprise unifying theory and praxis. As an enterprise, philosophy has suffered from the pervasive historical tendency, which has been intensified with the rapid development of advanced capitalistic-technological society (in this country particularly, in which the highest form of this development has been realized to date), toward increasing specialization and the concomitant development of narrowness, overconcern with methodologies and other discipline-focused matters, and in many cases toward forms of scienticism. Moreover, as a response to prevailing schemes of values of a capitalistic-technological society, the study of philosophy (i.e., participation in studies in the history of some ideas, almost wholly Western) has increasingly suffered from the pervasiveness of the "performance principle," which would have us judge our primary activities, particularly formal education, in terms of their performance potentials, namely, the accumulation of capital. Thus are philosophy students constantly struggling with the question (and its implied criticism that philosophy is not useful for anything in terms of "making a living") "What are you/am I going to do with philosophy?" Like most else in our society, the study and practice of philosophy are now often assessed by their market value, and we who "teach" it its market managers: professionals, higher degreed and salaried.

While the enterprise of philosophy has its rightful place in the overall scheme of things, it has nonetheless suffered from its professionalization, and we along with it. To the question "How do philosophers exist in the modern world?" William Barrett answers:

Philosophers today exist in the Academy, as members of departments of philosophy in universities, as professional teachers of a more or less theoretical subject known as philosophy. . . . The profession of the philosopher in the modern world is to be a professor of philosophy; and the realm of Being which the philosopher inhabits as a living individual is no more recondite than a corner within the University. . . . The price one pays for having a profession is . . .professional deformation. . . . As a human being, functioning professionally within the Academy, the philosopher can hardly be expected to escape his own professional deformation, especially since it had become a law of modern society that man is assimilated more and more completely to his social function. And it is just here that a troublesome and profound ambiguity resides for the philosopher today.[2]

This deformation reveals itself in other ways as well. It deforms the historical development of philosophical thought, evidenced by the degree to which the "problems" in philosophy continue to be, even in these very problematic times, discipline immanent, thus without foundation beyond the boundaries of the discipline itself. They have not emerged from the practices of life. Prior, therefore, to the resolution of the issue regarding "Black philosophy," the issue of philosophizing, its possibilities in the West, are in need of clarification.

III

The very debate itself is thus seen to rest on unclarified grounds. We black folks who would involve ourselves in it would be wise to be cognizant of this situation in its fullness: not only its present condition of deformation but the distorted historical development of the West in general. Our rush to uncritical intellectual "integration" in a problematic situation might prove to be our undoing: that is, we might fail to be sufficiently aware of historical tendencies and possibilities that we might struggle with others to realize and, in so doing, help to bring about historical developments that might lead to enhanced conditions of life for all, but for the presently "marginal" peoples in particular.

But isn't this very debate regarding "Black philosophy," the struggle on the part of some black (and white) folk (with the sideline support of others, black, white, and otherwise) to define such an enterprise, an attempt that aims at avoiding or correcting the pitfalls of deformation? My response: no, not necessarily. And judging by some of our present endeavors (and our history as a class of educated black folks), again no. The adequacy of our involvement in the debate will depend on how we attend to a number of crucial factors, the awareness of which must be reflected in our philosophizing.

We black folks must, first of all, be clear as to our own being, not only individually but, most importantly, collectively, viewed in its historical sweep and cultural, socio-political, economic complexities, our future possibilities. Our reflections on our future possibilities as a people must be particularly insightful. The achievement of a seemingly integrated position within the ranks of professional academic philosophers and teachers of philosophy must not leave us blind to the general condition of black people in this country and elsewhere and, most importantly, to the realities of the basis of political-economic power in this country in various groupings that are not sufficiently grasped by traditional theory regarding the class structure of capitalistic society. An appropriate grasp of this situation must in turn be reflected in our struggle to come to grips with the activities that constitute philosophizing. Our personal situations as a class of black people characterized as such to a large extent by our levels of formal study must not lead us into a form of philosophizing that would imply that reason has been realized in contemporary history, that reasonableness has come to pervade relations among men and women, among different racial, ethnic, religious groups and economic classes in this society and relations among nations.

We must not be guilty of a premature leap into universal peace and brotherhood without the historical realization of the same for all. Black people are still an oppressed racial group in this society and are still struggling against colonialism and neo-colonialism in other parts of the world. So too are other peoples. And there is ample indication that major powers, particularly the U.S., are neither moving nor are willing or capable of moving, toward a world of peace and increased liberation for all peoples, a movement grounded in a politics and ethics involving political, economic, cultural, and social democracy. The struggle of our people continues to be that of seeking progressive liberation at a level capable of being shared by many given the level of development of the culture as a whole. It is too a continuing struggle for many who are non-black, including many whites. It is, overall, the struggle to harness and direct the capabilities of the society as a whole in the maximum utilization of resources with minimum waste and environmental destruction toward the satisfaction of essential human needs with minimum exploitation and oppression — that is, toward the achievement of forms of life based increasingly on reasonableness democratically envisioned and realized.

Toward this end, however, the concrete realities of the politics of the past, present, and foreseeable future demand that we approach the struggle from the level of a group, i.e., racial and ethnic (or nationalistic, as some would say), position, the only viable position in terms of which to achieve limited goals within the present order of things. In order to realize ends beyond the present order of things, to pursue progressive tendencies and possibilities that might lead to the realization of greater reasonableness and thus to the transformation of the present order of life with greater benefits for greater numbers of people, we must move beyond the limited program of group-centered politics as the only mode of political activity. Still, we cannot be premature even with regard to this.

IV

A very serious phase of our preparation for philosophizing in the interest of black people (and others) includes coming face to face with the history of the relationships of black thinkers to the historical efforts of black people and, most importantly, with where this history leaves us today. We must, in other words, become transparent to ourselves as a class in terms of our history, our responsibilities, our possibilities.

Many very significant insights into the history of black thinkers are to be had in the work by Harold Cruse, *The Crisis of the Negro Intellectual.*[3] A controversial book, to say the least, still its uneven but very often penetrating analyses and its prescriptive projects harbor a core of truth (both historical and as future possibility) which is, in my judgment, very substantial. On the historical side there emerges from his analyses a picture of essential failure on the part of black intellectuals (i.e., writers, social critics, artists, etc.) in not having forged a collective vision for black people based on an appropriate grasp of social, political, economic, and cultural realities. For Cruse this failure rests fundamentally on the erroneous commitment on the part of many black intellectuals to the ideal of racial integration. Even more the failure of left-looking "radical" black intellectuals, in his judgment, has been/continues to be a uncritical commitment to Marxism-Leninism and to the sufferance of intellectual apprenticeship to white, particularly Jewish, liberal and left-wing intellectuals. The pervasive reality of American life, says Cruse, is that its politics, cultural systems, and economics are group based: power resides in racial-ethnic/national groupings primarily. The struggle for integration on the part of black people without having developed, cultivated, and consolidated our own nationalistic or racial solidarity has resulted in—and will continue to result in—the unsuccessful realization of the struggle for equality and "freedom" within the present scheme of things. The struggle, for the most part, has not been revolutionary either in separatist schemes (which, says Cruse, seek to avoid the problem via escape) or those seeking systemic reform.

The arguments advanced by Cruse call for serious review and critique. Still a number of things are clear. First, our need to be clear as to our grounding as black thinkers. That ground, given present realities and the near and mediate future, is the long history of struggle on the part of our people for an increasingly liberated existence. Out of this grounding emerges our first task: the effort to achieve a critical understanding of our situation: of our real needs and the means by which they might be met. In working to meet these mediate responsibilities we must struggle against the tendencies leading to deformation and particularly we must be prepared to commit "class suicide" in order that our energies be given unequivocally in service to the historical struggles of our people, here and elsewhere. In this regard there is a particular turn that we must make in our development, a turn whose importance is heightened by the debate regarding black folks and philosophy and its context. That turn of development and its ground of necessity is clearly set out by Cruse:

> Every other ethnic group in America, a "nation of nations," has accepted the fact of its separateness and used it to its own social advantage. But the Negro's conditioning steered him into that perpetual state of suspended tension wherein ninety-five per cent of his time and energy is expended on fighting prejudice in whites. As a result, he has neither the time nor the inclination to realize that all of the effort spent fighting prejudice will not obviate these fundamental things an ethnic group must do for itself. This situation results from a psychology that is rooted in the Negro's symbiotic "blood-ties" to the white Anglo-Saxon. It is the culmination of that racial drama of love and hate between slave and master, bound together in the purgatory of plantations. Today the African foster-child in the American racial equation must grow to manhood, break the psychological umbilical ties to intellectual paternalism. The American Negro has never yet been able to break entirely free of the ministrations of his white masters to the extent that he is willing to exile himself, in search of wisdom, into the wastelands of the American desert. That is what must be done, if he is to deal with the Anglo-Saxon as the independent political power that he, the Negro, potentially is.[4]

The insights of Cruse make clear our historically conditioned *vocation,* which is fixed for us even more specifically by Vincent Harding:

> The fact still remains that for the life and work of the black scholar in search of vocation, the primary context is not to be found in the questionable freedom and relative affluence of the American university, nor in the ponderous uncertainties of "the scholarly community," nor even in the private joys of our highly prized, individual exceptionalisms. Rather, wherever we may happen to be physically based, our essential social, political, and spiritual context is the colonized situation of the masses of the black community in America.[5]

The vocation of the black intellectual/scholar thusly grounded structures, in Harding's words, our *calling*:

> To speak truth to our people, to speak truth about our people, to speak truth about our enemy — all in order to free the mind, so that black

men, women, and children may build beyond the banal, the dangerous chaos of the American spirit, towards a new time.[6]

V

Still, the struggle to hear our calling and to respond, in part by taking a pilgrimage through the desert in search of wisdom, in part by speaking the truth, all directed by the concern to contribute to the historical movement toward the realization of a more reasonable life, takes us beyond the limited goals that emerge from group consciousness (i.e., nationalism, ethnicity). It will, in fact, drive us beyond the boundaries of the present order of life and, necessarily, bring us into serious conflict with it. Again, many of the more fundamental needs of black people are shared by many others. And there are, on the other hand, needs to be met in the lives of others that we don't suffer at all or with the same intensity, but they do require our concern and attention in the struggle to realize a life of progressive liberation. This world historical struggle thus draws us beyond limited peoplehood to a generalized peoplehood that recognizes peoples in their diversity. It makes for a struggle to achieve unity in diversity: reasonableness in life as a unity based on democratically agreed-upon notions of "reasonableness" in a diverse, pluralistic world.

Judged against these goals, the vocation of philosophizing takes on decisive meaning: it is to share in the refinement and perpetuation of critical intelligence as a practice of life that has as its goal raising to consciousness the conditions of life, historical practices, and blocked alternatives that, if pursued, might lead to life experienced as qualitatively — progressively — different. So conceived, "Philosophy explores and evaluates the *totality* of the human condition in society. It represents society's most general and most fundamental theoretical-critical self-consciousness. No other form of human intellect is as condemned to aspire to totality as is philosophy."[7] Thus, the social function of philosophy is to develop critical, dialectical thought, according to Max Horkheimer: "Philosophy is the methodical and steadfast attempt to bring reason into the world,"[8] a crucial moment of this process being the radical critique of what is, at a given time, prevalent:

> By criticism, we mean that intellectual, and eventually practical, effort which is not satisfied to accept the prevailing ideas, actions, and social conditions unthinkingly and from mere habit; effort which aims to coordinate the individual sides of social life with each other and with the general ideas and aims of the epoch, to deduce them genetically, to distinguish the appearance from the essence, to examine the foundations of things, in short, to know them.[9]

And the "dialectical" aspect of critical thought? As Herbert Marcuse has characterized it:

Dialectical thought starts with the experience that the world is unfree; . . . man and nature exist in conditions of alienation, exist as "other than they are." . . . Dialectical thought thus becomes negative in itself. Its function is to break down the self-assurance and self-contentment of common sense, to undermine the sinister confidence in the power and language of facts, to demonstrate that unfreedom is so much at the core of things that the development of their internal contradictions leads necessarily to qualitative change: the explosion and catastrophe of the established state of affairs.[10]

VI

For us black folks who would philosophize, that is to say, who would live life conditioned primarily by the activity of critical, dialectical thinking, a very first task is to bring this activity to bear on the practice of "philosophy" today to the extent that we are to have any contact with the traditions and practices of philosophy in the academy. Beyond this, however, the need to be grounded in the historical struggles of our people, in particular, and the struggles of men and women toward more reasonable forms of existence, in general, sets the tasks we must be about. While I cannot list all of the tasks to be performed in realizing the goals in either set of struggles, still it is possible to indicate some.

On the one hand, there is a need for a hermeneutics of the experiences of black folks directed toward a number of ends: the recovery of history, of historical meanings, as a means of radicalizing our own present and future possibilities as a people; the restoration and repair of broken communication among the various groupings of our people; the mediation of our people's traditions; and, most importantly, the achievement of increased self-transparency. In toto, such hermeneutical endeavors would aim at the full disclosure of the life-worlds of black people, our life praxes, and help us in formulating our projects.

On the other hand, there is the need, in terms of the efforts of others in the world, to increase the degrees of freedom, happiness, and well-being that they might enjoy, to be in solidarity with them in these struggles in our own life-practices and our own struggles. The increasing realization of the interdependence of all our lives on this planet, an interdependence grossly and distortingly exaggerated by monopolistic, imperialistic capitalism, reveals the broad directions we must take in the struggles of oppressed peoples throughout the world to increase the range and quality of their well-being. As beneficiaries of the high levels of cultural development in the West, in general, the U.S. in particular, based as it is in large part on the oppression and dehumanization of others, our responsibilities to ourselves and to these peoples are clear and immense.

In terms of all of this, our struggle as black folks involved in "philoso-phizing" is but a moment in the whole. We must be therefore clear where and how we come down in this debate. For in doing so — or in failing to do so — we will significantly condition our histories: as a class, as a people, as people in struggle in world history.

❧

2

PHILOSOPHY, AFRICAN-AMERICANS, AND THE UNFINISHED AMERICAN REVOLUTION

Light and Dark: Philosophy and the African Holocaust

Historically, what has come to be called "philosophy" has developed as a collection of thinking and discursive efforts devoted to knowledge about, among other things: what it is to be human; what human existence *ought* to be about: at what levels of achievement, on what conditions, and for whom; what it is to have *true* knowledge about these matters. Since such knowledge was thought to be *fundamental*, i.e., first in—foundational to—a properly ordered hierarchy of subjects, fields, and methods of acquisition, certification, and distribution of particular kinds of knowledge, philosophy came to be regarded as the realm of the architect (or discoverer) and custodian of the specifications of what it means to be human (individually and collectively), and the executive director of the disciplinary practices that employed them. Further, for some "philosophers," this knowledge and its deployment and realization in concrete social practices were to be found in the historical development of the peoples of Europe. Supposed certainty regarding matters epistemological and ontological often provided the basis for rank-ordering human groups, with rationalizing support from particular philosophical anthropologies (i.e., descriptions and prescriptions of models of and for human existence). Those who knew what knowing is were thought to be— thought themselves to be—the only persons capable of knowing *fully*. Consequently, assured certainty of knowing the "foundations," thereby the meaning, of the cosmos and of human existence, the certainty of having grasped *the* Truth, provided a great deal of rationalizing support for the intellectual (and social-political) projects of some thinkers and actors who were both arrogant, ethnocentric, sometimes racist epistemologists and social, political, and cultural imperialists.

In the "Western" intellectual traditions that have been mediated to us as "philosophy," the key conceptual vehicle for this epistemological-social project has been (and continues to be) the idea and ideal of *reason*, a con-

❧

cept that covers both the most basic structuring and ordering principles (laws) of the cosmos, and one of the most definitive aspects—the *essence*—of humans. A dominant commitment of philosophy thus became that of describing/prescribing, in the guise of "understanding," the nature of reason (cosmic and human), the conditions for its full and proper exercise by humans, and its realization in human affairs in terms of social (political, economic, cultural) organization and practices.

With the Europeanization of philosophy, particularly during the modern, Western Enlightenments, this agenda became part of the project of a rising bourgeoisie struggling to free itself from feudal domination. A philosophical anthropology was articulated that linked *freedom* to reason as a necessary condition for the latter's proper exercise, with further specifications of the economic, social, and political conditions for the organization of life that would be requisite for and conducive to the concrete (historical) realization of the exercise of reason in freedom. (The supposed historic precedent of the reason-freedom link was in political life in the polis of Athens during the fifth and fourth centuries B.C., supposedly the historic source of Western philosophy.) Among those articulating this new agenda were Kant, Hegel, Rousseau, Mill, Locke, and Marx. The modern French and British revolutions (as well as political developments that gave rise to democracies of various kinds in other places) provided concrete examples of its political actualization.

This agenda rode the Mayflower to the shores of what was to become known as "the United States of America" and fueled the revolution that launched the experiment to build a republican government with maximum social, political, and economic freedom for certain males of the "white race." For some persons, this was the playing out of the God-ordained destiny of peoples of Western Europe to spread Christian civilization and secure wealth within the framework of liberal, decentralized, representative democracy; capitalist slave and "free" labor economies; and social orderings involving class, racial, ethnic, gendered, and regional stratifications. Philosophers played significant roles at important points in the unfolding of this experiment, especially as various persons and groups struggled to forge, articulate, and legitimate a distinct national identity.[1] That struggle was waged on many fronts, often dealing simultaneously with both exogenous factors (e.g., the agenda of Britain and the King for the colonies) and endogenous factors (e.g., struggles involving Jeffersonian versus Jacksonian conceptions of "democracy," liberty versus union, the matter of slavery). This initial complexity accounted, in part, for the pluralism in philosophical articulations and practices that helped shape American history as it unfolded toward 1776 and beyond.

We should note that the term "philosophy," when used to identify particular intellectual efforts in the founding historical context, does not refer to the thought of professional teachers and scholars who were formally educated in an established discipline and ensconced in institutions of higher education. In the accounts of Schneider and of Flower and Murphey,[2] America's philosophical traditions do not have their origins in the academy but are to be found in the efforts of those who were occupied with thinking through and arguing various prescriptions for the nation being born, and with their own efforts, or those of others, to realize their programs in local, regional, and national institutions and practices.[3] The academic institutionalization and, subsequently, the professionalization of philosophy as a discipline relatively independent of reigning political, theological, and economic systems of thought were developments that would occur in the last quarter of the nineteenth century.[4]

Still, a number of persons who have been canonized as American "philosophers" were actively engaged in one of the most glaring contradictions of the American democratic revolution: rationalizations of the oppression of African peoples and their descendants. In particular, the formulation, launching, and maintenance of the agenda to create a nation-state that included legalized, race-focused slavery and, later, apartheid (with the 1896 Supreme Court decision in *Plessey versus Ferguson*) was accomplished with the support of intellectual constructions from some of the best "philosophical" minds in the country.[5] And virtually all of the canonizations of American philosophy published up to the very last few years give no consideration to the articulate voices of black Americans, or anything that might come from African-American traditions, as serious subjects worthy of study in philosophy.[6] The institutionalized collections of persons, texts, practices, organizations, and traditions that are commonly referred to as "philosophy" and sometimes taken to be the "guiding light" for human existence and development have been resources for the oppression of African people. Moreover, among philosophers in America, historically there has been a virtual total silence about the African holocaust and about the complicity of so much of "philosophy" in both the holocaust and the silence.

America at the Crossroads

The struggle to achieve a life of reason-guided liberty and prosperity for African people in the United States of America is yet to be won fully, a story to which additional chapters are added with each round of battle occasioned by crises in the social order.[7] In what follows I shall offer a brief characterization of the contemporary historical situation and that of African-Americans as a case study of an instance of America's unfinished revolution.

The Contemporary Historical Situation
While we must never take for granted the enormous achievements that are represented by existing democratic political institutions and processes, even in their imperfect realization, at the same time we must not be blind to

the significance of the changes and possibilities occasioned by recent shifts in the alignment of political forces. In general, we can see the manifestation of these changes in shifts in the direction, and reduction in the character and intensity, of federal intervention in civil, political, and economic areas of the society. In popular terminology this shift is described as a change from political, social, and economic "liberalism" to "conservatism." For the general public, the term "liberal" has referred to persons, groups, and positions committed to "change" in the social order guided by notions of freedom, justice, and equality. The "conservative," on the other hand, has been regarded as the persons or persuasions committed to "not changing" the way various aspects or dimensions of the social order are structured or oriented. Even further, "conservatives" are often regarded as persons who have attempted or advocated altering the direction of historical development along paths more in keeping with some previous period of history when, it was thought, the country was "properly" oriented and functioning.

While these popular conceptions of "liberal" and "conservative" are insufficient, they are supported, nonetheless, by a good deal of historical justification. Certainly since the decade following the Great Depression, America's political, economic, and social history has been dominated by ideas and ideals that have championed governmental intervention, especially at the federal level, in virtually all areas of life in order to achieve concrete objectives: a more stable economic order; better working conditions; civil rights for racially and/or ethnically oppressed peoples; an economic floor for the less well-off members of society; greater equality of opportunity and result in education and work; better living conditions for those most in need; improved health care and living conditions for the elderly; etc. On the other hand, during this same period the "conservatives" worked intensively to prevent, or to limit as much as possible, the realization of each of these objectives.

Generally, people of African descent in America are intimately familiar with this period of America's history, for in many respects it has been a second Reconstruction for us. Moreover, it is well understood that the "reconstruction" would not have taken place if not for the fact that more "liberal" forces held power — people who judicially, politically, and socially were open to the arguments, and could be moved by organized struggles, for redress being advanced by black people, or by others on our behalf. It is out of the experiences of this history that many African-Americans have viewed with concern the return of conservatives to political dominance at the federal level in conjunction with their ascendency in other areas, the election of Ronald Reagan in 1980 being the most compelling indication of what was to come.

This conservative wave, articulated in the domestic political economy, was signaled by the goal of gaining control over and altering the direction of the nation's economy, first and foremost, by, among other means: breaking the power of labor unions; restricting governmental involvement in the economy, leaving business and the market to steer the economy; and redistributing wealth into the hands of the wealthy, who are thought to know best how to save and invest to fuel economic development, supposedly to the greater good of all. In terms of the global political economy, the conservative agenda was devoted to being able "to control events where they happen," as then Secretary of State Henry Kissinger is alleged to have said, in order to provide stabilized conditions for capitalist economic activities. Preparations were made to return to a situation of readiness—ideologically and militarily—for intervention and dominance in world affairs whenever and wherever the economic and political interests of North America were thought to be at stake.

In many respects, the concern to intervene was generated by major political and economic imperatives: the strains in the U.S. and other capitalist economies brought about, in part, by the struggles for independence on the part of many peoples whose domination ensured the economic success of the capitalist nations. In addition, America now has to compete fiercely with other countries (Japan, Germany, France), and, in some cases, to accept positions other than first place in the design, production, and marketing of products that this country once dominated (e.g., steel, automobiles, ship building, clothing, electronics). In short, North Americans of the United States have had to come to terms with a much changed global political economy no longer under our relative control and, in many cases, much less under our direct influence.

These changes have necessitated a redefinition of "America," especially of its future prospects. The shocks and dislocations they have produced have had serious ramifications on individual and collective life. The rise of the conservatives must, therefore, be understood in part as a response to these conditions, and others more endogenous. This is especially visible in the increasing politicization of religion as various so-called conservative groups have worked to gain the dominant position from which to decide the values which will govern civil, political, economic, and even private life in the country. These changes, coming as they do on the heels of—and in large part in response to—the cultural inflections of the 1960s, the loss of the Vietnam War, and the overall loss of consensus regarding the agenda for America's development, represent a major attempt on the part of many to "get control" of the evolution of the country.

African-Americans: A Case Study

While a long view of America's history should lead us to an understanding of these recent political changes as forces that have been in the making for some time, and should thus condition us against resignation, poor judgment, and incorrect or misguided actions, still, that same study of U.S. history, when measured against our real needs and our ideas and ideals mane existence, should give us cause for serious concern about our ~~future~~ in particular, and that of large segments of the globe in general. For the achievement of political power of the "conservative" forces means that North America (and, to some extent, the rest of the world) stands at an axial point in its history.

By "axial point" I mean "major turning point" in history. We have come, in short, to a crossroads where our choices and actions will take us along paths of historical development that are of major significance, affecting our lives qualitatively and quantitatively. The conjunction of the achievement of political power by conservative forces in the body politic and their control of the economic institutions and processes of the society, guided by a plan to alter North American and world history along paths we must seriously question, means that all of us in this nation are faced with the responsibility of becoming seriously engaged in discussions regarding the country's future.

For people of African descent, this is a matter of such consequence, in view of our present situation as well as our anticipations for the future, that it cannot be taken for granted. As a matter of first priority, we need to inquire into the nature of our existence. Clarifying this question requires that it be addressed anew: What do we intend when we seek "justice," "parity," or "our rights" in behalf of individual and collective lives of decency and well-being? What would their realization on our part mean for this nation and other African peoples, other oppressed peoples? How should we go about realizing our idea of the "good life"?

In addition to the pressing nature of these questions, we black folks must be aware of the awesome and unavoidable responsibility we have with regard to them: whether we take them up responsibly or not, we shall live the consequences. Moreover, to whatever degree we engage ourselves in fashioning a history while conscious of our responsibilities, we have no guarantees of success. That is a fundamental aspect of the openness of human history. Nonetheless, for those of us who suffer in history, as well as for those who profit, it is fundamental to any hope for a different future that we realize the necessity of taking responsibility for shaping as best we can the future we wish to have. And that process of realization begins with the effort to understand clearly our present situation.

Thus do we come to the crossroads of contemporary American history. It is a time of great challenge and risk. For people of African descent, a people still struggling against the legacies of enslavement, oppression, and invidious racial discrimination, it is a time for serious, critical reviews of our situation. The revolution has not been realized for millions of us. In the words of Derrick Bell: "and we are not saved."[8]

Nor are we about to be. "Benign neglect," at best, has been the watchword, apparently, with the rise to hegemony of conservative political forces, a situation exacerbated by the agenda of stabilizing the economy, in large part by reducing federal expenditures in areas other than the military budget. This agenda has had major impact on people of African descent. To the extent that the majority of black people are not persons most well-off in the society, the program of helping those most well-off, on the theory that this, in turn, will condition greater productivity and "keep the economy going" and thus ensure that an important few will enjoy the good life of material affluence which, eventually, will "trickle down" to the rest of the society, means that many in this nation have experienced severe economic dislocation, the long-running bull market notwithstanding. We have more than abundant knowledge and living evidence of the devastating effects of poverty and economic inadequacy on all aspects of life: self-esteem; family life; educational opportunity, performance, and development; the physical development of the very young and the elderly; community life; etc.

Further, a major development during this period has been the much increased economic and social stratification among African-Americans. This is the result, on the one hand, of successful economic mobility (and all that goes with it) on the part of a significantly increased minority of black folks during the past three or four decades. This enhancement of life for recent generations of black Americans has been made possible by both the successful, heroic struggles for freedom and justice waged by thousands of black folks and others, and by the period of relative prosperity and rising standards of living that have been experienced periodically by the general population since the Second World War. On the other hand, there are segments of the black population that continue to occupy the lowest levels of the socio-economic pyramid, so much so that poverty and all that goes with it continue to be intergenerational, the promises of equal opportunity and upward mobility notwithstanding. Moreover, in every period of economic downturn, these segments of the population are pushed down even further and become even more dependent on governmental support. More profoundly, however, this support has been seriously curtailed even as the number of persons most in need has increased, persons who now comprise a socio-economic category of persons referred to as a permanent "underclass."[9]

We have, then, a complex set of social-economic dynamics that include:

1. generations of segments of the population of the least well-off among black and other folk becoming locked into the welfare system; and others beyond the welfare system, including increasing numbers of children, who inhabit our streets, doorways, parks, culverts, subway and train stations or "live" wherever they can;
2. a significant few becoming relatively (and, in some cases, absolutely) more well-off;
3. overall, a widening of the gap between the material conditions of existence, hence between life chances and life situations, of peoples of African descent and peoples of European descent, relatively; and

4. a struggle to regain and/or not lose control of schools and other key institutions of community life, such as businesses, the historically and predominantly black colleges and universities, etc.

Still, there are bright moments: the labor, civil rights, Black Power, and women's movements, combined with changes in the global historical context that continue to be consequential for us, have produced something of a mixed democratic, socialist, capitalist society, though the tensions of the mixture threaten to "tear us asunder." While the achievements are partial—though not, because of that, insignificant—the present situation, nationally and internationally, in many ways calls for the further practical realization of developments generated and guided by critical, emancipatory interests at work: in the founding of this nation (though their pervasiveness was limited); in its continued legitimation and the legitimation of actions undertaken in its name; and—from time to time—in the motivations driving philosophical praxis.

Agenda for the Future: Consolidating, Enlarging, and Completing the Revolution

Having arrived at the crossroads of a world historical situation of potential breakdown and new possibilities, crucial tasks must be accomplished if anything can or is to be done to realize greater "freedom," "justice," and "equality"; if the commitment to critical, emancipatory interests, and to praxis aimed at their concrete realization, are not to be abandoned; and if the enterprise of philosophy, at least in modes shaped by this commitment, is to play a role in this doing.

First, those of us in philosophy who share this commitment must become clear to ourselves about the responsibilities that fall to us as guardians of particular notions and practices of "critical reason." Furthermore, we must combine this clarity with an equally critical understanding of historical and cultural particularities of raciality and ethnicity, for example, that mitigate a false universalism and abstract essentialism often promoted by philosophers that mask various forms of oppression or, at the very least, foster arrogance regarding the lives and histories of peoples of color in particular, on the basis of which too many of us attempt to walk across oceans of ignorance.

Second, we must find ways to join with others who share these commitments, and with those involved in concrete struggles to realize a "better, more progressive" life—or who intend the same by the daily struggles of their lives—to clarify what such a "more progressive" life might entail, and what the concrete possibilities are for realizing it, for the good of all involved.[10] Crucial to these efforts will be to determine needs and prospects for moving from present situations to qualitatively new arrangements.

Third, we must be clear why the revolution of 1776 has not been finished (and the roles played by the philosophical enterprise in various moments of that failure), including the parts played by temporalizing compromises; bad faith; capitulation to the forces of capitalism, racism, ethnocentrism, and sexism; or commitments to hopes that were not realized because of factors that could not have been anticipated. But this effort must also take care to identify those achievements that could or ought to be preserved and carried forward in any struggle for a reformed social order. Not the least of these will be some of the conditions and practices of liberal democracy that make it possible to engage in such a venture in the most open and free fashion possible. The new order must be born in the very efforts to bring it about.

What will be the agenda for America's future? And who will set it? It seems the answers have been given in the results of recent elections. Consequently, one of the more probable future trends will be a continuation of the conditions sketched for African-Americans. More generally, we should not expect efforts to be forthcoming to complete the revolution for the millions least well-off.

Further, we must be aware of the dangers inherent in the present situation: the uncertainties and challenges to the collective American self-image, particularly to the notion of Manifest Destiny resurrected in the recent past by the Reagan administration, and the subtle yet powerful and quite effective manipulation and exploitation of the invidious race-focused passions of many persons of European descent by George Bush and his organization during the 1988 presidential campaigns. America's political culture is again skewed by such factors in large part because, more and more, many of us have relinquished our responsibilities as citizens to take up the hard task of transforming ourselves as the prelude to demanding efforts to realize a more just society. Instead, when we don't drop out altogether, we often capitulate to others ("leaders" and elected "representatives") who offer us simplicities and palliatives laced with scapegoats, the acceptance of which threaten us all. Virtually all areas of political life are now shaped by the search for a messiah who will show us the way. Our suffering tolerance of the "imperial presidency," made more comfortable for many by the skills of "the great communicator" Ronald Reagan, may well have helped to pave the road to an authoritarian state.

Some would tell us that a strong leader is needed to correct for the policies — some would say excesses — of liberals over the past few decades and to "stay the course" of the "recovery" fashioned by the policies and actions of the Reagan administration. Within this charge is a partial truth: some of the practices of liberal democracy have led to potentially socially disruptive conditions (e.g., the "desegregation" of "segregated" schools, which has resulted, generally, in the elimination of institutions vital to the cultural particularity of African-Americans). I would argue, however, that this has been the result, in part, because the *form* of democracy has, in fact, been excessively *liberal* democratic, and not yet consciously politically, economically, and culturally *social* democratic.

The neo-conservatives now in power are classically "liberal" with their emphasis on the primacy of the individual (and the nuclear family), on minimum intervention on the part of the federal government in economic matters, and on "free enterprise" capitalism to the exclusion of all else as the appropriate form of economic life. The "mess" created by the liberals is really the effect of policies based on "liberalism with a social conscience," to some extent modified by the interests of the powerful and conservative. We have been promised that the latter groups, by a return to classical liberalism, are setting things in correct order. They have failed to tell us, however, that classical liberalism (or, in today's terms "conservatism") has held power previously, and that the rise of today's "liberals" was made possible by their failures.

We cannot go forward by going backward, the admonitions of Reagan, William Bennett, George Bush, and similar others notwithstanding. We must face up to the responsibilities of taking up anew the fundamental questions of life and citizenship within the context of a historical period that is unique, even as it is structured by much that comes with us from our pasts. We are faced, in short, with setting a new agenda for America's future. And the process by which we go about this task must not be prejudiced by any unchecked assumptions.

Moreover, this task must include as one of its vital moments our full understanding of our historical situation in all of its complexity, even as we remain cognizant of the finitude of our understanding and of our efforts. And we must be prepared—armed with our best knowledge of where we are and where we have come from, and with where we think we ought to go in terms of realizing a democratically fashioned and shared vision of a collective life of humane existence—to chart and walk radically new paths carrying forward with us the positive, progressive features of our history. I offer to this effort the commitment that notions of a social order that preserve—but go beyond—liberal democracy toward a social (or socialist, if you will) democracy, of a form yet to be realized in any nation to date, ought to be near the top of the options seriously considered.

Once again: How will such an agenda be set? Who will set it? How will it be carried out? These are just a few of the many crucial questions that must be asked and answered. I do not have the answers to them. More importantly, however, it is not incumbent on me, nor on any single person or small, self-selected group of persons, to provide the answers. My call, in fact, is for *all* of us to become involved in the process of asking and answering them. Simply put: each of us must understand and accept the responsibilities of citizenship; each of us must understand the extent to which we are all potential "leaders" as well as "followers." Furthermore, our lives are already organized in many ways, at all levels: in various levels of schooling; in neigh-

borhood and community groups; in the workplace; professionally; religiously; racially and ethnically; around gender, age, and sexual orientation; etc.
From all of these places and more, _many of them overlapping_, we will have
to take charge of our lives and choose our collective history, fully conscious
that as humans responsible for others and the global environs as well as for
ourselves, we are involved in the awesome tasks of making the choices that
will determine our futures.

A New Social Movement?

How might the collection of intellectual praxes called "philosophy"
contribute to the discussion of these questions? When the philosopher —
myself, in this case — is also a person of African descent, and looks closely
and critically at the commitments grounding and structuring Euro-
American philosophy in its dominant modes, and at the agendas set for it (by
rather restricted groupings of men, for the most part, of a particular class
and of various lines of European descent whose commitments grounded and
structured its various modes and institutionalizations) in the face of the
stark realities of the enslavement and continued oppression of people of
African descent; when it is noted that the formation of the African holocaust
took place while philosophers went about their business of illuminating the
darkness of the "wilderness" of the New World frontier as Guide to the spread
of "civilization" for those who would be _free;_ when one sees that, in the face
of the glaring realities of the screams and resolute strengths of the enslaved,
then "freed," masses of African peoples and the well-cadenced, articulate
voices of the "race men" and "race women," slave and "free," who risked —
and often gave — their lives to speak for and realize the truth of our humanity; when one understands, feels, the depths of this lived history of African
peoples and our struggles against the highly rationalized degradation and
reduction of our being to thinghood, to _property_, to ontological invisibility
and marginality while, simultaneously, we were made beasts of economic
burdens, and too many of us continue living some of the worst of this nation's
exploitation and systematic underdevelopment . . . when we realize that
Euro-American philosophy responded to all of this with an almost total conspiracy of virtual _silence_, then, perhaps, we must tread carefully in drawing
on intellectual traditions or disciplines in which the overseers, apparently,
were struck deaf and blind by over-indulging themselves in listening to their
own presumptuous voices narrate inflated pictures of themselves that whit-
ed out the agenda for America's organization and development while rele-
gating African peoples to the vital role of superexploited laborers.

And there are other reasons for caution. There is no privileged role for
those of us involved in philosophy — in critical questioning in general — in
addressing the questions regarding the future and well-being of African-
Americans and this nation. We must be tempered by an understanding of
the limits as well as the possibilities of philosophical praxis, especially in its

academic institutionalization. Moreover, philosophical praxes shaped by Euro-American traditions are heavily conditioned by agendas that are often quite out of sync with social, transforming struggles, though they need not be. In their better moments these praxes can assist us in becoming clearer about humane and just enhancements to life that matter most to us, and about the ways we might go about securing them. As a brief example, I shall turn to a question that is constantly before us, and generally follows any consideration of the legacy of Martin Luther King Jr., and what we might or ought to do in the future to realized "the beloved community": the prospects and basis — the theoretical and practical dimensions and foundations — of a new black social movement.[11]

"Foundations" of a New Black Movement

The "theoretical and practical dimensions" of a "new" black "movement" admit of *many* possibilities. The following is at least one way of formulating a consideration of what is involved: the theoretical articulation of the historical basis (i.e., "foundations") of an organized contemporary movement of black people that

- is fully cognizant of the imperatives and possibilities of the present and of immediate and medium-term futures (i.e., "new");
- involves our having thought through and chosen — as critically, democratically, and systematically as possible, supported by a critical appropriation of our histories — which option(s) we should struggle to achieve, with whom, and by what means.

For many years many black thinkers, and others who are not black, have been concerned with trying to articulate a better "theory" of and for black struggle (in America in particular). Like a number of persons, I have shared the position that, in general, social struggles *need* theoretical guidance: ("practice without theory is blind"); that black struggles, in particular, need *better* theoretical guidance: for understanding the past, the present, and possible futures, and for organizing and guiding struggles to realize emancipatory social projects. In summary, we have justified these claims of need by offering critiques of our present situations, critiques which lead to judgments that the situations are undesirable and can and should be made better; critiques of the strategies and tactics that led or contributed to our being in such situations; and critiques, ultimately, of the ideational (or theoretical) complexes that we think spawned and sustain the strategies and tactics that led or contributed to the development and/or continuation of the undesirable situations, or at least failed to guide us through the successful correction of them. In doing all of this we have taken up certain commitments regarding theory and its relation to social praxis that are part of Western intellectual traditions, a relationship that is well captured in the architectural metaphor of "foundations": social movements should be guided by and have as their "foundation" correct theory.

44

Recently, however, the commitments and assumptions that structure this orientation, gathered up in and conveyed by the metaphor of "foundations" (hence "foundationalism"), have been the subject of much discussion and critique within certain quarters in Western philosophy and other fields of discussion. A brief review of some of the key points, drawing on the discussion of philosophy with which this discussion began, may be of value in this context.

In the "foundationalist" project, true or correct knowledge was required to stand (like a building) on an *invariant* base or "foundation" (e.g., ideas about human beings, about societies, about knowledge, etc.) and thus, in the context of social theorizing, to provide the most secure position from which to script social agendas. Theorizing about social developments or social changes was supposed to be connected to a "foundation" that was secure and unshifting, and to which the rest of the "structure" (e.g., arguments for particular social arrangements and for the strategies and tactics to realize them) was thought or required to be connected in the strongest possible fashion. Generally this meant that the connection was to be *necessary,* the knowledge *demonstrative,* or in nineteenth-century terms "scientific."

What recent critiques have pointed out is that the foundationalist tradition itself stood on certain notions that, when looked at closely, were seen to defeat the foundationalist project. These notions included ideas about the nature and power of human thinking, thus about human beings — really about *certain* human beings. In the foundationalist tradition, *true* knowledge (or theory) was *necessary* and *universal:* i.e., it held for any one, any time, any place since it followed the essential *laws* of thought, which themselves were said to be identical or isomorphic to, or of the same kind as, the laws of the universe. Further, it was often claimed that only certain people were capable — or were *meant* to be capable — of achieving such knowledge: generally, men of Greco-Roman, later European, descent. Many of these persons, having declared themselves successful in realizing the foundationalist project, quickly appointed themselves to the positions of ultimate definers of knowledge and, thereby, guardians and perpetuators of "civilization" (*European* civilization, that is). Within this tradition, philosophers appointed themselves the sole guardians and keepers of the human self-image, its exclusive franchisers and distributors, and likewise the exclusive certifiers of the definition and exercise of human reasoning. The foundationalist project, it turns out, itself rested on *social-cultural* bases of particular class, racial/ethnic, and gender groupings of people, thus on the agendas they championed. This project became hegemonic, to a significant degree, with the successes of European imperialism. Foundationalism, in many efforts — though not all, by any means — became court rationalist to racism and ethnocentrism and their globalization as imperialism (or, at the very least, was an inadvertent accomplice to imperialist projects).

Though this is, admittedly, a greatly simplified picture of a complex of traditions of intellectual history and social practice, one that, in drawing it, exposes me to great risks, there is still, I think, much to consider in it. What might we have in mind when searching for "foundations" for a "new black movement"? The critiques of foundationalism have, among other things, made the very idea and ideals of "rationality" and of theorizing problematic, in part by forcing us to look closely for the cultural (historical, racial/ethnic, gender, class, etc.) bases and colorations, and subsequently for the agendas, involved in them. Certainly, such critiques have been influenced, in significant part, by the struggles of oppressed peoples to be free from European domination, and free to assert — and have respected — their particularity within intellectual (and social-political) domains and practices. (They have also been influenced by critiques within discussions of the theory and practice of "science," the enterprise once thought to be the epitome of foundationalist thought.) This was the case in the critiques of Euro-American intellectual histories and practices during and after the Black Power movement.

Have we black theorists fully consolidated the insights from those critiques? Have we, in fact, carried the critiques far enough, in the light of more recent developments, such that our concern to discuss "foundations" is sufficiently critical and self-conscious? On the theoretical side, these issues have to do with our understanding of theorizing (i.e., with thought, talk, and writing about "foundations"), of the situation of the theorist and his or her relations to others over whom they theorize, and with the social objective in behalf of which, or with implications for which, we theorize. One of the major questions we must face is that having to do with our understanding of ourselves *as theorists,* across the full range and depth of our personal and shared identities, in terms of race/ethnicity, class, ideological commitments, our institutional and social situations, etc.

These matters are of particular importance when we consider questions of the relations of intellectuals and leaders to social movements, and, in particular, when we review the history of organizational formations in movements in which, for example, a self-selected group of persons has taken it upon themselves to be the "mind," the avant-garde, of the movement since, because of the superiority of the intelligence of individual members, and thus of its collective intelligence, this group knew best "what was to be done" to realize the "true" interests of those for whom (and by whom) the struggle was being conducted. I am a stern opponent of this tradition of leadership.

In searching for "foundations," then, do we overly privilege our own thinking? Have we identified and critiqued our own commitments and aspirations, compared them to the commitments of those over whom we theorize, subjected our commitments and aspirations to *their* review, and done so with openness and solidarity and according to public principles of democratic self-management? How does our theorizing stack up against the history of black thought and the complexities of different traditions and programs carried by different organizations and institutions that include assimilation, accommodation, bourgeois-capitalist pluralist integration, Left-nationalism, separatism, Marxist-Leninist proletarian internationalism, Nkrumahist and other forms of Pan-Africanism, and religious nationalism of various sorts?

Answers to these questions about ourselves and about organizing a social movement cannot be derived from theorizing itself. Nor can theory tell us what we should theorize about, or which theory is best, nor which provides the better articulation or grasp of the "foundations" for a new movement. These answers involve *choices* based on *commitments*. The choices have to do with whom we understand ourselves to be, and with what we want for ourselves and/or those in whose interests we claim to theorize and organize. As thinkers about matters of movements and their foundations, we are responsible for being as clear as we possibly can about our situations and roles as theorists.[12]

One of the most important ways to work at being clearer about these issues is to involve ourselves in a critical review of the history of black thought in this area. Such a review will, I think, reveal a number of problems. First, there is the problem, for many of us, of continuing ambivalence with regard to our identity: are we African or American? Or both? The root of this confusion is, in part, the uncritical acceptance of the ideology of America as a "melting pot." Though this notion is to some degree progressive (for example, it promotes the mediation of differences that might block the achievement of a unified society of diverse peoples), it has tended to mask the realities of ethnic, racial, and national pluralism and the hegemony of Anglo-Saxons.[13]

Another difficulty is the fact that the framework of thought that has been the foundation of much black protest has been, and continues to be, that of traditional American political democracy, civic privatism, and capitalist economics. It is argued by many that the unencumbered participation of people of African descent in national life is to be achieved and maintained through the political successes (via demonstrations and voting, primarily) won through the combined efforts of blacks, liberal whites and Jews, and organized labor (a combination that is much too often erroneously touted as a "coalition").

This strategy makes sense in some situations, but not as an exclusive orientation. Except for some among black nationalists and socialists, black thinkers have seldom broken the chains of this framework to question it radically and to risk conceiving and promoting an alternative, even while preserving the positive achievements that have been won through efforts guided by it. A key to this blockage of critical thought remains our failure to define for ourselves what would constitute full, liberated existence that does not presuppose present capitalist and liberal-democratic arrangements. Dropping this presumption would provide us with the necessary distance we need to critically assess our situation, our progress (or lack of it), and provide us the means for setting more appropriate goals.

Again, it is clear that in this country, African-American theorists, for the most part, have not come to terms with the realities of the American social order as a *capitalist* social formation and its manifest blockage of the liberation of black people. A full understanding of this system is necessary to secure that liberation. Grasping the multi-dimensionality of the American society is a first step toward realizing a full understanding.

Practical Dimensions of a New Black Movement

And there are the practical dimensions. Theorizing is itself a form of social praxis. Thus, the situation of theorists, when we are insufficiently self-critical, is always a serious matter, and is so indeed when we are concerned with setting out the "foundations" for a "new black movement." How shall the theorizing be conducted? Under what institutional and organizational arrangements? With what relations to which groupings of black people?

There is another sense of "foundations" that is still very much related to theoretical issues but is "practical" in a rather straightforward way: namely, the *people* who will be the human embodiment of this "new" movement and in behalf of whom it shall be made. *Who* are these people? How will we go about organizing a movement in which our people have been able to review and express their choices for orientations which best capture their interests, aspirations, and commitments? And who among our people shall decide these matters: The middle class? Workers and the unemployed? Students? Combinations of all of these? In what organizational and institutional contexts?

In the absence of presenting a full-blown plan in response to these questions, suffice it to say that, for me, the important point from which to begin is a commitment to those among us who are least well-off.[14] However, this commitment entails that we come to a radical and critical understanding of how those in such a state came to be that way. The result of such efforts, I am convinced, will bring us up against the American political economy, its configurations and agendas, and up against the distributed concentrations of power that sustain these agendas and configurations in their deployment, and make for our places and the conditions of our lives in the overall scheme of things.

A determination to move against this scheme will be no simple matter and will require, on the theoretical side, critical insights into, among other things, factors of race and class. And on the practical side, it will require us to move beyond the boundaries of our own communities in terms of sharing in the building of multi-racial, multi-ethnic organizations and movements. I am convinced that, while we must continue to live the lessons of our nationalist traditions that we must take responsibility for our own liberation, we cannot achieve that liberation through our efforts alone. The principles that must be put in place to secure our liberated existence *as people of African descent* would also support other racial and ethnic groups. This reality demands practical attention and must influence even our theorizing.

Also demanding an account are the demographic factors brought on by developments in the social order as a whole and within our own communities in particular. I have in mind the levels of unemployment and underdevelopment we suffer in the context of a changing economy; the shifting structures of our families; crime, drugs, and imprisonment; teenage pregnancy; the culture of "manhood" among young black males, etc. There are some things we can do in these areas that we are not doing, are not doing enough of, nor doing well enough. And it will not do to kill the messengers who take us to task for our failures and challenge us to do more.

What shall be the agenda, the "movement," for dealing with all of these matters? Given the uniqueness of the historical period and conditions, certainly a "new" movement is called for. But, in many respects, the theme for what we seek will not be new: liberation from oppression and domination, and the enjoyment of life at levels made possible by the best achievements and possibilities of the social order, at the highest levels of its development, *as an African people!* We must be prepared to shape a movement guided by a critical orientation that combines, on my terms, cultural, political, and economic nationalism with democratic, humanistic socialism. Only then will we be able to secure our existence as a people even while we share the responsibilities of shaping a multi-ethnic, multi-racial, humane society. And if we would have that society "after the revolution" or movement be what we desire, then that society must be born *in*—that is to say, *during*—the movement. Again, the principles of the new society must guide and actually inform the practices that comprise the struggle to bring it into being.

There is no privileged role in all of this for those of us involved in philosophy. Thus, what I have sketched out here must be tempered by an understanding of both the possibilities and limits of philosophical praxis, especially in its academic institutionalization. While that is, for me, a significant arena of praxis, it has it limits. Moreover, philosophical praxis is heavily conditioned by an agenda which is often quite out of sync with social, transforming struggles, though it need not be. At the very least, this can be avoided, at one level, only if we recognize the difference between theorizing practice and *phronesis,* and understand—and act in accord with that understanding—which situations are appropriate for which.

Conclusion

In a very real sense, a sense that is consistent with the critical impulse at the base of revolutionary social transformation, social development can never be finished. On one reading of the situation, what becomes apparent are the limits to the playing out of various developmental possibilities in ways that require that new structural arrangements be realized if the possibilities are to be liberated. The struggle for cultural integrity and economic justice on the part of African-Americans indicates just such a situation: only the achievement of an economic, social, political, and cultural democracy — based on principles and practices that preserve bourgeois liberalism and institute cultural, racial/ethnic, and sexual democracy that secures group identity and integrity — will provide the necessary conditions for both. Theoretical insights into these necessary conditions are preserved in the traditions of humanistic Marxism, democratic socialism, the contemporary women's movement, critical hermeneutics, and Black Nationalism, among others. The practical realizations of these conditions have, as well, their moments — in the Civil Rights and Black Power movements, in many communities and organizations across the country, in various institutional settings. The question is whether we will recover the understandings of these practical realizations as additional insights for present and future praxis, and incorporate them into our philosophical praxis as part of our agenda in behalf of a commitment to an emancipatory interest.

We need not be so committed. There is no question but we philosophers and other intellectuals could spend our lives in our various institutions struggling with discipline-immanent "problems." There are, however, other legacies, thus other possibilities. One of these is to bring ourselves into a radical and critical confrontation with our personal, disciplinary, and institutional histories in search of clarity regarding our own identity as part and parcel of the present historical situation, and in relation to futures to which we might commit ourselves. Finding others likewise engaged, it might well be that shared personal choices will be to take up the unfinished legacies of the democratization of America and the securing of a life of decency and well-being for African-Americans. And for all others, as well.

3

AFRICAN "PHILOSOPHY"?

Deconstructive and Reconstructive Challenges

The Smell of Death

A forceful debate has been raging in intellectual circles in Africa and Europe over the past forty years (and has now emerged in America) focused by questions ranging from "Is there an African philosophy?" "Did [or do] traditional Africans have a philosophy?" "Can there be an African philosophy?" to "What *is* African philosophy?" While these might appear to be benign queries that initiate and frame legitimate intellectual inquiry and discourse, for me they convey the putrid stench of a wretchedness that fertilizes the soil from which they grow. Why have such questions been asked? Why is the matter of "African philosophy" nothing more than a simple truism, or at most a heuristic for empirical identification followed by description and interpretation? More importantly, who initiated such questioning? And to what end? We can answer these last questions only by identifying the source of the stench from the former ones. That identification is what I shall offer in what follows.

The focus of my concern is indicated, in part, by the title of this essay, but in ways not all of which may be immediately apparent. First, the word "Philosophy" has been set off by quotes to warn of a number of related problems. Without the quotes (or if read without noting the quotes), the title could be read as implying that, among the collections of traditions of thought, discursive practices, texts, and various forms of association that make up the discipline and profession of "Philosophy," an enterprise assumed by some to be unified by universal and necessary principles and procedures, there are modalities and traditions that can be distinguished by their being "African."

For a brief moment I do wish to invoke precisely this understanding of the title. But only for a moment, and not in order to settle on this understanding as the promissory note for what is to follow. Rather, I wish to provoke such an understanding only to center it as an object of discussion to be subsequently displaced or decentered (that is, "deconstructed"). This is the move I have in mind and wanted to indicate it by a title that, with the assistance of punctuation, attempts to render "philosophy" problematic. Or, more precisely, attempts to suggest how the term, as a referent for a discipline (as collections of traditions of concepts and conceptual strategies, practices, texts, and persons) is made problematic by the efforts of persons identified as "African" to articulate what many of us labor to constitute as "African philosophy." Furthermore, I shall use two versions of the term "philosophy": "Philosophy" and "philosophy."[1] The first will be used to refer to the enterprise as it has been characterized by some of the dominant voices, and as it has been practiced by many of the canonical figures in the dominant traditions, throughout its Western history. The second will be used to convey a conception of philosophizing as a venture not structured by universal and necessary norms, but by norms conditioned by social, historical contingencies. Such a conception of philosophy as an enterprise, in contrast to the first, opens up the possibility of identifying other modalities of discourse as appropriate instances of a refined notion of what constitutes philosophizing, especially when these modalities are situated in non-European cultures.

But I wish to go further. While the title does not problematize "African," there are ways that contemporary African ventures in philosophizing do raise questions, implicitly and explicitly, about what it means — what is required — to be "African," and does so in ways not always seen by those endeavoring to initiate distinctively African modes of philosophizing or who are involved in reclaiming and legitimating past intellectual achievements by Africans as appropriate instances of philosophy. Each of the terms in "African philosophy" is made problematic by the very efforts to carve out or recover distinctively African modalities and traditions of articulate thought as part of intellectually and historically complex, globally dispersed enterprises of philosophy.

In some respects this problematizing is not unique and is rather easily understood in its similarities with previous and contemporary ruptures in the history of Philosophy that have either occasioned or represented efforts to rethink and redefine the enterprise, either wholly or partially. However, there are ways in which the question of "African philosophy" challenges the very idea of Philosophy as it has been construed by some of those narrating the histories and setting the agendas of philosophizing in the West, and does so in a most radical fashion.

Just how radical is indicated, in all its wretched nakedness, in the very posing of the questions whether there is, was, or could ever be something legitimately termed "African philosophy." For the issues involved are only partially concerned with disciplinary matters. The deeper issue is one with much higher stakes: it is a struggle over the meaning of "man" and "civilized human," and all that goes with these in the contexts of the cultural and political economies of the capitalized and Europeanized Western world. And when considered against the backdrop of European incursions into Africa that resulted in the enslavement and colonization of Africans and domination by Europeans of African lands and resources, the efforts to fashion "African philosophy" pose both deconstructive and reconstructive challenges.

By calling such efforts "deconstructive" I wish to associate them with a particular collection of agendas and practices within the enterprise of Western philosophy and other disciplines (recent efforts in literary criticism in particular). One of the objectives of deconstruction is to critique and displace the absolutist metaphysics and epistemology that have been thought to identify, and provide knowledge of, a rational order of axioms, first principles, and postulates that are the foundations of all that is and of knowing what is. The point of deconstruction is to show that "all philosophical systematizing is a matter of *strategy* which pretends to be based on a complete system of self-evident or transcendental axioms."[2] Having their bases in philosophical strategies, such concepts are thus *constructions,* "a product of numerous histories, institutions, and processes of inscription," whose social and historical — thus their metaphysical and epistemological — contingencies cannot be transcended by being presented as absolute, self-evident, and axiomatic.[3] To *de*construct these concepts is to review them critically by situating them in the fabric of historicity, that is, the historical, socio-intellectual contexts, in which they have been shaped and those in which we, too, have our being.[4] In doing so we become involved in "the unmaking of a construct."[5] Thus, in drawing on practices from within Western philosophy, I attempt self-consciously to "borrow from a heritage the resources necessary for the deconstruction of that heritage itself."[6]

However, "deconstruction" is but another strategy by which to read "texts" of various kinds, though one guided by a decidedly different agenda, logos, and form of self-consciousness, and with different consequences. It is a strategy that, when called "deconstruction," is principally identified with the work of Jacques Derrida, among others (including Nietzsche and Heidegger). But by no means am I claiming — nor do I wish to imply — that efforts constituting "African philosophy" are Derridian in nature or have their source in his work. Derrida himself would, I think, disallow any claim that would make either him or his work a source, an *origin*, and, thus, an *authority*. A strategy of reading/understanding that displaces its "text" into the historicity of its construction and maintenance neither originates in, nor is confined to, the work of Derrida. Rather, it is my contention that contemporary discussions about "P/philosophy" in Africa have been "deconstructive" *as a function of the historical exigencies conditioning their emergence and their agendas.*

I shall begin with a sketch and a critique of what I shall refer to as a dominant tendency in Western Philosophy and attempt to show, first, how that tendency, when joined with other factors, structured the context and terms of debates regarding "P/philosophy" in Africa. Secondly, I shall characterize and discuss, under the headings of deconstructive and reconstructive challenges, responses by various Africans intellectuals, and others, to this complex and infected situation.

The crux of my argument is that, in decisive ways, a number of the discursive practices we now identify as instances of "African philosophy" have been deconstructive and reconstructive, especially in their attempt to sanitize African intellectual practices of their necrophilia: that is, their concern to construct a self-image out of a decomposing, putrid, Greco-European philosophical anthropology that has been embodied in dominant voices and traditions of Western Philosophy. In a number of ways, the development of African philosophy as a discursive and disciplinary enterprise involves efforts to displace the dominant Greco-Eurocentric notions of idealized "man" and "civilized human" by redefining these notions and expanding their denotative ranges, in part by particularizing them to African peoples such that it becomes possible to distinguish them in non-trivial ways from peoples of European descent and from the latter's intellectual and cultural projects. A key point of this essay, on the way to a discussion of the challenges of African philosophy, is to characterize this ideal human and the wretchedness that has resulted from its imperialistic deployment, and to locate the source of the stench that too often affects intellectual praxes concerned with African philosophy.

"Manhood" and "Rationality": "Philosophy" in Dominant Western Narratives

The source of the stench is the rotting corpse of a particular complex, multi-faceted, projected (self-)image: that of the Greco-Roman/European "rational man." This was a self-image that was made a paradigm through the efforts of dominant figures in Western philosophy to identify *the* human essence (the construction of a "philosophical anthropology"). The construction of this self-image has sources in the works of Plato and Aristotle, was revised and continued by Descartes, Kant, and others. Through all of their efforts Philosophy became a venture many of whose canonical practitioners appropriated for themselves the sole right, responsibility, and capability of rising high enough intellectually to *see* the foundational (that is, the absolute and unchanging) realities in terms of which this self-image was to be articulated.[7] They also appointed themselves the sole custodians and guardians of this self-image. (For example, note the role and responsibility reserved for the philosopher-king by Plato in his *Republic*. Others after Plato would share in the belief that Philosophy was the queen of the sciences, and philosophers, consequently, were the royal authorities among intellects.)

The fulcrum of this multi-faceted self-image is formed by the notions of *logos*[8] and *nous*[9] (or, in today's language, "reason" and "rationality"). Through these concepts, and with the help of others equally important (i.e., "truth," "goodness," "virtue," etc.), a fundamental, orienting, and "grounding" linkage was made between the microcosm of human existence and the macrocosm of the cosmos, between the divine mind and/or the governing principles and processes of the universe and the mind as the *essence* of the human being: the structure of the cosmos is rational; humans reason, through *nous* or mind, and thus set into operation a dynamic structure whose principles of operation are the same as those structuring the universe; hence, the highest and most appropriate exercise of human reason or *logos* is to see and grasp those most fundamental structures or principles, and to bring human existence into accord with them. *Logos* is thought to be the "code" of Being; the task of understanding (i.e., the proper and successful exercise of human *logos* or *nous*) is to grasp and decipher this code. Philosophy, over time, becomes identified with epistemology: the specification of the norms for reasoning correctly or truthfully, that is to say, for deciphering Being and, consequently, determining the rules for correct living.

This rationalistic facet of the self-image, and the practices that sustain and seek constantly to refine it, continue to be mediated through institutionalized discursive ventures — i.e., "disciplines" — with written texts functioning as a principal means of mediation, especially those of the "great masters," who, in retrospect, have been accorded important roles in the casts of various schools and traditions narrated as the history of Western Philosophy. This self-image continues to be predominant among competing views within Philosophy, and in other disciplines (for example, theology, psychology, art, literature, and the natural and social sciences). Since the rise of modern Philosophy, beginning with Descartes in particular, the dominant philosophical self-image has been shaped by this mirroring of ourselves in a nature governed by *logos* or reason. The dominant voices in philosophy have thus been infected with logocentricism or, in the words of Foucault, with "logophilia": that is, the distorted and distorting over-commitment to *logos* or rationality where the objective is to "know" with "certainty" (which means, in my terms, to grasp and "decode" the *logos* of Being). We are led to believe that the supposed certainty about matters of "Truth," "knowledge," and "certainty" elevates Philosophy to the status of "queen of the sciences." One of the consequences of this "logophilia" has been a constant attempt by many of the mainstream figures in Western intellectual history (and, in some cases, in social and political life) to identify human telos with this sense of "rationality" almost exclusively, a telos supposedly exemplified in the history and developmental trajectory of Western European peoples.

The heavily weighted logocentrism of the "queen" of ventures of knowing that constitutes mainstream Western Philosophy, so insightfully described and critiqued by Rorty (who continues a tradition of such critiques), is only a part of the problem, though a significant part. The assured "certainty" of knowing the "foundations" of the cosmos and of existence, the certainty of having grasped *the* Truth, has provided a great deal of rationalizing support for the intellectual (and social-political) projects of masters of Philosophy, which very quickly transformed these possessors of Knowledge into arrogant epistemologists and social, political, and cultural imperialists. Supposed certainty regarding matters epistemological has tended historically to provide the basis for rank-orderings within realms of human affairs, with rationalizing support from the philosophical anthropology of ideal, rational Man. Those who know what knowing is quickly became those — and only those — who could know *fully*. Thus, deeply submerged among the facets of the constructed self-image that became embodied in a number of the dominant voices of Western Philosophy is a generally unspoken, but nonetheless very much operative, key aspect of identity: *male, rational male*, of Greek and subsequently European descent! (The "queen" of the sciences is in drag!) Across centuries of Western European history this ideal of Rational Man became a predominant model in Europe. It became culturally and politically hegemonic in other parts of the world, as well, with the spread of European imperialism, throughout the continent of Africa in particular. The death of this idealized, imperial Rational Man has been brought about, in part, by the struggles of Africans (and others) for freedom from European domination and exploitation.

It is the rotting corpse of this idealized *homo rationalis*, supposedly a distinctive human type found only among persons of the appropriate gender and racial/ethnic pedigree but fashioned in the historicities of particular, complex traditions of discursive activities, that has cast such a choking scent over Africa and the African diaspora and continues to infect intellectual discourse, including discussions of African P/philosophy. For the ideal of the "Rational Man," all the methodological strictures governing its articulation through Philosophy in the mode of epistemology notwithstanding, has been, in fact, the carrier of key elements of a particular *cultural* agenda. The notion of "rationality" itself is always shaped and valorized by the discursive context within which it is given meaning. Neither this context, nor the supposedly successful efforts of Philosophy as epistemology to articulate a historically (and thus culturally) neutral and universally binding framework for "rationality" (as in the efforts of Plato, Aristotle, Kant, and Descartes, among others), are free from the agendas of the culture within which they are situated, nor from the agendas that guide the architects and builders of such contexts or the social practices that sustain them. In fact, such discursive contexts, particularly those of philosophers, have tended to be devoted to the self-assigned tasks of defining and overseeing a society's (or a country's, or the world's) cultural and historical agenda.[10] In addition, they tend to be structured by what Michel Foucault has called "rules of discursive control."[11] Under particular circumstances, the certainty of "grounded" Knowing (according to the terms of the discursive control of Philosophy in the mode of epistemology), embodied in a dominant and dominating male, Eurocentric voice, quickly degenerates into self-assured arrogance.

Such was the case with the European encounter with the different others of Africa. There the "Man" of Western Europe assumed His Position as paragon of human development, achievement, and existence, for Whom the resources and peoples of the world were to be made part of His private dominion. This self-image and posture were off-loaded to Africa from the decks and bridges of slave ships and from inland caravans through rationalizations of greed and imperialism under the camouflage of sacred texts and practices guided by the cross, the pseudo-science of the "other" (i.e., early anthropology), and the outright practices of near genocide and dominating exploitation. The most frequent rationalization offered was that European encroachments in Africa brought "progress," in the form of the spread of Christianity and "rational" *civilization*, which would lead to the improvement of individual and social existence. By then Philosophy had become the well-entrenched, self-appointed guardian — and thus the highest expression — of this rationalization (and would remain so until displaced by achievements in the nineteenth and twentieth centuries in the natural sciences).

The effort to realize this deep-rooted project of Western "civilization" was conditioned by a principle of discrimination the basis of which is the racial/ethnic-sexual-*cultural* identity of the self-image through which it was formed and articulated. For not all persons or peoples were thought to share the level of development and/or potential required to realize rationality, especially at its highest levels: only certain males of the white race of Europe were. When these criteria of invidious discrimination were constructed and employed by an influential number of the dominant voices in Western Philosophy, in its most stringent and explicit formulations it was averred that only certain restricted groups of individuals (for example, the free Greek male in Aristotle's *Politics*) or certain "civilizations" (that of Europe, as Husserl claimed in his "Philosophy and the Crisis of European Man") had the wherewithal to engage in philosophical praxis. In even more pointed and restrictive claims by Hume and Hegel, African peoples were explicitly denied the status of rational, historical beings (even though Hegel, to his credit, is the most important figure in Western philosophy in its post-Kantian developments to take history seriously as the inextricable context within which philosophizing takes place).[12] Says Hegel:

> Africa must be divided into three parts: one is that which lies south of the desert of Sahara — Africa proper — the Upland almost entirely unknown to us . . . ; the second is that to the north of the desert — European Africa (if we may so call it) . . . ; the third is the river region of the Nile. . . .
>
> Africa proper, as far as History goes back, has remained — for all purposes of connection with the rest of the World — shut up; it is the Gold-land compressed within itself — the land of childhood, which lying beyond the day of self-conscious history, is enveloped in the dark

mantle of Night. . . . The second portion of Africa is the river district of the Nile — Egypt; which was adapted to become a mighty centre of independent civilization, and therefore is as isolated and singular in Africa as Africa itself appears in relation to the other parts of the world. . . . This part was to be — must be attached to Europe. . . .

The peculiarly African character is difficult to comprehend, for the very reason that in reference to it, we must quite give up the principle which naturally accompanies all our ideas — the category of Universality. In Negro life the characteristic point is the fact that consciousness has not yet attained to the realization of any substantial objective existence — as for example, God, or Law — in which the interest of man's volition is involved and in which he realizes his own being. This distinction between himself as an individual and the universality of his essential being, the African in the uniform, undeveloped oneness of his existence has not yet attained; so that the Knowledge of an absolute Being, an Other and a Higher than his individual self, is entirely wanting. The Negro, as already observed, exhibits the natural man in his completely wild and untamed state. We must lay aside all thought of reverence and morality -- all that we call feeling — if we would rightly comprehend him; there is nothing harmonious with humanity to be found in this type of character. . . .

At this point we leave Africa, not to mention it again. For it is no historical part of the World; it has no movement or development to exhibit. Historical movements in it — that is in its northern part — belong to the Asiatic or European World. Carthage displayed there an important transitionary phase of civilization; but, as a Phœnician colony, it belongs to Asia. Egypt will be considered in reference to the passage of the human mind from its Eastern to its Western phase, but it does not belong to the African Spirit. What we properly understand by Africa, is the Unhistorical, Undeveloped Spirit, still involved in the conditions of mere nature, and which had to be presented here only as on the threshold of the World's History.

Having eliminated this introductory element, we find ourselves for the first time on the real theatre of History.[13]

This European, male-centered effort to construct a paradigm of human being and its developmental trajectory, a paradigm that both reflected and conditioned the self-image of those involved in articulating and institutionalizing it, involved another key element, one not discussed by Hegel, commitment to which is so deep that it is virtually taken for granted that its presence is necessary (though, perhaps, not sufficient) for a people to be termed "civilized": that is, *writing*. Western philosophy after Socrates continues to be mediated through written texts, principally. Thus, it has been argued, peoples who do not write cannot engage in Philosophy, in the strict and proper sense. (Even while this is argued, often by persons — including some contemporary African philosophers — who invoke Socrates and Plato as the founding fathers of *all*, not just of Western, Philosophy, a bit of selective amnesia is at work in the reconstruction of the history of Philosophy: missing from this argument is memory of the absence of any writings by Socrates, and of Plato's own suspicion of writing.[14])

This orientation to Africa so poignantly expressed by Hegel was widely shared by many of the earliest European visitors to "the Dark Continent" (explorers, missionaries, seekers after wealth and fame, colonizers, etc.) whose travelogues and reports served to validate the worst characterizations of African peoples. These are practices that V. Y. Mudimbe aptly characterizes as the European *invention* of Africa and Africans out of the racism and ethnocentrism infecting Europe's encounters with Africans as the different and black Other.[15] In the years leading up to the 1895 partitioning of Africa, this orientation served to substantially rationalize and legitimate European racism and imperialism in Africa. The discursive practices sustaining the "invented" African, combined with those of the dominant, logocentric voices narrating histories, forming agendas, and conditioning the practices in Western Philosophy which, in its male embodiment, was postured as the paragon of human development, were key elements of the historical context from which the discursive control emerged that set the terms of the contemporary debate about African philosophy.

"African Philosophy"? Deconstructive Ruptures

A Father's Legacy: Opening the Field of Discourse

The focus of the debate was the complex of questions that asked, in various ways, whether African peoples had (or could have) developed anything termed "Philosophy." But this was only the surface issue. The deeper and more pressing question was whether Africans were fully human as defined by the reigning Greek-cum-European paradigm.

This debate began in earnest in 1945, with the publication of Placide Tempels's *La Philosophie Bantoue*.[16] The book continues to be the subject of a great deal of controversy, to say the least. A careful reading of the work, conditioned by an understanding of the larger historical context in which it appeared (i.e., the then-Belgian Congo — presently the Republic of Zaïre — in the colonial mid-1940s), and of Tempels himself, a Belgian priest, particularly his fate after its publication, should leave little doubt as to why. *Bantu Philosophy* is a deeply problematic and ambiguous book, further complicated by the intentions of its author. Consistent with one element of European projects in Africa, Tempels was concerned with "raising" the Bantu, through education and Christianization, to "civilization." On the other hand, Tempels advanced the then-revolutionary (and even humane) claim that this "civilizing" project could succeed only if Europeans understood the Bantu on the latter's own terms, that is, in terms of what Tempels regarded as their indigenous "philosophy." Further, Tempels argued that African peoples should be respected, part of the necessary way of relating to people one seeks to "civilize."

Reactions to Tempels were swift, numerous, and momentous. Colonial authorities were not pleased, for in a fundamental way Tempels's approach challenged their rationalizations of the colonization, enslavement, and exploitation of Africans and the resources of Africa. For the same reason, however, a significant number of African intellectuals were *very* pleased that, in their view, the humanity of Africans was defended and vindicated: Africans, too, were reasoning beings, thus were human. Even more importantly, perhaps, a *European* said so. Third, a number of Europeans who were more knowledgeable of, sympathetic to, and, even, more respectful of Africans than was Tempels were happy to see their views confirmed in Tempels's recapitulations of African achievements in Philosophy, that most learned of modes of Western thought. Furthermore, there was the hope that Tempels's book would lead to positive influences in relations between Africans and Europeans.[17]

Bantu Philosophy was thus an axial work. But its impact was such that it significantly influenced the terms of the debate it initiated: the conceptual strategies, the logocentric ideal, and the anthropological paradigm vested in its narrative voice were all from the cultural matrices of Europe. These were consciously mediated by Tempels (though not without serious ambiguity), and later by many African intellectuals who were socialized (i.e., "educated") in European institutions and organizations (sacred orders, for example) or institutions and organizations in Africa that were under the intellectual tutelage and administrative direction of Europeans. The continuation of this discursive control is revealed by the fact that what Tempels challenged through his work (as did others following him who continued to explore the matter of the "philosophy" of particular African peoples, or all Africans in general, guided, in a number of important cases, by the approach he had taken) was the claim that Africans were inherently (or, according to a more generous and paternalistic criticism, "due to their lack of development") incapable of the level of thought required for "true Philosophy."

The standards for "true Philosophy" were those operative in the discourses of mainstream European philosophy. An excellent example of a work invoking these standards is "Conceptual Take-off Conditions for a Bantu Philosophy," an essay by Franz Crahay that is the published version of a 1965 lecture he delivered to a predominantly African audience during a conference held at the Goethe Institute in what was then called Leopoldville, Belgian Congo (now Kinshasa, Zaïre).[18] Crahay was deeply critical of the extent to which Tempels's book, in his judgment, had been mistakenly and widely accepted as a work of Bantu philosophy, rather than as an "impetus" for such work. What he termed a "frank appraisal" of *Bantu Philosophy* required answers to two questions. The first: "Does a Bantu philosophy, within the admissible sense of the term 'philosophy,' currently exist?" This "admissible sense" of philosophy he defined as "explicit, abstract analytical reflection, sharply critical and autocritical, which is systematic, at least in principle, and yet open, dealing with experience, its human condition, and the meanings and values that it reveals."[19]

Crahay's second question was predicated on a negative answer to his first: "In case the answer to the first question is negative, under what conditions could a Bantu philosophy be founded?" In his judgment, there were certain "conceptual conditions" necessary for the development of philosophy, conditions that, he said, were not then fulfilled by Bantu peoples: (1) dissociation of subject and object through reflection; dissociation of I and others; (2) dissociation of the natural from the supernatural, of technical action and acts of faith; dissociation of the concrete and the abstract leading to dissociation of the named object and the term; (3) dissociation of time and space; (4) development from a limited concept of corporeal freedom to a "mature" concept of freedom involving a synthesis of corporeal freedom, the faculty of decision, and the "assumption of responsibility for one's actions and their rationally recognized consequences"; and (5) a desirable attitude, i.e., the avoidance of temptations of "shortcuts" or the "cult of difference."

At the heart of Crahay's argument is his notion of "philosophy within the permissible sense," even while he "tak[es] into account some innovations of contemporary philosophy and what makes for the originality of great philosophical traditions, other than the Western." When defining philosophy, in reality a complex history of differing traditions conditioned by the self-conceptions of their shapers and practitioners, he still manages to regard these as though philosophizing were a timeless unity the essence of which is captured in his definition, the differences of innovations within and among the various traditions of philosophy in Western and non-Western traditions notwithstanding. His definition, however, is a particularly modernist recasting of the meaning of philosophizing that, with Descartes, Locke, and Kant (among others), once again declares (as did Plato and Aristotle) that Philosophy in the mode of rationalist epistemology is the highest expression of human rationality and thus both identifies and exemplifies human essence. Further, Crahay's "conceptual conditions" for philosophizing are more than "conceptual." They have to do with structural features of a group's life-world and thus with their life-practices, with fundamental alterations of the ways persons or groups might go about their lives as indicated, for example, by his repeated demand for "dissociation." Philosophizing on these terms requires a particular kind of person: a radically "rational," "free," isolated "individual" in an abstract, idealized form exemplified by the decidedly Cartesian *cogito*.

Thus, it was within the context of a debate structured by these parameters that strategies emerged for establishing the humanity of Africans: it was to show, contrary to the picture of the "invented" African, that Africans also had produced "Philosophies," i.e., "rational "accounts of the world of lived experience, of the group or person, of the relations between the world and human existence, and "rational" articulations of principles for guiding social existence. In short, the task was to establish that Africans, too, were appropriately to be placed in the premier category of European philosophical anthropology, that of "Rational Man," a task that involved challenging the category's denotative limits as set by the rules of control at work in the discursive practices of European Philosophy and in their implementation in European colonialism. One of the merits of Tempels's *Bantu Philosophy* was its forcing of these issues.

The strategic, though limited, Tempelsian attack on the European "Man" as the sole embodiment of human rationality was supported by the work of other scholars, European anthropologists and historians especially, who, during the same period (1930s–1940s, and more recently), were themselves shedding light on the systems of thought of various African peoples.[20] It was in this context that the voices of Africans concerned with the liberation of African peoples from colonial domination in general, and with the reclamation of African character and being as exemplified in various fields of endeavor in particular, including that of "Philosophy," were raised in challenge to the European caricatures of black peoples, some of which efforts are now framed by the phrase "African philosophy." This framing gives identity to a new field of discourse which, simultaneously, is heavily conditioned by its European heritage (e.g., in calling itself "Philosophy") while, in many instances, challenging this very heritage and its claims to Truth, exclusivity, and, thus, predominance.

Harvesting the Legacy: Hybrids and New Strains

The business of identifying these challenges and discussing their deconstructive implications is enhanced by having "maps" of the developing field and its contours. One sign of the relative maturity of African philosophy as a disciplinary field, its youth notwithstanding, is the extent to which critical self-consciousness on the part of several persons working the field with regard to its development has been displayed in the form of articulations of various taxonomic overviews. But such efforts are not merely taxonomic orderings; they are also intended — or, even if unintended, they come to function — as normative rules conditioning discursive practices and the placement or distribution of labor in the field. For at the foundation of such efforts are definitions of what constitutes "Philosophy" or "philosophy." At the very least, they attempt to recapitulate the meanings various thinkers give to the term, either through explicit thematizations or as implicitly operative in their articulations. Thus, while we appreciate the usefulness of these taxonomies, we must not forget that they are themselves *strategic accounts* the objectives of which are achieved through their actualization: African philosophy as a *field*, that is, as a bounded *unity* with determinate contours and subregions (to play out the geographical metaphor), is to a significant degree constituted as such through taxonomic/cartographic efforts as these provide orientations for practitioners.

Yet there is a further move usually made by taxonomists/cartographers of the field: they include in the domain practices and traditions of discourse that were not themselves conditioned by an explicit sense on the part of the practitioners that they were involved in "philosophy," however broadly or narrowly conceived. The delineation of the field as an explicit discursive context is thus achieved *ex post facto*. And, to that extent, the maps and taxonomies that provide the boundaries and contours of the field themselves become part of that which they seek to define and describe. In what follows I shall briefly survey several of these efforts at overviews as a way of coming to see the field and its contours as defined by the "grid" the "cartographers" have employed (that is, the terms and strategies they use for description and analysis) to distribute the forms of African philosophy based on analyses and interpretations of the articulations (oral and written) of various persons.

H. Odera Oruka has offered an interpretation that distinguishes four "currents" in African philosophy.[21]

1. *ethno-philosophy* — works or books that "purport to describe a world outlook or thought system of a particular African community or the whole of Africa";

2. *philosophic sagacity* — the thought of "rigorous indigenous thinkers... (sages) who have not had the benefit of modern education. But they are none the less critical, independent thinkers who guide their thought and judgements by the power of reason and inborn insight rather than by the authority of the communal consensus";

3. *nationalist-ideological* philosophy — the contributions, mostly, of politicians and statesmen who led the struggles for independence and "the creation of a genuine humanist socialist order," though some of the works in this group are not, "in the strict sense, really philosophical";

4. *professional* philosophy — "works and debates of the professionally trained students and teachers of philosophy in Africa."

These categories are useful for initial surveys of the field of African philosophy, but they only provide a very rough view of the landscape. Alphonse J. Smet[22] and O. Nkombe[23] offer more insightful and nuanced mappings in their discussions of philosophical "trends" in Africa.[24] The first (in the order in which Smet and Nkombe discuss them, not in the order of either historical appearance or importance) they term *ideological*. It is a trend that, for them, includes the works and figures Odera groups in his *nationalist-ideological* current (but for Smet and Nkombe this trend includes persons he might otherwise place in the *professional* trend) as well as other "currents," "traditions," or "schools" of discourse: "African personality"; [25] Pan-Africanism;[26] Négritude;[27] African humanism;[28] African socialism;[29] scientific socialism;[30] Consciencism;[31] and "authenticity." [32]

The rule for inclusion in this trend is that all of the works and discussions are geared primarily to redressing the political and cultural situation of African peoples under conditions of European imperialism, enslavement, and colonization.

Smet and Nkombe's second trend includes works that recognize practices of philosophizing in traditional Africa, examines the philosophical elements found in various manifestations of these practices, and systematically explores these as having resulted in the development of repositories of wisdom and esoteric knowledge.[33] The principal criterion for placement in this category is the shared motivation to contest the pernicious myth that Africans have a "primitive mentality."

Smet and Nkombe's third trend, exemplified by the orientation and practices of a collection of *critical* thinkers, is characterized by the participants' reacting to the theses and projects of the *ideological* trend and those of the trend that recognizes the existence of traditional philosophies. It is from this critical group that we get the label "ethno-philosophy" applied to the modes of philosophizing of the first and second trends as a way of questioning their relevance and, especially, their validity as instances of philosophy proper.[34] However, some in this third group also critique Western conceptions of science and philosophy.

Finally, the Nkombe-Smet taxonomy includes a fourth grouping, one they term the *synthetic* current. Here are to be found the works and practices of persons who are involved in, among other things, the use of philosophical hermeneutics in explorations of issues and in the examination of new problems, some of which emerge in the African context.[35]

This map of the field of African philosophy is given even greater detail by Mudimbe's intimate, critical discussions. He identifies a first group (the principle of placement which Mudimbe uses being the idea that the participants make use of a "wide sense" of the term "philosophy"[36]) that is made up of two subgroups: the *ethno-philosophical*,[37] which includes "works arising from the need to express and to render faithfully the unity and the coherence of traditional philosophies," and the *ideologico-philosophical*, which includes works "qualified by an explicit intention to separate and to analyze present constraints of African society, marking the present and future situation, while remaining true to African ideals."[38]

Finally, Mudimbe's second group is made up of persons whose works are structured by the notion of Philosophy "in the strict sense" (i.e., in the sense articulated by Crahay). Again there are subgroupings. One comprises persons (e.g., Fabien Eboussi-Boulaga, Marcien Towa, and Paulin Houn-tondji) who are involved in reflections on the conditions of possibility of African philosophy; another, persons who reflect on the significance of Western science for African contexts (Stanislas Adotevi, Binda Ngoma, Mudimbe himself). Writings in a third group (those of Atanganga, Njoh-Mouelle, and other writings of Eboussi-Boulaga), which involve reflections on philosophy "as a critical auxiliary to the process of development," Mudimbe regards as "high points" in the field. Finally, the works of Nkombe, Ntumba Tshiamalenga, I. P. Leleye, John Kinyogo, and others Mudimbe includes in the subgroup of writings that share a concern for philosophical hermeneutics.[39]

Oruka, Smet, Nkombe, and Mudimbe each employs some notion(s) of the meaning of "P/philosophy," even if, on their interpretations, they attempt to employ the term as it is used by those whose philosophizing they endeavor to characterize. Nonetheless, in every case — whether through the meaning(s) they give to the term, or on the basis of their interpretations of the works of others, or in terms of the actual efforts of those who *do* "African philosophy" — the consequences are the same: the *deconstruction* of Philosophy.

Oedipal Moments and Maturation: The Unmaking and Remaking of P/philosophy

When read in the context of the history of Western Philosophy as narrated by predominant voices and practiced by predominant figures in general, and against the explicit derogations of African peoples by a number of these figures in particular, the advent of discussions about "African" P/philosophy is, by the force of historical contingencies, *necessarily* deconstructive: Philosophy, both as practice and accomplishment, had been reserved for the most capable few among the peoples privileged to be the "agents of the universe," peoples who had realized — in fact, were the embodiment of — the Greco-European paradigmatic forms of rational contemplation and understanding as the highest, most definitive, and most divine activities of which *true* humans are capable. Africans, in the mirror of this paragon of "Rational Man," were not truly, fully human. Thus, each instance of African philosophy — whether ethno-philosophical, ideological-nationalist, critical, or synthetic — is, at the outset, a deconstructive challenge: it decenters the concept of "Philosophy" and its discursive practices into the history of their construction and maintenance, into the historicity of the philosophical anthropology that forms the fabric of their textuality and thus of the race/ethnicity, the gender, and the cultural agenda of the voices in which they became embodied and the practices through which they were constituted and institutionalized.

This is clear in the case of works in the category of ethno-philosophy (though not without serious problems). The discursive practices and texts grouped in this subfield have their source in, among other things, the desire to replace the caricature of the invented African with an image reconstructed (and rehabilitated) through the extension of the denotative range of the privileged category of "rational human animal" to "traditional" Africans. The effort to fulfill this agenda involves the explicit representation of the conceptual insights and practices of particular ethnic groups.[40] Here one concern — certainly a major effect — is to show the *particularity* of philosophy while supporting, at the same time, arguments in behalf of a reconstructed sense of its *universality*. But the historical contexts within which many of the works in this subgroup emerged as well as the agenda of the challenge were to significantly influence the choice of strategies employed in the construction of the arguments supporting the presentations of African "philosophies" or African "thought." Even when the arguments were not advanced by anthropologists themselves, the proponents tended to make use of ethnographic findings and/or the techniques of ethnographic description to identify the practices (linguistic, intellectual, and otherwise) and concepts of particular African peoples which, it was argued, embodied their "P/philosophy." Thus did works of this genre come to be labeled "ethno-philosophy."[41]

This ethno-philosophical challenge was given a tremendous boost by other historical developments: i.e., the struggles for the liberation of the colonial states of Africa from European hegemony, struggles which were to culminate, beginning in the early 1950s, in the establishment of politically independent African nations. These developments had a profound impact on philosophical praxis in Africa. For the struggles harnessed into powerful political, social, and cultural movements the challenges on the part of many Africans and people of African descent (and some Europeans) to the "invented African." As part of this challenge, a number of important African thinkers/activists took up key terms in European discourses (socio-political, cultural, and disciplinary, including anthropology, religion, and philosophy) and challenged both the historical and social range of their applicability, and challenged their very foundations.

An important example of such a challenge is the critical examination of that central motif of Western Philosophy — the characterization of the fully developed human being as "Rational Man" — and the reconstruction of the different, yet fully human, African by the proponents of Négritude, one of the most deconstructive forms of African philosophizing. In the words of Abiola Irele:

> A distinctive vision of Africa and the black man, and of his relation to the world . . . stands at the very heart of the literature of Négritude and informs it in a fundamental way, provides what can be said to constitute the "mental structure" . . . that underlies the imaginative expression of the French-speaking black writers, and which emerges with a sharp clarity in the ideological writings. The rehabilitation of Africa which stands out as the central project of Négritude thus represents a movement towards the recovery of a certain sense of spiritual integrity by the black man, as the definition of a black collective identity, as well as of a new world view, derived from a new feeling for the African heritage of values and of experience.[42]

In this we have a major challenge to the notion and ideal of what it means for *Africans* to be human. Further, we have the reclamation of the place of Africans on the stage of human history, but now cast in roles defined by Africans who have structured those roles out of what *they* take to be the meanings of African histories and existences, both of which are seen as decidedly different (or ought to be) from the histories and existences of peoples of Europe.[43] But the complex of strategies that we now refer to as Négritude involved much more than the rehabilitation of Africa. In addition to the construction of a philosophical anthropology carved out of African ebony, there was also an effort to displace from its dominating position the paradigm of rationalist epistemology championed by proponents of Philosophy by arguing in favor of an epistemology that had its basis in African racial/bio-cultural life-worlds. In the words of Léopold Senghor, one of the initiators and chief theoreticians of the Négritude movement: "European reasoning is analytical, discursive by utilization; Negro-African reasoning is intuitive by participation" and "Knowledge . . . is not the superficial creation of discursive reason, cast over reality, but discovery through emotion: less discovery than re-discovery. Knowledge coincides, here, with the *being* of the object in its discontinuous and indeterminate reality."[44] In addition, for Senghor and other Négritude writers, African historical-cultural life-worlds are shaped by values and aesthetics particular to African peoples. Part of the Négritude agenda was to identify the elements and practices constituting these life-worlds and to reclaim and rehabilitate them from the twisted amnesia resulting from European colonialism and enslavement. Thus, in addition to arguments in behalf of an African epistemology, Négritude bequeathed African-centered aesthetics, axiology, and socio-political philosophies.

Like all discursive ventures, Négritude was not a homogeneous unity, nor is there consensus regarding the meaning of the term.[45] And there continue to be powerful (and sometimes persuasive) criticisms of Senghorian Négritude. Nonetheless, the Négritude arguments, fundamentally, involved a profound displacement of the African invented by Europeans. It is this African challenge and displacement, through radical critique and counter-construction, that have been deconstructive in particularly powerful and influential ways: involving direct attacks on the assumed embodiment of the paragon of humanity in whites of Europe, an attack that forces this embodiment back upon itself, forces it to confront its own historicity, its own wretched history of atrocities, and the stench of the decay announcing the impending death of the hegemonic ideal of the Greco-European Rational Man. Perhaps no other European has articulated this experience better than Sartre:

> Here . . . are black men standing, black men who examine us; and I want you to feel, as I, the sensation of being seen. For the white man

has enjoyed for three thousand years the privilege of seeing without being seen. It was a seeing pure and uncomplicated; the light of his eyes drew all things from their primeval darkness. The whiteness of his skin was a further aspect of vision, a light condensed. The white man, white because he was man, white like the day, white as truth is white, white like virtue, lighted like a torch all creation; he unfolded the essence, secret and white, of existence. Today, these black men have fixed their gaze upon us and our gaze is thrown back in our eyes; black torches, in their turn, light the world and our white heads are only small lanterns balanced in the wind. . . . Being is black, being is of fire, we are accidental and remote; we have to justify for ourselves our customs, our techniques, our "undercooked" paleness, our verdigris vegetation. By this steady and corrosive gaze, we are picked to the bone. . . . If we wish to escape this fate which closes in upon us, we can no longer count upon the privilege of our race, of our color, of our techniques. We shall be able to rejoin the human hegemony only in tearing off our white underclothing and in attempting simply to be men.[46]

The reconstructive aspects of this challenge are to be found in the self-definition, the specification and reappropriation of an African authenticity and legitimacy, in the disproving — the displacing — of the inventive discourse, and, most importantly, in the efforts to reclaim control over African historicities and the interpretation of African histories in general, and African philosophical histories in particular (though it must be noted that there were and are persons in Africa for whom the task is that of proving themselves and other Africans to be worthy of assimilating into a humanity defined in Eurocentric terms).

The same is true for many of the other strategic projects grouped together as *nationalist-ideological* philosophy, and for a number of those which are part of the *critical, professional, synthetic* groupings. In each of the complex of activities comprising these approaches to philosophizing are particular works and strategies that in very real ways are characteristically deconstructive in a Derridian sense: they preserve (are constituted by) relations of difference. For in each case the object of the strategy — the articulation of a "text" of "African philosophy" — is constituted *within* the bounds of that which it challenges (i.e., Philosophy), but as both *similar* (philosophy) and *different* (African). Such works have their distinct identity, through the rules governing discourses of/about P/philosophy, only in their difference, a difference gained through an ineliminable relation with that from which they differ.

Other examples of what I have been calling deconstructive challenges to Western Philosophy can be drawn from the various subfields or trends of African philosophy. On the way to closing off this discussion, I shall at least identify what I take to be other ruptures in the history of philosophizing in terms of the efforts of various thinkers of African descent to reconstruct histories of African philosophizing, efforts that are self-conscious in challenging the received wisdom of white lies about both Philosophy and Africa. Suffice it to say that the arguments in support of these claims are deeply problematic and are far from settled.

The reconstructive work of three persons is noteworthy here. First, that of George G. M. James.[47] According to his ground-breaking but poorly presented arguments, Ancient African (i.e., Egyptian) philosophy was the precursor to and source of much or all of Greek philosophy. Henry Olela continues this line of argument and adds a second claim, namely, that "black [American] philosophy" is (and should be) reducible to African philosophy.[48] Finally, Lancinay Keita proposes the following periodization of African philosophy: (1) the *classical* period — a time, supposedly, when Egypt was peopled and governed by black Africans;[49] (2) the *medieval* period — one of Islamic influence on literate expression in North and Central Africa during the time of the medieval states of Mali, Ghana, and Songhay; and (3) the *modern* period: "less well developed than its two preceding moments, since philosophical traditions have become somewhat distorted as a result of the colonial experience. As a result, the best works, as is expected, are political and literary in nature."[50]

The significance of these works, their limitations and controversial agendas notwithstanding, lies, in part, in the concern of the authors to take up the tasks of reconstructing the history of Western Philosophy in a direct challenge to the dominant narratives which have claimed Greece as the site of Philosophy's singular origin. In the narrative reconstructions of James, Olela, and Keita, we are taken back to Egypt — *African* Egypt, not the Egypt of Hegel that was annexed to Europe — as "source." In light of the untruth racking the embodiment of the mainstream narratives of Philosophy, this possibility is an issue of very real importance. It is to be hoped that it will soon receive the disciplined, systematic attention it deserves and requires. Martin Bernal's *Black Athena: The Afroasiatic Roots of Classical Civilization* has contributed a great deal to our understanding in just this way.[51] It remains to be seen whether professional philosophers will study this provocative text, which seriously disrupts longstanding genealogies of Western philosophy, and revise their understandings, their intellectual genealogies, and thereby their identities.

A Logic Come Full Circle

I will conclude by taking up, very briefly, one of the lines of development that indicates quite well something I referred to near the beginning of this essay: namely, the way in which discussions of African philosophy render the notion of "African" problematic.

The different strategies grouped together as *ideological-nationalist* philosophy — especially those of the Négritude authors — have been most concerned with addressing the question of the meaning of "African," especially through efforts directed at reconstructing and rehabilitating "African" while forging identities and notions of authenticity thought to be appropriate to the exigencies of modern existence. And, as I have attempted to show, these efforts have their locus in, and thus derive their meanings from, the historical context of the institutionalization of the practices, and their rationalizations, of European racism and imperialism in the colonization of the African continent, the enslavement and dispersal of Africans to the New World, and the mediation of these rationalizations through the self-appointments of mainstream figures of Western Philosophy and its historians.

But the concern has not been limited to nationalist-ideological discussions. Even for those persons less concerned with rehabilitation and the formation of identity, and who are generally not concerned to deconstruct Philosophy (e.g., persons grouped in the categories of critical, synthetic, professional philosophy), there is, nonetheless, a need to circumscribe the (for them) proper meaning and bounds of "African," a need to explain — if not to justify — the meaning and use of "African" to qualify "P/philosophy," a need that emerges with the very initiation of the discourse about "African philosophy," a need, finally, that is required by the rules (and anthropological commitments) controlling the dominant traditions in Philosophy.

The ostensible issue is the meaning of "philosophy." And often it is the Crahay-type of definition (more or less) that is accepted as appropriate. For some persons the field of "African" philosophy is distinctive only to the extent that the persons involved in it "just *happen*" (accidentally) to be African. Philosophy proper, it is said, is, as praxis, the same regardless of where it is engaged in, or by whom: i.e., it is characterized by "rationality" (in the mainstream sense) or "science" (in an equally mainstream positivistic sense) and is thus *universal* in both its unity and singularity and its empirical manifestations. While we might refer to the mainstream characterizations of philosophy as "European," rationality is not the birthright of Europe, nor of the Greeks, but is a capability shared by all persons, their race or ethnicity notwithstanding. "African" philosophy, then, by this argument, is distinguished only by the *geographical origins* of its practitioners, not by a content somehow made different by their "Africanness" (*à la* the proponents of Négritude). Hountondji is representative of persons holding this view:

> What is in question here, substantially, is the idea of philosophy, or rather, of African philosophy. More accurately, the problem is whether the word "philosophy," when qualified by the word "African," must retain its habitual meaning, or whether the simple addition of an adjective necessarily changes the meaning of the substantive. What is in question . . . is the universality of the word "philosophy" throughout its possible geographical applications.

My own view is that this universality must be preserved — not because philosophy must necessarily develop the same themes or even ask the same questions from one country or continent to another, but because these differences of *content* are meaningful precisely and only as differences of *content*, which, as such, refer back to *the essential unity of a single discipline, of a single style of inquiry* [emphasis added].

The essential point . . . is that we have produced a radically new definition of African philosophy, the criterion now being the geographical origin of the authors rather than an alleged specificity of content. The effect of this is to broaden the narrow horizon which has hitherto been imposed on African philosophy and to treat it, as now conceived, as a methodical inquiry with the same universal aims as those of any other philosophy in the world. In short, it destroys the dominant mythological conception of Africanness and restores the simple, obvious truth that Africa is above all a continent and the concept of Africa an empirical, geographical concept and not a metaphysical one.[52]

I find this view particularly disturbing. But it is an excellent example of the manner in which the historical forces mediated in the language and discursive practices of Philosophy explode the limits of its structuring rules. As Hountondji plays out his argument, it quickly unravels. It takes only a few probing questions to uncover the fact that Hountondji uses "African" as a signifier not just for *geographical* origins, but also for race/ethnicity. This attempt to circumscribe "African" is frustrated by the play of forces that brings on a deconstructive encounter with the "white mythology" infecting Philosophy. At the core of this mythology is a substance-accident metaphysics grounding a supplemental philosophical anthropology: the soul, consciousness, or the person is regarded as the *essence* of the human being; their race, ethnicity, or gender is secondary or accidental.

This is at best naive. No living person is accidentally or secondarily African or European, that is to say, is of a particular race or ethnicity "accidentally" while being a "person" or "human" *substantively*. While some important gains have been realized in the political arena with the help of the "substance-accident" and "universal-particular" strategies of Western metaphysics, to forget that they are precisely *strategies* and then use them to conceptualize concrete persons or peoples as though they capture and express differences of our effective history is to succumb to some of the worst seductions of the dominant voices of mainstream Western Philosophy: the premature, false, abstract universality of an equally false and abstract "humanity" invoked prior to the holding of appropriate conversations in which all of the key issues, including "rationality" and "human," are themselves the first matters of discussion.

Again, there is serious naiveté with regard to the notion of philosophy as a "single discipline" having an "essential unity" and a "single style of inquiry." No serious, critical encounter with the history of Western philosophy can leave one with this view — unless, of course, this encounter is led by the historians of Philosophy. On the contrary, what a critical review of the various traditions grouped together as philosophy reveals is that many different strategies have been employed often with each claiming to be *the* correct and most appropriate form. Thus, the history is rich with palace revolutions. What is consistent is the use of "philosophy" as the signifier for particular discourse/strategy candidates, and, sometimes, the sharing of family resemblances among various candidates. Only from the vantage point of great distance, with the perspectival distortion, and loss of cultural detail and particularity, that accompanies it, do we group all of these candidates together and regard them as a single discipline. The basis of what unity there is, perhaps, is that the participants in these discourse/strategy ventures, using what passes for them as appropriate definitions, regard what they do as "philosophy," or those of us constructing the history of such ventures do so in hindsight using *our* definitions. There is no timeless *essence* or "essential unity" that characterizes all philosophizing, certainly no *single* style of inquiry, as Hountondji would have it.

Philosophy has been (and continues to struggle to be, in the rearguard actions of various incarnations) one of the most privileged of disciplines, especially in its self-appointed role as guardian of the self-image of the brokers of Western history and culture. Were this not the case, there would have been no debate about "African philosophy." Thus, any discussion of *African* philosophy involves, *necessarily*, confronting this privileged self-image. It is this confrontation that problematizes "African" and forces its deconstruction/reconstruction in its relations of difference with "European." But this confrontation leaves the complex fields and histories of philosophizing in the West — past, present, and future — forever altered, in ways similar to (because part and parcel of) the alterations of socio-political landscapes involving the West, Africa, and the African diaspora. The fraudulent Greco-European monarchy *philosophia* is no more.

Does this mean that Philosophy is left without universality and unity? Yes. Does this mean that philosophy is without universality and unity? "Yes" again. But philosophizing never had these characteristics in the sense proclaimed by Philosophy. What the ruptures and challenges of African philosophy do mean is that unity and universality can be achieved only through consensus regarding discursive practices. And such an achievement, if realized, will always be tentative, a result of *phronesis*. It is my hope that we find our way to this and other important universals-through-consensus by way of open, "edifying" discussions, in the words of Richard Rorty, discussions in which all of the world's peoples are participants and which are conducted according the best possible realization of Habermasian conditions for undistorted communication, not through an attempt to escape from key elements of our historicity — our race/ethnicity and gender included — no matter how well intended or how well rationalized through methodological moves fashioned while looking at ourselves in the mirror of nature, a mirror so captivating that it sometimes blinds us — or we allow ourselves to be blinded — to the inextricable historical, cultural, racial/ethnic, and gender components that give our philosophizings their prismatic character.

4

AFRICANA PHILOSOPHY

Introduction

Just over fifty years ago it was proposed by some persons—in important instances persons of European descent—that certain modes of thought of African peoples should be regarded as "philosophy."[1] Very quickly this proposal became a matter of serious and intense debates. Both the debates and the contexts out of which they emerged and in which they were waged were structured by the domination and exploitation of Africans by peoples from Europe in whose behalf some among them rationalized their inhumanity using terms and strategies infected with racism (that is, rank-ordering distinctions among types and groupings of people on the basis of their raciality) and assisted by the efforts of particular European philosophers. That Africans could philosophize was for many persons, then, a very bold declaration or proposal, at the very least. In light of the rationalizing redefining and attempted refashioning of African peoples into subordinates to the "civilized" peoples of Europe that were part and parcel of the enslavement and colonization of Africans, it was all but unthinkable that modes of thought of persons African and of African descent could be appropriately characterized as instances of philosophy: as achievements of the intellect that exemplified rationality at its best, that most definitive characteristic of the human species. Such achievements were long said to be possible only for the most developed of persons, namely, certain males among peoples of the white race of Europe.

Today, of course, there are a significant number of formally trained African philosophers throughout the world. And to a great extent the *explicit* development of discursive formations within the discipline of philosophy that are distinguished as being "African" or those of persons "African-descended" has been unfolding through efforts to identify, reconstruct, and create traditions and repositories of literate thought, both oral and written, as forms of philosophy by persons African and African-descended. In the context of such endeavors, persons past and present without formal training or degrees in philosophy are being worked into developing canons.[2]

Similar (and related) circumstances and developments condition efforts to give shape and meaning to a distinct disciplinary enterprise of African-American philosophy. For example, a review of the tables of contents of collections of writings organized under the heading of "American Philosophy" will disclose that, in virtually every case, *no* writings by persons of African descent have been included. And histories of American philosophy tend to be equally silent about the articulate thoughts and writings of Africans-becoming-"Americans" as instances of philosophizing. There are, of course, long, rich traditions of critical thought by women and men of African descent articulated in speeches and writings of various kinds. Many of these are now being appropriated as instances and traditions of philosophizing.[3] And during the last two decades in particular, with the significant increase in the number of Americans of African descent with formal training in philosophy (nonetheless, still a very small number: fewer than one percent of professional philosophers in America), many of whom underwent this training during the highly charged periods of the Civil Rights, Black Power, and African independence movements, efforts to construct a disciplinary formation and to identify and refine traditions of intellectual praxis as distinctively African-American philosophy continue to be a major concern of several engaged and determined persons.[4]

"Africana philosophy" is the phrase I use as a "gathering" notion under which to situate the articulations (writings, speeches, etc.), and traditions of the same, of Africans and peoples of African descent collectively, as well as the sub-discipline- or field-forming, tradition-defining, tradition-organizing reconstructive efforts which are (to be) regarded as philosophy. Use of the qualifier "Africana" is consistent with the practice of grouping and identifying intellectual traditions and practices by the national, geographic, cultural, racial, and/or ethnic name for the persons who initiated and were or are the primary practitioners — and/or are the subjects and objects — of the practices and traditions in question (e.g., "American," "British," "French," "German," or "Continental" philosophy). However, "Africana philosophy" is meant to include, as well, the work of those persons who are neither African nor of African descent but who recognize the legitimacy and importance of the issues and endeavors that constitute the philosophizing of persons African or African-descended and who contribute to discussions of their efforts, persons whose work justifies their being called "Africanists."

But what is it that is characteristic of the philosophical practices, and the results therefrom, of African and African-descended thinkers that distinguishes — or should distinguish — the efforts *by virtue of their being those of persons African and/or African-descended*? Is there, or can there be, a properly determined field of philosophy that is constituted by the efforts of persons of a particular racial or ethnic group? Further, given the global dispersions and migrations of African peoples and the subsequent development of regional (e.g., Caribbean), complex local-national (e.g., African American), and nation-state socio-political and ethnic groupings ("Nigerian," "Kenyan"), can we speak cogently of the philosophizings of persons from such historically, culturally, and socially diverse locations by using "Africana philosophy" as a covering notion?

These are some of the questions I wish to explore. In the process I hope to clarify, for myself especially, the extent to which it makes sense to continue using "Africana philosophy" as an "umbrella" notion under which can be gathered a potentially large collection of traditions of practices, agendas, and literatures of African and African-descended peoples. I propose to review, briefly, developments in what is now referred to as African philosophy and particular instances of African-American thought as examples of philosophizing. As well, however, I shall set the stage for exploring whether it makes sense to speak of Africana philosophy in even stronger terms: namely, as a venture that should be bound by *particular* norms appropriate to discursive practices by and/or in the interests of African and African-descended peoples, norms that have their origins, justification, and legitimacy in the life-worlds of African peoples, first and foremost, in contrast to norms from the life-worlds and agendas of people who are neither African nor African-descended. At issue is whether raciality and ethnicity have any normative saliency for the production of various forms of knowledge, for philosophizing in particular.

African Philosophy

The publication in 1945 of Placide Tempels's *La Philosophie Bantoue*, one of the earliest characterizations in modern history of African intellectual efforts as philosophy, initiated contemporary discussions regarding African philosophy.[5] Emerging during the apex of European colonization in Africa, the discussions were much influenced by this context and by anti-colonial struggles. The focus of the discussions was whether African peoples could *have* or *do* philosophy. But this was only the surface issue. The deeper and more pressing question was whether Africans were fully human as modeled by the then-reigning Greek-cum-European philosophical-anthropological paradigm centered on the capacity for reasoning.

Tempels evoked strong reactions, both positive and negative, because the major thesis of the book, that Bantu Africans were guided in their living by a distinct "philosophy" (though they were not aware of it as was Tempels who, using the resources provided by his knowledge of Western philosophy, had the ability to engage in a hermeneutic of the language and practices of the Bantu and extract for analysis and presentation the operative constitutive epistemology and axiology), challenged the rationalizations of the colonization, enslavement, and exploitation of Africans and the resources of

Africa. A significant number of African intellectuals felt that the humanity of Africans as beings of reason was defended and vindicated, all the more so by a European. Even further, particular European researchers and scholars with years of contact with various African peoples were happy to see their positive assessments of Africans confirmed in Tempels's report of Bantu Africans having a philosophy, an achievement only made possible by the proper exercise of a relatively highly developed capacity for reasoning.[6]

There were, of course, those who challenged Tempels's claim. As noted in the previous essay, Franz Crahay, in his criticism of *La Philosophie Bantoue*, argued against what he regarded as the mistaken acceptance of the book as evidence of Bantu philosophy, rather than as what he termed an "impetus for" philosophy. His "frank appraisal" of the book led him to conclude that Bantu Africans were not yet capable of philosophizing "within the admissible sense" of "philosophy." Crahay went on to specify certain necessary conceptual conditions that had to be satisfied by Bantu thinkers in order to qualify their thinking as philosophizing.[7]

Other scholars who have investigated thought systems of various African peoples have made substantial contributions to this discussion.[8] In addition, it was in the context of this debate that Africans concerned with the liberation of African peoples and the reclamation of their indigenous cultures from colonial domination challenged the caricatures of black peoples perpetrated by many peoples of European descent. Efforts to identify or to elaborate an instance of articulate thought as distinctively "African" philosophy have to a large extent been part of this challenge and have come to be part of efforts within a particular field of discourse (i.e., philosophy) that continues to be conditioned in various ways by European legacies while, in many instances, challenging the claims to truth, exclusivity, and predominance that for centuries have been constitutive aspects of these legacies and driving forces in the imperialist encounters of European peoples with peoples in Africa and elsewhere.[9]

The debate about whether African or African-descended peoples have philosophies or can philosophize has now given way to explorations of a broader range of concerns. On the African continent, pursuit of these concerns has resulted in the emergence of different philosophical trends or schools of thought; a growing, diverse body of philosophical literature; the formation of national and international professional philosophical organizations; the hosting of national, regional, and international conferences; and the development of programs of study in African institutions leading to advanced degrees in philosophy with strong emphasis, in a number of instances, on African philosophy.

African-American Philosophy

The crucible for New World Africans has been (and continues to be) life thoroughly conditioned by various forms of systematized oppression and class exploitation motivated and rationalized by white racial supremacy, and further complicated by related matters having to do with sexuality and gender. In a dialectic of racist imposition and creative response in the struggle to survive, reproduce, and flourish, New World African descendants-become-Americans have had to form and perpetuate new ways for getting on with their lives. In doing so we have had to face a recurrent and always decisive aspect of life in the racialized crucible: the struggle to resolve tensions affecting identity-formation and all that is related in important ways to identities, tensions involving the ambiguities and ambivalences of being, in important senses, both "African" and "American." Historically, how these tensions were confronted by particular persons and communities in the forging of identity was crucial to forming or sharing agendas and exercising strategies devoted to securing *freedom*, for the person and the race. For this and other important reasons differences have always existed among thinkers of African descent in the U.S., which have resulted from and led to distinct foci, strategies, and objectives of discursive traditions and practices. A brief review of several complexes of socially engaged thought will provide examples of what today is being recovered and reconsidered by several persons as instances of African-American philosophy that, in the words of Leonard Harris, were, indeed, "philosophy born of struggle."[10]

First a bit of historical context. From the earliest presence of Africans as slaves in the portion of the New World that was later to become the United States of America, militant anti-slavery agitation was a prominent endeavor among "free" persons of color in the North and East (early 1600s through the Civil War of 1860–1865). Frederick Douglass was one of the most well-known participants in the movement to abolish slavery. (The movement had its foundations in the efforts of black folks, though white abolitionists came to play dominant, controlling roles.) Two decades of post-Reconstruction separatist and emigrationist activity followed the Civil War (mid-1860s–1880s) but was soon eclipsed by a period during which the accommodationist strategy of Booker T. Washington was predominant (1880–1915), though not without "radical" challenges from W. E. B. Du Bois and others who initiated the Niagara movement to counter the effects of Washington's agenda and to press for full and immediate citizenship rights for African-Americans. The National Association for the Advancement of Colored People (NAACP), which grew out of the Niagara movement, and the National Urban League were organized toward the end of this period (in 1909 and 1910, respectively) and would play major roles in promoting the melioration of racial apartheid by utilizing legal attacks and organized protests to combat invidious racial discrimination in schools, work places, and public transportation and accommodations.

Booker T. Washington's death in 1915 occurred during a period when the American economy (and economies in other countries), influenced by the First World War and other momentous developments, was undergoing major transformations: in the North and Northeast, industrialization created historic opportunities for work; in the South, agriculture was being transformed by mechanization and subsequent decreasing reliance on the labor of peasants and tenant farmers while the region was undergoing greater industrialization. These developments, combined with hopes for life unrestricted by violent racial segregation, prompted millions of black folks in the defeated Confederate South to migrate north, east, and west into America's industrial heartland. With their settlement in these regions in large numbers, conditions developed that became the nurturing soil in which various forms of nationalism flowered once again (during 1916–1930), and Washington's accommodationist approach declined in significance. The organizational activities and achievements of Marcus Garvey and the Harlem Renaissance were two of the most significant nationalist developments. Further, recovery from the Depression and its dislocations, spurred by the Second World War and, later, the Korean War, conditioned several decades of economic expansion that led to rising prosperity for urban, industrial workers in particular. Among these were a significant minority of black persons who ushered in the rise of the modern black middle class. A significant number of these persons would rise to prominence and to historical significance as leading players in various segments of the Freedom Movement, particularly those areas in which "civil rights" and "integration" were objectives of black struggle, as the influence of an earlier generation of nationalists waned (1950s to mid-1960s). The integrationists would be strongly challenged, and momentarily eclipsed, by young Turks, inspired by the likes of Malcolm X and Frantz Fanon, who initiated yet another resurgence of black nationalism in what came to be known as the Black Power movement (mid-1960s to the early 1970s).[11]

Within this 300-year sweep of history it is possible to identify several philosophical-political orientations. *Assimilation*, broadly conceived, is the name for projects that would have one racial and/or ethnic group absorbed, physically and/or culturally, by another, the former taking on the defining characteristics of the latter and relinquishing its own racial and/or ethnic distinctiveness. For African-American assimilationists, the "official" cultural, social, political, and economic ideals of the American republic, which have emphasized pursuit of the good life "without regard to race, creed, or color," have been accepted as sufficient and appropriate goals for African-American life. Frederick Douglass was one of the most well-known of African-American assimilationists.

As noted, *accommodation* was the prevailing agenda and strategy during the period when the influence of Booker T. Washington, its most successful purveyor, was dominant. For Washington, the economic and political hegemony of white folks was not to be challenged directly but was to be finessed by subtle strategies of seeming accommodation while black folks prepared themselves for economic self-reliance and eventual full political citizenship that was to be "earned" by forming and exercising good character and responsibility through education for and the practice of honest work.

Washington's strategy was fervently opposed by W. E. B. Du Bois.[12] One of the foremost intellectuals in American history, Du Bois was a proponent of what I term *pluralist integration*: that is, the commitment to achieving a society that is integrated socially, politically, and economically though made up of a plurality of racial and ethnic groups that maintain and perpetuate their racial and ethnic distinctivenesses to the extent that doing so does not threaten the integration of the social whole. Du Bois was thus something of a *nationalist* in being committed to the proposition that black folks should articulate and appropriate a racial identity based, in part, on biological descent but, more importantly, on shared history and culture.[13] In this respect Du Bois might best be classed as a cultural nationalist. Other forms of nationalism include economic (capitalist or socialist) and political nationalism (democratic, socialist, or dictatorial) either of which might — but need not — promote varying degrees of racial and/or ethnic integration or separatism.[14]

In contrast to those who have been called "left nationalists" (i.e., nationalists committed, as well, to socialist or communist agendas and strategies, such as C. L. R. James and Grace and James Boggs[15]), are those African-American thinkers who have been committed socialists or communists for whom "race" is at best an epiphenomenon secondary to the primary contradictions of class-conflicted capitalist societies. For such persons racial (or ethnic) distinctions will disappear with the transformation of capitalist social formations into self-managing socialist or communist societies in which neither race nor ethnicity will be of any social significance.

Such thought/praxis complexes are among some of the most ready candidates for being regarded as instances of African-American philosophy. Of course, organizing, examining, and re-presenting the articulations of these persons and movements as "philosophy" involves positioning them in ways and contexts not intended by the "authors" themselves. W. E. B. Du Bois was one of the very few to study philosophy formally; he even considered pursuing it professionally.[16] Alain Leroy Locke was one of the first persons of African descent in America to earn a doctoral degree in philosophy (Harvard University, 1918). Over the last half-century, a small number of African and African-descended Americans joined the ranks of professional philosophers. Starting in the early 1970s and continuing into the 1990s, several of these persons, influenced by the Civil Rights and Black Power movements in responding to the need and desire to identify and otherwise forge philosophical traditions, literatures, and practices distinctive of black peoples, began the work of calling for and setting out "Black," or "Afro-American," and later "African-American" philosophy.[17] During annual meetings of divisions of the American Philosophical Association (APA) a number of sessions, organized by the APA's Committee on Blacks in Philosophy, were devoted to the tasks. (APA recognition of these efforts as having opened a legitimate subfield of philosophy was accorded in 1987 with the decision to include "Africana Philosophy" as a specialty in the discipline.)

Leonard Harris has been an invaluable contributor to these endeavors over the past twenty-five years as an editor of collections that make widely available important texts that otherwise would not get the attention of researchers and scholars concerned with the philosophizing of black folks. His edited *The Philosophy of Alain Locke: Harlem Renaissance and Beyond*[18] provides ready access to twenty-two distinctively philosophical essays from among Locke's more than two hundred and nineteen published, and fourteen unpublished, essays and ninety-six published book reviews. *Philosophy Born of Struggle: Anthology of Afro-American Philosophy from 1917* remains the only widely available, somewhat historically organized collection of writings by African American philosophers. (An important earlier collection is Percy E. Johnston's *Afro-American Philosophers*.[19]) Today the work of developing African-American philosophy as a distinctive subfield is hampered by the very limited availability of a number of ground-breaking articulations from the early 1970s, many of which have not been published. A significant number of these were presented during conferences held, for the most part, at historically black colleges and universities (e.g., Tuskegee University and Morgan State University) during the early 1970s, others during the special APA sessions and conferences held from the mid-1970s through the early 1990s. Examples: "Value and Religion in Africana Philosophy: The African-American Case" by Robert C. Williams (deceased); George Garrison's "Afro-American Philosophical Thought: The Early Beginnings and the Afro-Centric Substratum"; and Cornel West's insightful critical survey "Black Philosophers and Textual Practice," in which he examines what he terms the "ideological character" of the textual practices ("academic dovetailing," "professional criticism," and "counterhegemonic praxis") of black philosophers in the twentieth century.[20] However, not all of this effort has been lost from view thanks, especially, to the invaluable contributions of two persons in particular. Marx Wartofsky, as editor of *The Philosophical Forum*, twice has devoted entire special issues of the journal to philosophical explorations of the experiences of black folks, with African-American philosophers serving as guest editors.[21] (I know of no other journal in philosophy in the U.S. managed almost wholly or exclusively by persons who are neither African nor African-descended that has followed the lead of *The Philosophical Forum*.) And Alfred Prettyman, a publisher who lives and works in New York City, has devoted considerable time, energies, and other resources, including his home, to initiating and nurturing an organization of black philosophers and other interested black and non-black scholars (originally The New York Society for the Study of Black Philosophy; presently The Society for the Study of Africana Philosophy) and to publishing their work (principally through the now dormant *The Journal* of The New

York Society for the Study of Black Philosophy). The sustaining support of Wartofsky and Prettyman must not go unacknowledged.

Other recent texts that are part of the growing collection of efforts by African and African-descended philosophers in America are the lengthening list of writings by Cornel West; Charles A. Frey's *From Egypt to Don Juan: The Anatomy of Black Studies* and *Level Three: A Black Philosophy Reader*;[22] presentations and discussions of the writings of such persons as Alain Locke by Leonard Harris and Johnny Washington;[23] and writings in ethics, social and political philosophy, and other fields of philosophy by Laurence Thomas;[24] Bill Lawson and Howard McGary;[25] Bernard Boxill;[26] Anthony Appiah;[27] Tsenay Serequeberhan;[28] Anita Allen, Adrian Piper, Michele Moody-Adams, Frank Kirkland, and Tommy Lott;[29] Robert Birt;[30] Lewis R. Gordon;[31] Blanche Radford-Curry;[32] Charles W. Mills;[33] and others.

Until quite recently there was a notable aspect to the work of professionally trained African-American philosophers: much of it had been conducted with little or no knowledge of, or attention to, either the histories or the forms of philosophical activity on the African continent or elsewhere in the African diaspora. At the very least, this lack of awareness and attention may well have contributed to deficiencies in the historically informed self-understandings of African-American philosophers and, to that extent, have had important implications for our work whether or not we take that work to be distinguished, or at least conditioned in significant ways, by our being persons of African descent. African philosophers have generally been much more successful in advancing the enterprise of philosophy, theoretically and practically, as a venture conditioned by explicit commitments and linkages to the histories and historical situations and to the interests of African peoples. In contrast, the development of distinct traditions of thought by African-American professional philosophers has been seriously curtailed by our not having labored together more, conditioned by a critically informed sense of shared identities, shared histories, and a need to work together to help realize possible shared futures of enhanced liberation for ourselves and others, to develop refined, shared agendas and practices to guide and structure our work.

A comparison of instances and traditions of philosophizing of African thinkers in various African countries to those of African-American thinkers reveals significant differences in the degree to which philosophical praxes and legacies have been institutionalized that have been conditioned by commitments and orientations growing out of "black consciousness" movements in the U.S. and Africa (the Civil Rights and Black Power movements in the U.S., the Négritude movement in France and its colonies, the Pan-African movement throughout Africa and the African diaspora). African-descended philosophers in North America are perhaps long overdue for coming together for sustained, systematic, critical reconstructions of intellectual histories that might serve as resources for our work. Still, in doing so we must take care: historical connections among, and similar as well as shared experiences of, persons of African descent in the United States, in the African diaspora, and throughout continental Africa will not warrant uncritical appropriations and celebrations of a presumptive univocal and shared raciality, nor of glorious longstanding philosophical insights and traditions of the African Motherland to which we can and should turn to be guided to our futures by primordial, ancient wisdoms that simply wait to be reclaimed by us. It is into the thicket of raciality that I will now move on the way to clarifying further what is intended by "Africana philosophy."

Africana Philosophy

Drawing on the preceding brief and incomplete survey of philosophizing by African-Americans, the question to be answered now is whether what has been gained from the survey, when combined with the descriptions and analyses of African philosophy in the preceding essay, are sufficient to provide an idea of what would be required in the way of commonalities in the philosophizing of persons African and African-descended to warrant grouping the practices and articulations under the heading of "Africana philosophy." However, an even more vexing question arises: can adequate reasons be given to warrant efforts to set out distinctive agendas, practices, ends, and norms as characteristic, even intellectually and morally *compellingly* so, of the philosophizing of African and African-descended thinkers *because* they are African or African-descended?

"Africana philosophy," while working as an umbrella notion, harbors two sets of complexities. The first set is covered by the term "Africana," which is a covering term for some of the intellectual activities, and the "products" resulting from them, of persons identified as members of the various ethnies of a widely dispersed geographic race.[34] Anthropologically, then, the range of coverage of "Africana" is determined by the existence, the situated experiences and practices, of biological and socio-cultural descent groupings of persons who, collectively, constitute a fuzzily bounded racial population. The constitutive raciality involved in characterizing this population as African or African-descended is not provided by shared genetic homogeneity but by varying combinations of particular characteristics that are functions of locally conditioned bio-cultural evolutions of peoples whose origin and development were in a particular geographical location (i.e., Africa) and who, over long expanses of time and continental spaces, have shared lines of increasingly diverse biological and cultural ancestries that have been continued, to varying degrees, through descent, dispersals, and migrations. Persons comprising the various ethnie of the race have tended to share relatively distinctive characterizing gene pools and cultural economies, traceable, in part, to the "ancestors" that determines the relative frequencies of various physical attributes and cultural practices, even throughout the

African diaspora. In turn, geographical, cultural, and social factors as well as forces of natural selection have influenced the shared pools of genes and cultural resources and thus conditioned processes of *raciation*: that is, the formation and evolving influences of biological and cultural factors that collectively characterize the changing ethnies of the race. It is this raciality—collections of biological and cultural characteristics that make for shared family resemblances among widely dispersed, similar, and different peoples—that is referred to by "Africana": that is, persons African and African-descended.

This understanding of "Africana" provides only an initial circumscription of a primary distinguishing feature of the discursive practices of persons philosophizing, or who are the subject matters of others' philosophizing. The strategy of circumscription is so far at best a point of departure. To avoid undue simplicity—or, worse still, fallacious biological or racial essentialism—more is required, namely, to identify the features that make certain intellectual practices and legacies of persons African and African-descended instances of "philosophy," features characteristic of, though not necessarily *unique* to, these persons *as members of a dispersed race.*

While I have offered a sketch of several orientations of African-American thinkers as candidates for inclusion under the heading of Africana philosophy, a key commitment influencing my discussion is the belief that there are no timeless, essential, thus definitive logical and epistemological characteristics shared by any and all forms of thought called "philosophy." A serious study of the articulations of persons included in canons of Western philosophy, for example, will disclose that these are the same only in the most general sense of involving reflections on thinking, moral and ethical matters, political life, etc. The agendas, motivations, strategies, and achievements that are involved and that characterize the philosophizing are quite diverse. What is the case universally is that there have been and are persons among all peoples who have engaged and do engage in praxes of reflection. It is these praxes, in various forms, that constitute what has come to be called philosophizing. The capacity for the activities constitutive of philosophizing are species-specific. To that extent they are universal anthropologically. However, as philosophizing is socially and historically situated, it is inherently grounded in and thus conditioned by social life, not regulated by ahistorical transcendental rules governing reasoning above and beyond concrete social and cultural life. When we view philosophical practices historically, sociologically, culturally, and comparatively, we are led inescapably to conclude that "philosophical practice is inherently pluralistic," and "all philosophical ideals are local" to communities of thinkers.[35] We mislead ourselves if we require that there be something more than family resemblances common to all the practices and articulations we propose to recognize as instances of "philosophy." The important common features that characterize intellectual praxes as "philosophizing" is that they involve "systematic" *reflections* and *articulations* with regard to various aspects and areas of life, to the end of helping create ordered, meaningful existence.

The *situated* actualizations of species-specific capacities in response to the need for reflection and articulation in order to ensure survival guarantees diversity in the philosophizings of persons who are members of a large race that is geographically dispersed and ethnically diverse. Furthermore, to the extent that "Africana philosophy" is invoked to identify a distinct discursive venture or "field," this field, as a collection of endeavors, is constructed, in large part, *ex post facto* through the collecting efforts: that is to say, through discursive strategies (my own, in the present case) which seek to organize and study instances of articulated reflection by persons African and African-descended, and accounts of these reflections, in particular ways. Further, it must be noted that in important cases the gathering of practices and traditions of discourse under the heading of "Africana philosophy" will involve assembling some which were not conditioned by an explicit sense on the part of those engaged in them that they were involved in something called "philosophizing" or "Africana philosophy" (or any of the many other subgroupings such as "African," "Akan," "Nigerian," or "Afro-Brazilian" philosophy). Further still, important aspects of the ethnic and geographical diversities of African and African-descended peoples are consequences of imperialism in Africa on the part of European and other peoples. However, even before these imperialistic incursions and subsequent colonizations and dispersals of Africans, there were diversities among the peoples of Africa. Thus, the practices, traditions, and literatures comprising "Africana philosophy," because they are tied, in the first instance, to the life-worlds of numerous African peoples, have diverse histories, sites, and conditions of emergence. Therefore, Africana philosophy, as archeology, cannot but be constituted by diversity. This is the second set of complexities that is harbored by "Africana philosophy."

How, then, to speak of "commonalities" or "unity" sufficient to underwrite Africana philosophy as a disciplinary field of studies with distinct boundaries and intellectual and praxiological coherence? The only appropriate way of doing so is by first recognizing that the unifying commonalities sought for are provided through the third-order organizational, classificatory, or archeological strategies involved in "gathering" people and discursive practices under "Africana" and "philosophy," respectively. I say "third order" because the gathered discursive practices are themselves "second order" in that they are reflections on "first order"—that is to say *lived*—experiences of the various African and African-descended persons and peoples. Crucial existential, meaning, and ontological differences exist between what are here distinguished as first, second, and third orders of reality: lived experiences (concrete life: first order), reflections on lived experiences (philosophizing: second order), reflections on reflections on lived experiences (Africana philosophy: third order). In addition, we must remember that the identification of commonalities sufficient to support gathering the practices and articulations of persons of a dispersed race under a single heading proceeds initially by disregarding other factors in terms of which both the persons and the practices differ. Identification of similarities and commonalities while disregarding differences are agenda-bound activities carried through by particular strategies according to particular discursive rules. Thus, in important senses the third-order subject matters or "objects" of Africana philosophy *as objects of a discursive field* are constituted as such retrospectively through the discursive rules employed to regulate a disciplinary venture. (To the extent that persons take themselves to be philosophizing they do so on the basis of some understanding of constitutive discursive rules and norms, and in this way these rules and norms come to have proscriptive effect.)

Examples of this retrospective, third-order making of a field can be seen in the efforts of V. Y. Mudimbe, Alphonse J. Smet, and O. Nkombe, discussed in the previous essay, to identify commonalities in the philosophizings of various African intellectuals that have made for trends or schools of thought.[36] So, too, my discussion of examples of social and political orientations of a number of African-Americans. There are, of course, other examples. In each case it is the extent to which the philosophizing shares aspects that are more or less common to the intellectual labors of African and African-descended peoples that warrants including it under the heading of Africana philosophy. Kwame Gyekye's approach with respect to African philosophy is worth considering:

> I believe that in many areas of thought we can discern features of the traditional life and thought of African peoples sufficiently common to constitute a legitimate and reasonable basis for the construction (or reconstruction) of a philosophical system that may properly be called African — African not in the sense that every African adheres to it, but in the sense that philosophical system arises from, and hence is essentially related to, African life and thought. Such a basis would justify a discourse in terms of "African philosophy."[37]

For Gyekye, the commonalities identified in comparative studies of "traditional" African thought are to be found in the customs, beliefs, traditions, values, socio-political institutions, and historical experiences of African societies.[38] However, a momentous rupture of tradition-bound life occurred when millions of Africans from distinct ethnic groups were thrown together in systems of colonization, enslavement, and dispersion fashioned by powerful organizations of people from that racial and ethnic cultural complexity referred to as "European civilization." Consequently, this search for commonalities or unity in the cultures, experiences, and philosophizings of African and African-descended peoples is both complicated and complicating. The quest for unity among African and African-descended peoples has been a longstanding political project exemplified in that complex tradition of endeavors known as Pan-Africanism, a project devoted to freeing African and African-descended peoples from racialized domination. But is the search for unities or commonalities in the philosophizings of African and African-descended peoples as grounding for speaking of Africana philosophy but a case of romanticism or political adventure (or both) that distorts the enterprise of philosophy? That remains to be seen. Each case of an appeal to, or purported demonstration of, unity or commonality in the philosophizing of persons African and African-descended requires an appraisal on its own merits. What makes it possible and appropriate initially to group diverse intellectual endeavors of diverse persons under a single heading is the extent to which the persons share racial-ethnic identities as African or African-descended, thus share socially and culturally conditioned biological attributes, cultural traditions, and historical experiences more or less distinctive of the African race and its ethnies.

Yet, this collection of characteristics is sufficient only for making an *initial* distinction that allows for grouping persons by raciality and ethnicity. Doing so, however, provides no immediate and/or necessary insight into the forms, agendas, strategies, or ends of the persons' discursive traditions and practices—that is, their philosophizings. We must turn to these traditions and practices of philosophizing—along with the agendas and strategies structuring their formation and deployment, situated in the contexts of the cultural life-worlds of the persons who engage in them—to answer questions regarding commonalities and differences. Only there are to be found whatever shared unities that will be sufficient to support "Africana philosophy" as a comprehensive concept for an encompassing disciplinary field. We must take particular care to avoid conflating the quest for unity among African and African-descended peoples as a form of political mobilization with a search for unity in their philosophizing.

Though "Africana philosophy," as a field of discourses, is initially constituted through third-order surveying and arranging of discursive practices and literatures according to agendas played out in the arranging, surveying, and naming of the field, the practices and articulations arranged and named do not require these field-constituting activities to secure their meaningfulness or integrity or their validity. Their meaning, integrity, and validity are determined, initially, by the prevailing norms in the local contexts within which they emerged, not to the third-order endeavors. The latter are conditioning only of those practices that are engaged in self-consciously as instances of Africana philosophy. It is not decisive, then, that many of the discursive traditions and practices included under the heading of "Africana philosophy" were not identified as such by those involved in them, and in important cases were not even called "philosophy." That some of us now regard these as instances of "philosophizing" is a matter of historical, cultural, social, and political circumstances affecting intellectual practices.

Those of us in professional philosophy must free ourselves of any concerns for pernicious ordering and privileging that too often have guarded and administered "philosophy" as an honorific term reserved for certain practices of certain persons of a particular geographic race and its ethnie who have been thought to be, by nature, more capable than others.

Still, is there anything beyond raciality and ethnicity that is common to and constitutive of the philosophical that in being covered by "Africana philosophy" helps to identify the philosophizing as characteristic of endeavors of persons African and African-descended? In general, for a great many post-traditional African and African-descended thinkers, this shared characteristic has been and continues to be the effort to forge and articulate new identities and life agendas by which to survive and to flourish in the limiting situations of racialized oppression and New World relocations. It is, as well, the effort to recover or reconstruct life-defining, identity-confirming meaning-connections to lands and cultures of the African continent, its peoples, and their histories.

These efforts have motivated critical reviews and reconstructions of histories of Western philosophy and the relations of these philosophizings to peoples on the African continent, to endeavors to recover and rehabilitate African-descended thinkers from earlier periods as precursor and pioneer black philosophers, and to significant moves to deconstruct and revise narratives of the histories and agendas of philosophical enterprises in the West. The recent vintage of these efforts notwithstanding, they have been of major significance for the self-understandings and identities of many African and African-descendant thinkers, and increasingly those of non-African or African-descended thinkers. When considered against the context of the history of Western philosophy as narrated and practiced by some of its dominant figures, in general, and against the explicit derogations of African peoples by a number of these figures, the advent of discussions regarding African and African-American philosophy has been *necessarily* "deconstructive." Thus, for example, each instance of an attempt to identify and/or articulate a philosophizing effort as distinctively African or African-American is, at the outset at least, an important challenge that situates the very idea, as well as the discursive practices, of "philosophy" into the historicities of their construction and maintenance, and into the historically conditioned philosophical anthropology that has informed them via the valorized and racialized notion of "Rational Man." Furthermore, efforts to articulate the norms and boundaries of distinctly "African" or "African-American" philosophy expose the agendas of the persons who constructed that philosophical anthropology and the practices through which it was institutionalized in service to interests and objectives that were more than simply "philosophical," in some restricted academic sense, but were intimately connected to social-political projects. In this regard the reconstructive efforts of a number of persons, and the issues raised in and by their work, demand serious attention:

George G. M. James,[39] Henry Olela,[40] Lancinay Keita,[41] and the work of various persons in the Association for the Study of Classical African Civilizations, especially *Kemet and the African Worldview: Research, Rescue and Restoration*[42] editied by Maulana Karenga and Jacob H. Carruthers; and Carruthers's own *Essays in Ancient Egyptian Studies*[43]; and more recently Martin Bernal's multi-volume *Black Athena: The Afroasiatic Roots of Classical Civilization*.[44] Along with the precursive work of William Leo Hansberry[45] and Frank M. Snowden Jr.,[46] all of these efforts deserve attention.

So far the discussion has focused on Africana philosophy as a third-order venture devoted to identifying and organizing for study discursive objects, that is, the articulated reflections of various African and African-descended persons. Are these endeavors sufficient to constitute a *disciplinary* venture? Yes indeed, as with all work in philosophy (and other disciplines) that have the form of archeology. But major challenges are still to be faced: first, in settling the questions whether there can and should be norms and practices, as well as agendas, that are or would be definitive of any philosophizing appropriately identified as instances of Africana philosophy; second, in specifying the requisite agendas, norms, and practices. For decades similar challenges and questions have been addressed by scholars in such disciplines as literature and literary theory, sociology, history, art, and music, especially in contributing to various efforts that collectively constitute the inter-disciplinary and multi-disciplinary ventures of African Studies, Black or African-American Studies, and Africana Studies. Each of these disciplines and collections of disciplinary efforts has established traditions of normatively guided efforts and accomplishments that structure ongoing work. It will be important to study several of these for possible assistance in thinking about Africana philosophy. Especially pertinent is the work of Molefi Asante, who is the leading proponent of an "Afro-centric" or "Africa-centered" approach to "Africalogy," Asante's name for his attempted recasting of Black or African-American Studies.[47] Asante's is one of the most prominent and contested current attempts to take up the challenges of setting out definitive agendas, norms, and practices for the production of knowledge regarding African and African-descended people.

In preparation for this review it would be helpful to consider the following complicated questions: how shall the intellectual praxes of Africana philosophy be shaped to serve the best interests of African peoples, first and foremost, and thereby provide those philosophizing with normative guidance while, at the same time, abiding by norms intended to secure propriety and truthfulness in discursive practices on conditions of warrant that are open to and can be confirmed by persons who are neither African nor African-descended? Are such concerns appropriate conditioners of philosophical effort? As an enterprise within the modern academy that seeks to speak knowledgeably to black folks and to others for and about black folks, the rules of discourse for Africana philosophy will have to satisfy certain institu-

tionalized criteria governing scholarly practices even as those of us committed to the development of Africana philosophy contribute to critiques and
refinements of a number of these same criteria while we devise and propose
others. In participating in discussions of African and African-American philosophy, we have helped to change the rules of discourse in contemporary
academic institutions and organizations. However, as long as we consent to
share in these social ventures and to participate in national and international publics — whether academic or non-academic — our discourses cannot be conducted according to exclusionary racialized rules.

Of course, some black cultural nationalists argue that the values and
norms that should ground and structure the study of black folks exist in "the
way of life," "the collective worldview and belief system," or "the African cultural system" that, supposedly, have existed in their original forms throughout history and are shared by all African and African-descended peoples.
The rhetorical force of these claims has much to do with the emotional, even
psychological, rehabilitation and satisfaction they provide the persons
advancing them as they endeavor to cultivate identities necessary for struggling against the racialized domination and hegemony of white supremacy.
Still, the cultivation of such identities must not come at the expense of
responsible, critical thought. Already a number of critics of efforts to produce knowledge by and about black folks that would challenge prevailing
knowledges have successfully challenged the abstract naiveté and romanticism often involved in such sweeping and unfounded declarations, which
tend, among other things, to disregard very important factors such as class
stratifications, gender (black women's experiences, for example), and serious disparities in values and practices among the ethnie of African peoples.
Declarations of this kind, to the extent that they seek to gain normative
authority by appealing to questionable historical reconstructions of the values, practices, and accomplishments of ancient civilizations in Africa, also
tend to disregard the complicating fact that no ancient Egyptian or Nubian
shared our historical and cultural worlds, nor we theirs, thus in ancient
times and places shared our senses of what it means today to be "African."

Given the complicated meanings that have been invested in this term
following Europe's imperialist incursions into the continent, resulting in the
death of tens of millions of Africans and distortions of the lives of millions
more, we must inquire whether "African" is always an appropriate term of
reference when speaking of the Ancients. For "African" is problematic when
we move to apply it to ancient history as well as to concrete persons, as is
always the case with general terms weighted with meanings from more
recent history. Asante, for example, in *Kemet, Afrocentricity and Knowledge*
(p. 9), takes the following approach in applying the term to persons: "By
'African' I mean clearly a 'composite African' not a specific discrete African
orientation which would rather mean ethnic identification, i.e., Yoruba, Zulu,
Nuba, etc."[48] But what is a "composite African"? The unity such a concept

harbors is gained at the price of abstracting from many vital aspects and details of historical and daily existence of living African peoples, an abstraction accomplished by we intellectuals who do so, supposedly, in the interest of others who have little or no recall on our efforts. Can real persons and peoples living throughout the world who are identified (many of whom identify themselves) as "African" or "African-descended" find themselves in our concepts, in our reconstructions of their histories and our prescriptions for their futures? Are these reconstructions and prescriptions justified by our taking ourselves to be in solidarity with "the people"? Have we gone too far some times, while rightfully criticizing the racism and ethnocentrism that have historically conditioned many of the norms and justificatory strategies of knowledge production of many Europeans and Americans of European descent, in discarding such strategies completely, or in doing so without having fashioned new ones to replace them—perhaps more importantly, without having clarified for ourselves that norms and justifications for the production of knowledge are not the invention of "white" folk?

A critical stance toward the endeavors we would have constitute a distinctive disciplinary venture focused on the philosophizing of African and African-descended peoples requires that we review the presuppositions and requirements often invested in using "African" and/or "black" in totalizing fashion: that is, as names for racial and ethnic identity formations presumed to involve singular forms of subjectivity and orientation shared by all persons African and African-descended. Such a presumption follows, I think, from a too easy conflation—or explicit identification—of knowledge production and articulation with psychic rehabilitation and political mobilization: for example, taking cultural *commonalities* shared by diverse African and African-descended peoples as *prima facie* evidence of an a prioristic *cultural* unity taken to be foundational to *political* unity. It is true that, in important senses, "all knowledge is political" in terms of the situatedness of the production and distribution of what passes for "knowledge" in the complexities of historically specific social formations. Still, the truism says nothing about the variety of forms and ends of politics, or about the variety of ways in which the production and distribution of knowledge stand toward and are related to the complex social formations in which these processes take place. Contemporary Black and African Studies developed out of particular historical circumstances and in service to particular political agendas. Black Studies, in particular, was a venture that, in many of its instantiations, was devoted to fashioning identity formations in black recipients of knowledge, identities that were thought to be appropriate to and prerequisite for the politics. However, with Stuart Hall we must recognize:

> The extraordinary diversity of subjective positions, social experiences and cultural identities which compose the category "black": that is, the recognition that "black" is essentially a politically and culturally

constructed category, which cannot be grounded in a set of fixed trans-cultural or transcendental racial categories and which therefore has no guarantees in Nature. . . . This inevitably entails a weakening or fading of the notion that "race" or some composite notion of race around the term black will either guarantee the effectivity of any cultural practice or determine in any final sense its aesthetic value.[49]

Neither politics nor scholarship can be properly conducted by the simple reversal of replacing, in Hall's words, "the bad old essential white subject" with "the new essentially good black subject."

Of course, culturally informed personal and social identities are vital to the well-being of individuals and peoples. How such identities are formed, revised, maintained, or overthrown is always a matter of importance, especially in historical situations conditioned by racialized domination and hegemony. Stuart Hall is especially insightful and helpful in thinking about how we might approach the business of cultural identity formation: either as a function of a shared ancestry, history, and culture that provide continuous and unchanging frames of reference and meaning out of which is formed a collective "one true self" shared by all; or, more appropriately, as risk-prone ventures of recurrent, historicized "becoming." He notes: "Far from being grounded in a mere 'recovery' of the past, which is waiting to be found, and which, when found, will secure our sense of ourselves into eternity, identities are the names we give to the different ways we are positioned by, and position ourselves within, the narratives of the past."[50] Put slightly differently, our identities are the relatively stable but changing constellations of meanings of social and self-definition that are functions of how we are recurrently positioned by, and position ourselves within, narrations of pasts, presents, and anticipated or desired futures. Hence the need for critical intellectuals to review the legacies and practices shaping a people's reproduction of itself and to mediate the results of the reviews as "knowledge" meant to assist social ordering and reproduction. It is important, then, to attend to the matter of the self-identifications of thinkers and scholars involved in knowledge production and distribution as contributions to the formation of identities and thus to social and cultural reproduction—attend, that is, to both how their identities are influenced by, and how they influence, the production and distribution of knowledges and socio-cultural reproduction.

Given the racially motivated mistruths that have infected the predominant histories of Western philosophy, the advent of Africana philosophy is of very real importance to this productive and reproductive work. A compelling need exists to give greater respectful attention to raciality and ethnicity (as well as gender, sexual orientation, and other constitutive aspects of our personal and social identities) as conditioners of philosophical praxis without thereby invalidating reconstructed notions of proper reasoning. Of course doing so would cut against the grain of central convictions of modern Western philosophy, among which has been that of providing the definitive characterizations of what it is to be human without explicit references to race, ethnicity, or gender. The modern Enlightenments were triumphant partial political realizations, to a large extent, of this project that made possible substantive progressive achievements without which, even with their shortcomings, many of our societies would not be much to the liking of many of us.

But with the achievements came much too exclusive focus in philosophizing on "universal" characteristics thought definitive of human beings with too little attention to the distinguishing characteristics of particular cultural groups for reasons other than invidious discrimination and exploitation. Often the invidious projects were facilitated by rationalizations that appealed to the normativity of universals which were, however, sometimes disguised norms of particular Europeans and European descendants. Increasingly today critical investigations are removing the disguises to disclose the ethnocentrism and racism, sexism, and class biases at the very heart of the Western philosophical enterprise.

Does this signal the complete inadequacy of what have heretofore been regarded as historic and praiseworthy achievements of ancient and modern philosophy and of European and American Enlightenments? Not necessarily. But the recognition and acknowledgment of inadequacies in basic notions in these legacies, and of histories of invidious appropriations and applications of them, open us to challenging possibilities for further revising our philosophical traditions and practices. Africana philosophy as an enterprise can contribute to a critical review of the "universalist" liberal agenda that has dominated so much of philosophical praxis in the West since the modern Enlightenments.

We are in the midst of a historical conjucture that is relatively new, one highly charged by efforts to achieve democracy in multi-ethnic, multi-racial societies in which much that is decisive in personal and social life is ordered by raciality and ethnicity. In light of this I join others in calling for a serious revision of our philosophical agendas and praxes. It is my sincere hope that the expansion of the enterprise of philosophy to include Africana philosophy is indicative of a movement in this direction and that, as a result, philosophizing will be practiced with much less pernicious racism and ethnocentrism than has been the case historically. It is also a sincere hope that the activities that are identified as constituting Africana philosophy will be nurtured in this revised context and make substantial contributions to it. Of course, all the persons who might share in the work of Africana philosophy need not be African or of African descent. Similarities and commonalities (and differences) in the *experiences* of the dispersed race of African peoples in their varied ethnicities are one thing; the intellec-- tual and sociological coherence of an *intellectual enterprise* are related to such experiences but are a different matter. The former must not be confused with the latter. Racial identity and common experiences, cultural commonalities and a site of common origin *do not*, automatically and necessarily, provide unifying intellectual and sociological coherence for a disciplinary enterprise or determine its norms, agenda, and strategies. "Africana philosophy" is indeed a "gathering notion," not a proxy for an immutable essence shared by all African peoples. Gathering together various traditions, practices, and literatures identified as "philosophy" is just an initial, though important, step. Then the real labor begins: interrogating works, learning from them, comparing and contrasting them with endeavors by African and other peoples as part of a larger, ongoing efforts to catalog and study the many creations of African peoples, their contributions to the treasure houses of human civilization.

5

AFRICOLOGY

Normative Theory

*Critical Prelude: The "Africology" Project
and Normative Theory*

Whatever the precipitating occasion, venturing into a discussion of "normative theory"—in addition to having to work through the difficulties generated by the ambiguities of the phrase—is more than enough to produce a serious case of trepidation. One must be mindful of the plurality of positions on the subject, thus of a complex history of conflicting efforts and agendas; and, in particular, mindful of the powerful, persuasive critiques that have been advanced against certain of those efforts that have sometimes dominated this field of discourse. For the subject of normative theory is a minefield that, once entered, is without a map that guarantees an unimpeachable way out: specifying norms is not a process that can be accomplished by way of the rigors of deductive logic with all of the certainty and absoluteness such a process is thought to secure. The anxiety is increased (at least for me) when one answers the call to contribute to a project by sketching a map to guide those involved to safe and solid ground on which to carve out and work an important—even historic—field, one that seeks to center itself in and devote itself to the most well-achieved understanding of all that matters with respect to Africa and its peoples. Maps to safety and solid ground can only be provided by surveying the (mined) field, noting the areas of danger, and marking a path to the desired destination. Of course, such maps will only be as good as the surveyor.

The metaphor of mined and safe "fields," with normative theory projected as something that can contribute to reaching, laying out, and working a field "safely," takes us to the heart of the matter (and, simultaneously, reveals my slant on it): there are many ways through a dangerous field, likewise many dangers to be negotiated, the "best path" being, to a considerable —and ultimately ineliminable—degree, dependent on *where* one wants to go and *how* one proposes to get there. The key insight to be grasped is that the "best path" is a matter of *choice*, conditioned by experience and understanding. And the choosing can never be formalized into an algorithm that systematically secures the selection of a correct path with rigorous and absolute certainty.

However, to the extent that our efforts to reconstruct a disciplinary field is a joint project to be shared with larger publics, then the choices involved cannot be capriciously arbitrary if we expect others to partake of what we do. At the very least, it must be possible for the partakers to understand both where we are going and how we would get there. This mutual understanding will only be possible if we all are governed by *shared* rules of reason and discourse by which we can and should *justify* our choices—that is, give "good reasons" for them. We intellectuals involved in such endeavors tend to do so by setting out the "principles" or "rules" according to which we choose, the principles and rules being what are in part meant by "norms" that help to order our theoretical work. But norms also require justification, and the justification can never be absolutely conclusive: that is, it will always be open to criticism and subject to revision. For "norms" are intended to tell us what we *should* do, what *ought* to be the case. As such they are oriented toward the future and thus function fundamentally to *guide* praxis (intellectual and practical) and to provide standards by which to *evaluate* our efforts.

But the future is open—there are many *possible* futures—and what is or was the case in the area of human activity *might* have been otherwise. All praxis (in the full, social sense of the term), whether in its conceptualization, initiation, or execution, must negotiate the crossroads of choice on the way to its completion. And since our choosing is always conditioned by experience and understanding—both of which are intrinsically and *fundamentally* conditioned by our historical/cultural development, with all of its vagaries—our choosing can never be axiomatized. This is why we *need* the guidance of norms.

But what of "normative *theory*" in terms of this project to rethink "Black Studies," efforts that our organizers have referred to as "essential parts of a first-order architectonic inquiry into the building of the discipline of Africology"?[1] First, the phrase "normative theory" is ambiguous. On the one hand, it can be understood as referring to *theorizing* about norms; on the other, as referring to theorizing that leads to *prescribing* particular norms. However, as with norms, so, too, with theorizing *about* and *prescribing* norms: there are no Archimedian points in the lofty heights of cognition on which to rest an absolute foundation from which we can derive, axiomatically, rules and principles to guide our theorizing or prescribing of particular norms. We can struggle to make the normative foundation of our architectonic strong, and, likewise, the prescriptions we make from it. But we can't make either of them impregnable.

Then what, or how, might I contribute to this discipline-building endeavor in light of my assignment? By way of a discussion *of* normative theory? By theorizing about—by suggesting, perhaps—norms to *guide* our theorizing? Answers to these questions are neither immediate nor obvious when considered in the context of the following list of interrelated (and quite complex) questions and issues it was suggested I might address:

1. the "fundamental, ontological axiomatic assumptions over time among peoples of African origin";
2. the "discernment of the relationship between ontological assumptions and the ethical/moral precepts that are grounded in those assumptions";
3. the "teleology of human conduct" that "emanates" from 1 and 2;
4. the "epistemology of human conduct as it emanates from 1 through 3";
5. "criteria for the ascription of approbation and disapprobation"; and
6. the question of the roles of each of the above in "the description, explanation, justification and prediction of human conduct."[2]

Obviously I am to identify "fundamental ontological assumptions" of African peoples; to connect those with ethical/moral precepts, and the latter with human conduct and its "teleology"; to identify criteria for ascribing praise and blame; and to connect all of this to describing, explaining, justifying, and predicting human conduct. These tasks involve both descriptive and prescriptive normative efforts. But with what connection to "Africology" as a discipline in the making? As one of its tasks, I think: that is, Africology should—or will—also assume the responsibilities of describing, explaining, justifying, and predicting the conduct of African peoples.

These are hardly small tasks. Not only are they fraught with the dangers mentioned above, but with potential others, not the least of which are those that lurk in the assumptions made regarding the relation of normative theoretical work—and, thereby, of normative theorists—to those with respect to whom this "describing, explaining, justifying, and predicting" is carried out, *supposedly in their best regard.* There is ample room here for the best of intentions to degenerate into presumptuous arrogance, into the imperial, self-justifying, paternalistic, and authoritarian dogmatism of a self-elected clique, which it passes off as the enlightenment needed—no, *required*—by "the people" or "the masses."

This treacherous ground must be explored first: namely, the norms conditioning "Africology" itself as a discipline in (re-)formation. My initial aim is to be clearer about how it is that disciplinary, discursive efforts (theorizing in particular) are connected to both their objects and subjects, overall how they are situated, and, in light of that, what the implications might be in terms of these efforts' normative conditions and conditioning. In other words, if I can be relatively clear about disciplines, norms, and normative theorizing in general, with respect to Africology in particular, then, perhaps, I will be in a better position to situate and take up the suggested issues and work toward the mapping out of possible paths where "we" might do well to go.

In pursuit of this goal, initial discussion will be devoted to setting out a working sense of a "discipline"—including possible components, the context of development and articulation, possible avenues to its formation—and of the roles of norms in the maintenance of a discipline and the deployment of the practices that constitute it. In discussing these matters (later to be characterized as efforts to "manage" a tradition of intellectual praxis) my concern is to achieve an understanding sufficient to bring into focus the importance of a concern with norms in the context of theorizing. The objective is to be critically self-reflective in moving to the discussion of "describing, explaining, justifying, and predicting the conduct of African peoples."

This initial discussion will be assisted by two approaches: the *archaeological* and *genealogical* investigations of Michel Foucault[3] and discussions of *metascience* by Gerard Radnitzsky.[4] This structuring context will then be used, first, to situate a review of endeavors that, for more than three decades now, have been variously referred to as "Black," "Afro-American," "African-American," "Africana," or "African" Studies[5] (though "African Studies" have significantly different histories, audiences, and "managers," in important cases); second, to situate a discussion of "Africology" as a particular discipline in (re-)formation in relation to the thematization of norms—their historical ground and range; their implications; their legitimacy or legitimization—at work in, and/or preferred for, Africology as institutionalized intellectual praxis. This will be followed by a critical discussion of the issues it was suggested I address.

Archaeology/Genealogy and Metascience: Understanding and Managing Disciplinary Fields

I think it best to begin by thematizing, once more, the agenda structuring this project: to pool efforts that are to constitute "essential parts of a first-order architectonic inquiry into the building of the discipline of Africology." Of course, in the effort to form this discipline we do not create *ex nihilo* as though nothing of the sort has come before. Rather, this is more an attempted *refinement*, a renovation, of Black Studies. These "fields of discourse" or "discursive formations" (to borrow the language of Foucault) emerged at particular historical moments in service to particular agendas: as struggles *against* the dominating racism of Euro-American establishment *logoi* institutionalized in various disciplines and, simultaneously, *in support of* the reclamation, rehabilitation, and celebration of African peoples properly resituated in our narratives of our histories. These ventures, later to be described as "Afrocentric" (in contrast to "Eurocentric"), were deliberately disruptive, intended to interrupt the continuation of the supposedly progressive, "evolutionary flow" of Reason embodied in the historical development of the peoples of Western Europe and their American descendants. This "progressive" advance of Reason has been argued by some to be manifested in achievements of the intellect as crystallized and systematized in key "disciplines," particularly the natural and social sciences, and, at the "highest" level, philosophy. Some have wished to conserve and legitimate these developments through attempts to base them on an "original foundation" that would make rationality "the *telos* of mankind," and, further, through attempts to "link the whole history of thought to the preservation of this rationality, to the maintenance of this teleology, and to the ever necessary return to this foundation."[6] Contemporary African-American Studies contributed to this critical, anti-(Euro-American) foundationalist legacy directed against this mythology of "progressive Reason" narrated in some reconstructions of European and American histories. It is this legacy, in part, that we seek to refine and continue as "Africology."

Yet what's in this name, offered as the essence-gathering concept and focusing lens for a complex of activities that are to constitute a "discipline"? A great deal, obviously. Most apparent is the deliberate shift from "Black" or "African-American" Studies to "*Afric-ology*": from a heuristic set that took its departure from color (but always involved more than color) to one that rests explicitly on peoples (and all that goes with them, as before) identified by the name given to the land of their origin (ultimately, the origin of all peoples?!); to a heuristic set guiding the efforts to achieve a conceptual capturing (recovery?) and recapitulation, interpretation, of the *logos* of Africa—that is, the collection of constitutive logic(s) and practices, the "spirit," of Africa that, in part, make up the "essence" of its peoples, thus distinguishes them from all (subsequent) others? This recovered *logos* is then to be used to guide and to measure the adequacy of all studies of Africa and her peoples, with Africology as discipline having become the systematization of such studies and evaluations. The anticipation of the existence and recovery of this *logos* is, I take it, what serves heuristically to guide the "architectural" work preparatory to discipline building.

I have elected to bring Foucault and Radnitzsky into this project because they are both concerned with the critical review of what Foucault refers to as "fields of discourse" or "discursive formations," and what Radnitzsky terms "sciences" or, generally, "X-ologies." Both are concerned, in significantly different but related ways, with the characterization, organization, and development of knowledge complexes. In this regard, both have something to say about "norms," that is, about the value-laden *rules* that structure "discursive formations" generally, and "sciences" as particular instances of them. Furthermore, Foucault in particular is especially critical of certain disciplinary practices, and his critique supports some of the criticisms of "Eurocentric" intellectual endeavors advanced in African-American Studies. On the other hand, Foucault's critiques, and Radnitzsky's insights, can—and should—be brought to African-American Studies and the efforts to refine its disciplinary practices and norm-setting power into Africology. Thus, an excursion through Foucault and Radnitzsky will help to clarify the norms that do—or ought to—*structure* Africology, on the one side, and Africology's concern to *prescribe* norms to guide intellectual and social practice, on the other.

Archaeology/Genealogy

Foucault has been concerned with critical examinations of a number of the discursive *logoi* institutions and practices of Europe, particularly with constructions of their histories and with how these historiographic efforts are conceived and carried out.[7] I regard his work as "critical" (though in *The Archaeology* he denies that it is critical "most of the time") because it questions previous narrations of these fields—as presented, for example, in approaches to the histories of medicine, science, or "ideas," and in philosophies of history, of science, etc.—by focusing on the *rules that* govern their emergence and development as "fields of discourse." Of particular relevance here are his efforts to carry through "archaeological" or "genealogical" reconstructions challenging those modes of articulating histories ("narrations") that attempt to provide, among other things, "the reassuring form of the identical."

> There is a reason for this. If the history of thought could remain the locus of uninterrupted continuities, if it could endlessly forge connexions that no analysis could undo without abstraction, if it could weave, around everything that men say and do, obscure synthesis [sic] that anticipate for him, prepare him, and lead him endlessly towards his future, it would provide a privileged shelter for the sovereignty of consciousness. Continuous history is the indispensable correlative of the founding function of the subject; the guarantee that everything that has eluded him may be restored to him; the certainty that time will disperse nothing without restoring it in a reconstituted unity; the promise that one day the subject—in the form of historical consciousness—will once again be able to appropriate, to bring back under his sway, all those things that are kept at a distance by difference, and find in them what might be called his abode. Making historical analysis the discourse of the continuous and making human consciousness the original subject of all historical development and all action are the two sides of the same system of thought. In this system, time is conceived in terms of totalization and revolutions are never more than moments of consciousness.
>
> In various forms, this theme has played a constant role since the nineteenth century: to preserve, against all decenterings, the sovereignty of the subject, and the twin figures of anthropology and humanism.[8]

To preserve, we should add, the "sovereignty" of the Greco-European–Euro-American *anthropos* in whose defense anthropology rose as "the science of the *other*"; to preserve the "sovereignty" of the Greco-European–Euro-American *man* whose "best" picture was painted as "humanism."

Foucault's aim, in contrast, has been "to define a method of historical analysis freed from the anthropological theme."[9] Further, his methods seek to be free of the "comforts of the grand abstractions" of universal truths which, in their apodicticity and permanence, allow those who have grasped them, secure in their sovereignty, to script human development. As Paul Rabinow notes, Foucault moves to *historicize* supposedly universal categories (e.g., "reason," "truth," "justice"): "For Foucault, there is no external position of certainty, no universal understanding that is beyond history and society . . . there is a consistent imperative . . . which runs through Foucault's historical studies: to discover the relations of specific scientific disciplines and particular social practices."[10] One of the most fundamental of these relations is that of *power.*

The insight undergirding this imperative has been basic to Black Studies. Still, Foucault is helpful. First, by way of the sophistication of his "archaeological," "genealogical" methods which, through the use of concepts of "rupture," "discontinuity" "threshold," "transformation," etc., "decenter" the established *unities* of the investigated discursive fields. An early requirement is that a number of heretofore key notions be suspended: "tradition,"[11] "influence," "development" and "evolution,"[12] "spirit."[13] Why? Because they function as "ready-made syntheses" that are accepted without examination, their validity recognized "from the outset," and are accorded "unqualified, spontaneous value." Other "unities" must be questioned, as well, such as the groupings that distinguish between the major types of discourse, or between such forms or genres as science, religion, history, philosophy, literature, etc.[14] And a final "precaution": that we take care to "disconnect" the unquestioned continuities by which the discourse to be analyzed is organized in advanced by our renouncing two linked but opposed themes. On the one hand, the theme that regards the historical analysis of discourse as "the quest for and the repetition of an origin that eludes all historical determination"; on the other, the theme that sees such analysis as "the interpretation or 'hearing' of an 'already-said' that is at the same time a 'not-said,'" a "truth" already spoken back at the "beginning" that lies waiting for reclamation through hearings held today. Both themes must be renounced. Instead, "discourse must not be referred to the distant presence of the origin, but treated as and when it occurs."[15] In short, the "tranquillity" with which these "pre-existing forms of continuity" are accepted without question must be *suspended* (though not rejected "definitively"); they must be shown to be *the result of a construction* whose rules must be known, their justifications scrutinized, the conditions and analytical points of view that establish their legitimacy defined, and "which of them can never be accepted in any circumstances" indicated.[16]

With these suspensions what one is left with is the "discursive field" (or "discursive formation"). In his investigations Foucault has focused on the rules governing the emergence and development of what he takes to be their key elements: *objects; enunciative modalities* (statements and ways of speaking about the objects; descriptions of *who* speaks and with what authority); the *concepts* employed in the discourse; and *strategies,* or the themes and theories guiding the deployment of concepts, the formations of objects, the invocation of modes of enunciation. Such efforts Foucault terms the "archaeology," the "genealogy," of a discursive field the point of which is to "grasp the statement in the exact specificity of its occurrence; determine its conditions of existence, fix at least its limits, establish its correlations with other statements that may be connected with it, and show what other forms of statement it excludes."[17] To what ends?

> In fact, the systematic erasure of all given unities enables us first of all to restore to the statement the specificity of its occurrence, and to show that discontinuity is one of those great accidents that create cracks not only in the geology of history, but also in the simple fact of the statement; it emerges in its historical irruption; what we try to examine is the incision that it makes, that irreducible — and very often tiny — emergence.[18]

The force of these insights from Foucault that situate disciplinary practices in discontinuous history will be amplified when joined to the critical studies of "metascience" of Radnitzsky.

Metascience
Radnitzsky's work in "metascience" is useful for similar reasons.[19] He studies the production of knowledge, in particular "the research-guiding interests institutionalized in intellectual traditions," in an effort to identify possible alternative models and paths of development. In the process he distinguishes a number of approaches to the study of a science: (1) studies of its logical, semantic, information-theoretical, epistemological aspects; (2) a *genetic* perspective that focuses on the production-and-product system, i.e., on how knowledge grows in a particular enterprise; (3) a focus on producers and users: on "sociological, psychological, historiographical, culturological, political, etc., aspects of science"; (4) a focus on *science, man, society* "as a total system which sets its own aims and can change these aims"; and/or (5) a "critical" perspective on a science that focuses on the *meaning* of science "for man" and an evaluation of its possible future impact.[20]

However, it is the focus of *Contemporary Schools of Metascience* that I find most relevant in terms of providing another critical perspective on efforts to fashion a discipline of Africology: the elaboration of an articulate, critical theory of research (hence, *meta*science). It is an elaboration that is primarily *normative* and *praxiological*: that is, it presents a *theory* of research, the intent of which is "to provide adequate models of the growth of scientific knowledge" that can then be used to "manage" or guide the emergence and development of intellectual traditions.[21] I shall exploit this relevance as it relates to Africology by briefly sketching Radnitzsky's theoretical overview of a research-scientific enterprise and discussing what he opts for as a fruitful "frame" for critiquing research-scientific (disciplinary) praxis.

On Radnitzsky's interpretation of a research enterprise, a research group operates in a certain "intellectual milieu" that supplies intellectual resources and in which certain ideals and "tastes" for certain concepts prevail and may influence the research group. A particular "research strategy," adopted by the group, steers the research process. The research is directed at certain sectors of "reality" and produces a "knowledge system" in regard to it, results of which are "reported" or mediated to "interessees": among others, colleagues working within the discipline; persons working in other disciplines; and intellectuals more generally who make use of the results of the work.[22]

This interpretation of a model of a research enterprise reconstructs it as a system whose components include various *persons* (researchers and those interested in the products of the research); *activities* or *processes* (research, reporting, etc.); a *territory* or subject matter; and *products* (symbolic systems, including knowledge and software instruments, hardware instruments, etc.).[23] The research process involves the transformation of complexes consisting of knowledge, problems, and instruments.[24] The options chosen, the direction in which the research is steered, and the sequences and stabilization of its development are all determined by the *research program*, which grows out of a "prospect": "a map sketched on the basis of foreknowledge and indicating the places where one thinks it would pay to search and research." Thus, the research program is the chief "system-constitutive" factor of a research direction. We get a *tradition* of research with the appearance of a sequence of research enterprises all governed by a common research program.[25]

We should look more closely at a number of the factors conditioning the research process. First, those that give direction to a research program are a combination of *cognitive* and *teleological* elements inherent in the "foreknowledge" that guides the mapping of the field of research: "a striving to achieve a certain end, a position-taking toward something, is already informed by or impregnated with partisan-foreconceptions about that something." The "core" of these are foreconceptions regarding the territory of research, whether that territory is part of the natural world (in which case the foreconceptions or assumptions will make up part of a "world-picture" of, say, the continent of "Africa") or, in the case of the humanities and social sciences, an image of human beings (i.e., a philosophical anthropology of "Africans"). This core, and the perspective it implicates, become the "earmarks" of a research enterprise or tradition. The tradition or enterprise can undergo evolutionary change, but it can be drastically altered only at the expense of transforming its identity.[26]

Among the originating assumptions that make up the core are "*conceptions about the type of research* in question, about the 'X-ology' to which the research enterprise belongs: i.e., a research-theoretical position." These "programmatic" notions reflect thoughts about what a discipline should be like, and will determine the *system of criteria* the practitioners will use to critique the discipline, and its "products," in its ongoing development.[27]

All of the foreconceptions constitutive of the research enterprise, Radnitzsky notes, when viewed historically or socio-psychologically, are in reality constitutive of the researchers themselves. He thus calls them "*internal* steering factors," collectively the *internal steering field*, a "dialectical unit" conditioned by inner tensions — or, even, contradictions. Further, the research enterprise, along with its Internal Steering Field, is embedded in an *intellectual milieu* made up of particular types of "climate" and "market":

> The *intellectual climate* contains above all world-picture hypotheses in the broadest sense: philosophical cosmologies (world views), and philosophical anthropologies (images of man, which are to a large extent evaluative). The *intellectual market* consists of other research enterprises and traditions. These provide virtual sources of knowledge, of instruments (and problems), and of paragons.
>
> Which of the components of the intellectual environment influence the research enterprise depends mainly *on the researchers themselves*. Hence it appears appropriate to consider the foreconceptions and the research program . . . as the *inner* part of the Internal Steering Field and that part of the intellectual environment that actually is made use of by the researchers as the *outer* part of the Internal Steering Field.[28]

Further, the wider social world in which a research enterprise is embedded impinges on researchers in various ways. Radnitzsky refers to this world as the *external steering field*. Its components consist of "extra-intellectual" factors that manifest, in particular, the interests of persons other than the researchers. Negotiating the dynamic feedback relations between the "internal steering field" and "external steering field" is a major task for those involved in structuring and managing a research enterprise. It is a task made even more difficult when the "external steering field" is as complex (historically, socially, politically, intellectually) as, say, America and its involvements in the global political economy in general, its involvements with Africa and the African diaspora in particular.[29]

On the way to a discussion of norms in Africology we should look more closely at the business of *foreconceptions*, for these provide the "foundations" and boundary conditions of the enterprise. Of particular importance are those foreconceptions that function as *criteria* in terms of which various aspects of research are determined. For with these criteria we can see how norms structure a discipline.

Among these criteria we must distinguish: (1) criteria researchers *claim* to use; (2) those that they *believe in;* (3) and those that *"de facto" govern* research activity. For there can be an enormous disparity between (1) and (3). Further, we must be able to locate those criteria of which we researchers might have insufficient self-understanding (e.g., "as a function of the influence of intellectual traditions that are not seen through") so we may subject them to critique.[30] Such critique is what Radnitzsky terms one of the *normative turns* of a theory of research: that is, a critical review of the norms that structure a research enterprise and govern its praxis. And to the extent that such "critical turns" are a part of the research tradition itself, governed by criteria from its internal steering field, the tradition can develop under the critical guidance of criteria relativized to it.

This "critical turn" is an important aspect of Radnitzskian metascience: "The way science grows is to a considerable extent determined by schools or intellectual traditions. Hence a metascience that is concerned with developing a theory of the growth of scientific knowledge must devote attention to criticism of tradition." Normally, "routine science" evolves or grows under the guidance of traditions: "they regulate what problems are dealt with, in what manner they are dealt with, what resources are utilized, etc. They establish a routine; and thereby they save efforts and energies that may be used for possible innovations."[31] However, when different traditions intersect within an enterprise, or when the dialectics generated by the cognitive dissonances inherent in it force it to develop in innovative, "revolutionary" ways, conflicts emerge and must be resolved if the knowledge acquisition and refinement processes are to continue.

Achieving this resolution of conflict is seldom simply a matter of following the dictates of (deductive) logic. The *better* method, for Radnitzsky, is "the long-term process of the criticist dialogue between various opposed intellectual traditions," for this is the *only* thing that "gives science what objectivity it has." Thus arises the vital need for the criticism of tradition intended to free us from bondage to *certain* traditions, since "we cannot stand outside all traditions," by "playing out one tradition against another, by engaging in the dialectics between opposed traditions."[32]

At the heart of this *Traditionskritik* (criticism of tradition) is what Radnitzsky refers to as the "criticist frame," an orientation for guiding and evaluating intellectual practices and products that includes a number of key commitments: (1) recognition of the "historicity" of the researcher: i.e., that one is *always* in some historical situation and tradition; that this is constitutive of who one is, what one does; (2) recognition that, given our historicity —our situational boundedness—there is, therefore, always "the problem of the practice of life": i.e., "the urgent need to connect theory and practice";[33] (3) recognition that our situational boundedness is unavoidable, an awareness that is the first step toward overcoming one's boundedness *as much as it can be overcome* (never totally); and (4) recognition that thinking, "although history-bound, has a certain autonomy, possessing a universally and humanly valid basis . . . e.g., logic; i.e., that there are inter- or super-traditional adequacy criteria."[34] The "criticist frame" is itself a collection of such criteria and is recommended by Radnitzsky as the most appropriate context in which to mediate competing traditions, in particular, and, more generally, to facilitate the practices of research enterprises.

I shall enlarge this frame by combining it with archaeological and genealogical problematizing strategies from Foucault. This enlarged frame will recover the critical insights of Foucault and Radnitzsky into a single perspective that can be deployed in a review of Black Studies as normative theory and in considering how Africology might be an improvement:

AN ARCHAEOLOGICAL/GENEALOGICAL CRITICIST FRAME
A. Historicist Postulate:
   1. Discursive formations (fields, disciplines) must be understood in the context of their historicity: i.e., they are constituted in contexts conditioned by historical developments such that there is no "evolutionary flow of Reason" that is realized in the practices and achievements of disciplines as a "progressive" and systematic accumulation of knowledge.
B. Anti-Foundationalist Postulates:
   1. Achievements of the intellect are *not* based on an "original foundation" that makes rationality the "telos" of mankind. Further, given the historicity of intellectual practices, the history of thought does not continue this teleology, thus does not preserve this rationality, via necessary returns to this foundation.
   2. The historicity of intellectual practices argues against historical reconstructions in the form of narratives that offer "the reassuring form of the identical" as a "privileged shelter" for the "sovereignty" of a particular form of consciousness, or a particular *anthropos*, even, that overcomes difference, thus overcomes time and space, in the "universal truth" of a "grand abstraction," no matter that, as in the proposed case of Black Studies and "Africology," the range of universality of the truth is thought to be restricted to persons of a particular race.
C. "Normative Turns" via Critical "Suspensions":
   1. Key notions in intellectual schemes that function as "ready-made syntheses accepted without examination" must be suspended: e.g., "tradition," "influence," "development" and "evolution," "spirit." Such notions must be deployed only after a careful examination that situates them in the historicity of their formation and use.
   2. Likewise, unquestioned continuities by which discourse is organized *in advance* must be suspended or "disconnected" by (a) *not* regarding

the historical analysis of discourse—or the formation or refinement of a discursive field—as "the quest for and the repetition of an origin that eludes all historical determination"; and (b) by *not* regarding such analysis as "the interpretation or 'hearing' of an 'already-said' that is at the same time a 'not-said'"—a "truth" already spoken back at the "beginning," if you will, which lies waiting for reclamation through our reconstructive "hearings" from today.

D. The "Exposed Field":

1. With these "suspensions" we are left, first, with the "internally steered" "discursive field" of the disciplinary enterprise within which *rules* govern the emergence and development of the key elements:

   a. the "objects": e.g., the "history," "norms," and/or "spirit" of a people;
   b. the "enunciative modalities" of the enterprise, i.e., statements and ways of speaking about the objects and other activities or processes. Included among these modalities are cognitive and teleological *foreconceptions* with respect to a "world picture," a "philosophical anthropology," "programmatic notions" about the discipline, and criteria for evaluating the discipline and its products. This "fore-knowledge" provides the boundary conditions and platform of the enterprise;
   c. descriptions of *who* speaks, and with what authority;
   d. concepts employed in the discourse (e.g., "Afrocentricity," "Eurocentricity"); and
   e. the *strategies*—i.e., the themes and theories—guiding the deployment of concepts, the formation of objects, the invocation of modes of enunciation (Foucault); in the language of Radnitzsky, the *research program* —the "internal steering field"—in terms of which options are chosen, the direction of the research is set, and the sequences and stabilization of the development of the field or enterprise are structured. The "strategic," "programmatic" rules govern the activities and processes, the subject matter, and the products of the field.

2. Second, there is the "external steering field": the wider social world in which the enterprise is embedded and which has a compelling impact on the researchers. Here, too, dialectical critique of this impact is called for—yet another important instance of a "normative turn."

Norms and Theory in Black Studies

The fruitfulness of the criticist frame is brought to focus in the characterization of the angle of view of the Radnitzsky theory of research: it involves what he terms a *praxiological* perspective, one that "views the research enterprise as a system of actions[,] of stratagems, moves, etc."[35] Such a perspective joins smoothly with insights that have been foundational to Black

Studies. Intended to fulfill agendas designed by, and in the interests of, black folks, Black Studies emerged, in its first moments, as reconstructions and critiques of particular research enterprises (history, sociology, political science, literature, art, music, among others) whose practices and products were thought to be racist—or deficient, at the very least—when Africans and peoples of African descent were the objects of concern.

The enlarged criticist frame makes possible an especially systematic characterization of research enterprises, one that allows for a more critical investigation of a particular instance of a tradition or school of research, whether the occasion involves the articulation of a critical stand *against* research enterprises or the *refinement* of a tradition or school to which one is committed. While efforts toward Africology necessarily involve both these strategies, the latter set is of most concern at present: the refinement of a tradition of teaching, research, and scholarship into a "discipline" with a particular configuration of agenda, practices, products, and projected consequences. The call is for the founding of a particular "school" of research with clarified normative and *praxiological* dimensions.[36] It is here, precisely, that the matter of research-guiding norms is brought into sharp focus.

The structuring norms of a discipline, we have seen, are localized in *foreconceptions* constitutive of the "internal steering field" of rules, thus of the practitioners, and constitutive of the "external steering field," i.e., the wider intellectual and social milieu that the practitioners share. Norms— rules—are thus foundational to a discipline: they mark off the field of its operation, set its boundary conditions, and steer the practices executed in its name. Thus, we come to a discussion of "normative theory" in the context of "Africology" already loaded with pre-conceptual baggage—regarding norms, theory and theorizing, disciplines, "Africology," etc. We would do well to take the normative turn proffered by the criticist frame and examine some of this baggage.

We might begin with the ambiguity of the phrase "Africology: Normative Theory." On the one hand, it can be taken to mean theoretical discourse *about* norms in general—what they are, their basis, etc.—but discourse steered by partisan foreconceptions about "Africans." On the other, it can be understood as referring to (or calling for) the specification of particular norms *for* Africology as a disciplinary complex. A third possibility is the notion that Africology should *conceptualize* (theorize) and *prescribe* norms by which persons of African descent ought to live, a "way of life." In each of these cases the concern is with the specification of *rules* to guide action— whether in the context of a research enterprise (i.e., rules to govern production, producers, the quality and distribution of the products) or the social, historical worlds of peoples of African descent more generally. I understand this conceptualizing and specifying of norms to comprise, in part, the *theory* anticipated in "Africology: Normative Theory."

However, the three possibilities are neither unrelated nor mutually exclusive. If we expect Africology to set out the norms to guide African peoples' living, then we must know everything important to know about norms in general, about the normative bases and parameters of Africology, about what *ought* to be the case for black peoples, and how we *ought* to go about achieving and/or maintaining what ought to be. Thus, what at first may have seemed a simple case of ambiguity in a title is really a matter of the inherent complexities involving two aspects of the basis and practices of a research enterprise: its *structuring* norms, and the norms it might *prescribe.* In other words, what is involved are the inherently related matters of theory and practice, knowing and doing.

Dealing with these two aspects requires that the insights summarized in the criticist frame be supplemented by clarifications with regard to the business of systematically establishing principles (or rules) for *determining* norms, and, thus, for prescribing rules for conduct. This is the business of normative ethics.[37] A brief excursus through this context of discourse will help to situate a review of Black Studies and anticipations for Africology as enterprises devoted to normative theorizing and prescribing.

Theorizing "Norms"

With normative ethics we move into the field of discourse of moral philosophy where concerns about normative matters (such as discussions regarding moral *principles* to guide action, moral *concepts,* and moral *reasoning*) are explored in a number of ways, toward various ends. Central to these discussions is, first, the question of *justification,* where the goal is "stating, elucidating, and defending a sound procedure for determining the truth of conflicting moral claims and the soundness of moral arguments."[38] (Implicit in this, of course, are rules for the "soundness" of procedures.) Also central is *objectivity,* that supposedly key rule for guiding the practices of science. According to Nielsen: "A moral judgment is objective if, and only if, it is either true or false and if its truth or falsity does not depend on the peculiarities of the person who makes the judgment or on the culture to which he belongs, but shall be determinable by any rational agent who is apprised of the relevant facts."[39] Finally, there is the all important matter of *truth,* which philosophers (and others . . .) have expended a great deal of energy and ink debating.

Across hundreds of years, no one position regarding either of these terms has been able to supplant all others. Regarding "truth," for example, a position that continues to be advanced is the claim that there is no single, universal definition, one that is valid for all persons and peoples, for all time. What Nielsen offers as a definition of "truth" is a position most acceptable to me:

> To be capable of being true, a statement need not state a fact or assert that certain empirically identifiable characteristics are part of an

object or an action. Rather, what is necessary is that the statement in question be publicly warrantable, that is, that it admit of some publicly determinable procedure in virtue of which rational men could come to accept it. . . . We can properly call a statement or judgment in any area objectively true if it would be endorsed without doubt by informed, reasonable, reflective, and careful observers.[40]

Of course, it takes only a few moments of reflection to realize that in trying to establish the truth of ethical-normative statements and have them "endorsed" by "informed, reasonable, reflective, and careful" observers, the meanings of these key terms are not—and, as I asserted at the outset, *cannot* be —fixed axiomatically. Nor, therefore, can the notion of "objective truth."

Along the same line, equally as much, if not more, energy has been expended debating whether—and/or to what extent—"objectivity" can be achieved on universalist, "foundationalist" terms. As with "truth," a similar position continues to be advanced: ethical norms are not "objective" *a priori* (i.e., prior, and thus not subject, to human experience); rather, "objectivity" is at best a matter of intersubjective agreement (consensus) achieved by adherence to shared rules, an adherence worked out, mediated, and maintained in particular social conditions.

Along these lines, then, the justification, objectivity, and truthfulness of ethical-normative statements fail the tests of ethical naturalism[41] and certain forms of ethical objectivism, such as ethical logicism,[42] intuitionism,[43] or objectivist theological theories which assert that "there is an objective criterion of what is right or wrong which is provided by what God wishes us to do, approves our doing, commands us to do, and so on."[44] Norm-setting discourse is a *practical* venture: "its primary use is not that of asserting, questioning, or reaffirming that something is the case but that of making something the case, of criticizing or appraising something that is the case, or of molding attitudes toward certain states of affairs or actions. This is what is meant when we say that moral discourse is essentially action-guiding and attitude-molding."[45] And, to invoke Foucault once again, this is ultimately the case for *all* discourse—not just for normative ethics; this is also the case for intellectual praxis in general, especially when it concerns the social world. In both cases—theorizing about norms for theoretical-disciplinary praxis, and theorizing about norms for "a way of life"—the concern with norms is the same: making rules to guide and control actions. We are involved with *strategies* to achieve ends and, thereby, with all of the vagaries and conditions of non-axiomatizable *choice* that are involved.

Insights such as these with respect to norms have served as major planks in the platform of Black Studies: "Afrocentric" research emerged as a *normative* turn vis-à-vis European- and Euro-American–centered research. It (Black Studies) is an explicitly *partisan* venture consciously and explicitly devoted to serving interests of black peoples by way of "the systematic study of black people . . . an examination of the deeper truths of black life . . . [Black Studies] will examine the valid part that black people have played in man's development in society . . . [and] differs from academic disciplines rooted in European tradition by relating to African history and culture."[46] Further, it is a venture that, from the outset, seeks an intimate and *necessary* connection between theory and praxis, between systematic knowledge development and social action, "science" and "ways of life":

> Currently, the two principal pillars which support theory building in Black Studies are the concepts of (1) knowledge development or consciousness raising and (2) the liberation of black peoples, translated as a change in the social, political and economic order. . . . The goal of Black Studies is not merely to seek knowledge for its own sake, but knowledge for the purpose of pragmatic manipulation. This is an instrumentalist view of theory building in Black Studies. That is, the significance of research and the uprooting of information lies in the actions they guide.[47]

In short, Black Studies is about *both* "science" and "ways of life," has both "an academic and social mission, and is, therefore, both an investigative and applied social science."[48]

In such statements we get a sense of the normative commitments of Black Studies. If Africology is to be its refinement, while consciously attending to norms in its (Africology's) theorizing and direction setting for black life, then it is imperative that we review these normative principles and commitments at work in — and advanced on behalf of — Black Studies in service to its partisan agenda.

Black Studies: A Partisan Venture

Nick Aaron Ford's *Black Studies: Threat-or-Challenge?* is one of the earliest surveys and analyses of Black Studies programs conducted.[49] In it he presents seven categories of objectives for Black Studies programs (drawn from a survey of two hundred programs with approximately two hundred objectives listed):

1. concern with "the need for the educational experience *to provide for black students a feeling of personal identity, personal pride, and personal worth*";
2. the programs are "based on the assumption that a study of black history and culture will aid blacks in understanding the basis for an identity that is satisfying and fulfilling";
3. "the need to promote sympathetic interest and dedicated involvement in the improvement of the black community (local, national and worldwide)" [Ford notes that, in the programs surveyed, more space is given to this objective than to any other];

4. *"the radical reformation of American education by attacking its basic racist assumptions and making it truly democratic and relevant to the current needs of blacks and whites"*;
5. *"to train black students in the philosophy and strategies of revolution as a prelude to black revolution"*;
6. *"preparation for career opportunities, including the professions"*;
7. *"the determination to encourage and actively develop intellectual growth and broad scholarly interests in their students."* [50]

But how are these objectives to be met? In the words of Maulana Karenga, one of the leading theorists of Black Studies, the matter of first priority is the elimination of our "ideological deficiency" by posing and answering "the fundamental question": "what ideology—coherent system of theories and value system—can give us a correct worldview and analysis of our situation, pull us together and weld us into the conscious and progressive *social force* we need to be in order to achieve in *struggle* and alliance with other oppressed and progressive people, the liberation of ourselves and all people?"[51] Such systems of theories and values, sanctioned as principles or rules to guide theoretical and social praxis, are *norms.*

In the effort to set out a "coherent system of theories and value system," one aspect has involved a revaluation of the notions of "objectivity" and of its corollary "disinterestedness." One of the stronger claims advanced by some proponents of Black Studies is that "objectivity," in the sense expressed by Nielsen, is not achievable, and any claim that it is in fact operative in conceptualizing and setting out principles for "ways of life" is at best an ideological cover for ethnocentric and/or racial—if not racist (and/or gender-based)—power moves. A less stringent—and, I think, more appropriate—view is expressed by Maurice Jackson:

> Objectivity in sociology cannot be taken for granted. Although scientific objectivity can be safeguarded, to a degree, by the scientific method, the sociology of Black Studies makes explicit the interdependence of science and society referred to by Max Weber. . . . [B]lack Studies follows the modern scientific view that facts do not speak for themselves, but are informed by perspectives and assumptions which are implicit if not explicit. . . . [B]lack Studies questions the presumed disinterestedness of much current knowledge and is explicit in its assertion that appropriate knowledge should be used for and by black people as well.[52]

The same is true, say some proponents of Black Studies, with respect to intellectual practices and their results in general: their justification, objectivity, and truth are ultimately *group* based, thus are not secured in disinterested objectivity and universality simply by their cognitive, epistemological character. Molefi Kete Asante, for example, argues that "all analysis is culturally centered and flows from ideological commitments"; therefore—to extend his argument—analysis serves *particular* agendas of *particular* persons.[53] Thus, values *cum* norms structuring the practices of a research enterprise, and, through their deployment, the explicit attempt to structure "ways of life," are not *objective* in the sense that the grounds of their truth, objectivity, and justification are without reference to *any* group, or any person as a member of some particular group. Rather, such norms can be justified only *relative to* some group(s) or to some person as a member of a particular group; hence they do not automatically and necessarily transcend historical social life-worlds. In the words of Philip Daniel:

> The whole emphasis on objectivity and empirical theory as opposed to normative theory is out of place in Black Studies and the arguments concerning it should be dropped. We scrutinize and act as we live. Analysis in Black Studies is a purposeful activity and the conditions of the black community involve questions of right and wrong.[54]

As "purposeful activity" also concerned with questions of right and wrong, Black Studies is to provide rules for answering such questions. Since it is in *lived* social worlds, in the rules structuring this living, that norms are at work, Black Studies must address such matters guided by the life-practices of the people comprising them. Norms, then, are "culturally relative":

> The cultural relativist emphasizes the cultural tradition as a prime source of the individual's views and thinks that most disagreements in ethics among individuals stem from enculturation in different ethical traditions, although he need not deny that some ethical disagreements among individuals arise from differences of innate constitution or personal history between the individuals.[55]

In contemporary Black Studies this position has been termed "cultural nationalism."[56] In fact, it has been the dominant orientation in contemporary Black Studies and accounts for much of its platform. Molefi Asante and Maulana Karenga, among others, are two of its leading proponents. A brief review of (some of) their arguments will be helpful not only for insight into the "ideology" of Black Studies that they offer, but also because both attempt to refine and advance the enterprise.[57]

"Afrocentricity"

Molefi Asante's contribution centers on the concept of "Afrocentricity," which, together with its corollary "Eurocentricity," have come to have a pervasive life of their own in Black Studies discourse. "Afrocentricity" is offered as the name for a perspective that is centered on "the African Cultural System" in which *all* African people participate "although it is modified according to specific histories and nations."[58] The core of Afrocentricity is *Njia:* "the collective expression of the Afrocentric worldview based in the historical experience of African people. . . . Incorporating Njia into our lives, we become essentially ruled by our own values and principles. Dispensing with alien views at our center, Njia puts us in and on our own center."[59] With Njia, we become Africa-centered, if you will, in our normative commitments and practices. Thus, "Afrocentric," "Afrocentricity."

Oriented and guided by Afrocentricity, Asante argues, a new criticism emerges. "It introduces relevant values, denounces non-Afrocentric behavior, and promotes analysis . . . the Afrocentric critical methods start with the primary measure! Does it place Africans in the center?"[60] For the present, the primary task of this new criticism is the "recapturing of our own collective consciousness. . . . It is reclaiming Egypt, deciphering the ancient writing of Nubia, circulating the histories and geographies of Ibn Khaldun and Ibn Battuta, and examining records of Africans in Mexico and other places in the new world."[61] On the way to this collective consciousness there are five levels of awareness:

1. *skin recognition*—"when a person recognizes that his or her skin is black and or her heritage is black but cannot grasp any further reality";

2. *environmental recognition*—seeing the environment "as indicating his or her blackness through discrimination and abuse";

3. *personality awareness*—"It occurs when a persons [sic] says 'I like music, or dance or chitterlings.'. . ." Even if the person speaks truthfully, this is not Afrocentricity;

4. *interest-concern*—"demonstrates interest and concern in the problems of blacks and tries to deal intelligently with the issues of the African people." This level is also not Afrocentricity since "it does not consume the life and spirit of the person";

5. *Afrocentricity*—is achieved "when the person becomes totally changed to a conscious level of involvement in the struggle for his or her own mind liberation."[62]

Further, once achieved, Afrocentricity allows one to predict the actions of whites and non-Afrocentric persons "with certainty." And, one does not refuse to "condemn mediocrity and reactionary attitudes among Africans for the sake of false unity."[63] Within an Afrocentric perspective, the "two aspects of consciousness" are operative: toward oppression, toward victory.

Specifically, what does this mean for the practices of Black Studies? It means, according to Asante, that Black Studies must become the discipline of *Afrology*. Pertinent to this discussion, the "outlines" of the normative base of the discipline are available: they are "rooted in the social, political and economic values of our people." And the discipline will be the crystallization of "the notions and methods of black-oriented social scientists and humanists" whose "basic qualities" will be *competence* ("the analytic skills with which the scholar investigates his subject"), *clarity of perspective* ("the ability to focus on the Afrocentric issues in the subject area and to interpret those issues in a way that will expose the essential factors constituting the subject"), and *understanding of the object* [sic] ("Understanding the subject means that the scholar knows something of the inter-relationship of his subject and the world context.").[64]

Asante offers two "theoretical propositions" that will "set the tone" for an analysis of the emerging discipline of "Afrology" with its Afrocentric core:

> Afrology is primarily pan-Africanist in its treatment of the creative, political and geographic dimensions of our collective will to liberty....
> A second proposition is that the Afrologist, by virtue of his perspective, participates in the coming to be of new concepts and directions. His perceptions of reality, political and social allow him to initiate novel approaches to problems and issues. Not being encapsulated by the Western point of view he is a person who is mentally as free as possible. ... In fact, the Afrologist ... is a person who is capable of participating in both the African and the Western point of view; however, as a practicing Afrologist he must act Afrocentrically. What he has learned is the value of every viewpoint.[65]

The future of Afrology?

> Since Afrology is based upon an Afrocentric interpretation and a particular conception of society, the results of our work will alter previous perceptions and set standards for future studies of African peoples. It is here that Afrology comes into its own as an organizing methodology, and a reflective philosophy, able to open the door to a more assertive, and therefore proper, consciousness of cultural and historical data. Such a proper consciousness is founded upon the genuine acceptance of our African past, without which there is no Afrological discourse or basis for peculiar analysis.[66]

Molefi Asante continues his articulation of Afrocentricity in *The Afrocentric Idea*.[67] Here Afrocentricity is further defined and deployed as "a critique that propounds a cultural theory of society by the very act of criticism" and proposes "a cultural reconstruction that incorporates the African perspective as a part of an entire human transformation." The object of critique: "Eurocentricism," that is to say "the preponderant ... myths of universalism, objectivity, and classical traditions [that retain] a provincial European cast." Afrocentric analysis will "reestablish ... the centrality of the ancient Kemetic (Egyptian) civilization and the Nile Valley cultural complex as points of reference for an African perspective in much the same way as Greece and Rome serve as reference points for the European world." Afrocentricity, as the foundation of the discipline of Afrology, will "expand ... the repertoire of human perspectives on knowledge."[68] The goal: "a post-Eurocentric idea where true transcultural analyses become possible."[69]

Sustained by new information and innovative methodologies, Afrology will transform community and social sciences, as well as arts and humanities, and assist in constructing a new, perhaps more engaging, way to analyze and synthesize reality. Perhaps what is needed is a post-Western or meta-Western metatheory to disentangle us from the consuming monopoly of a limited intellectual framework.[70]

"Afrocentricity," then, may be viewed as a covering term for *rules of construction* for the disciplinary field of Black Studies — or "Afrology" — guiding the formation of enunciative modalities (statements and ways of speaking about objects and practices in the field) and inclusive of foreconceptions that provide the field's boundary conditions and platform.

"Kawaida" Theory

Maulana Karenga has provided an even fuller articulation of what the disciplinary project of Black Studies should involve. His most complete discussion is presented in his *Introduction to Black Studies*. After setting out a number of objectives for Black Studies, he discusses, as well, a number of points of "relevance":

1. a "definitive contribution to humanity's understanding itself . . . Black Studies . . . becomes important because it is a study of a particular people which aids in the study of humanity as a whole";
2. "its contribution to U.S. society's understanding of itself";
3. as a logical consequence, "a contribution to the university's realization of its claim and challenge to teach the whole truth, or something as close to it as humanly possible";
4. "a contribution to the rescue and reconstruction of Black history and humanity";
5. "a critical contribution to a new social science which will not only benefit Blacks, but also the U.S. and the world."[71]

Both Karenga's objectives and his points of relevance are well represented in the categories of objectives, listed above, assembled by Nick Aaron Ford in his survey. Clearly they help to set the agenda for Black Studies and thus shape part of its normative platform. Other planks are added when Karenga discusses the "scope" of Black Studies as a discipline. It is to be

the scientific study of the multidimensional aspects of Black thought and practice in their current and historical unfolding. . . . Black Studies . . . is both a particular and general social science . . . [and] . . . as an interdisciplinary discipline has seven basic subject areas. . . : Black History; Black Religion; Black Social Organization; Black Politics; Black Economics; Black Creative Production (Black Art, Music and Literature) and Black Psychology.[72]

For Karenga, these subject areas constitute the "core" of Black Studies. However, an essential point to note is that he grounds this "conceptual framework" on a normative platform of his own articulation: *Kawaida* theory, "a theory of cultural and social change which has as one of its main propositions the contention that the solution to the problems of Black life demand critiques and correctives in the seven basic areas of culture . . . : mythology (religion), history, social organization, economic organization, political organization, creative motif and ethos."[73]

At the heart of *Kawaida* theory are seven principles advanced as the core of a "Black value system," the *Nguzo Saba,* provided to guide cultural and social change, and the organization of black life:

UMOJA (Unity) — To strive for and maintain unity in the family, community, nation and race.

KUJICHAGULIA (Self-Determination) — To define ourselves, name ourselves, create for ourselves and speak for ourselves instead of being defined, named, created for and spoken for by others.

UJIMA (Collective Work and Responsibility) — To build and maintain our community together and make our sister's and brother's problems our problems and to solve them together.

UJAMAA (Cooperative Economics) — To build and maintain our own stores, shops and other businesses and to profit from them together.

NIA (Purpose) — To make as our collective vocation the building and developing of our community in order to restore our people to their traditional greatness.

KUUMBA (Creativity) — To do always as much as we can, in the way we can, in order to leave our community more beautiful and beneficial than we inherited it.

IMANI (Faith) — To believe with all our heart in our people, our parents, our teachers, our leaders and the righteousness and victory of our struggle.[74]

These normative principles, combined with the objectives, relevances, and conceptual framework of Black Studies, support what Karenga terms a set of "core integrative principles and assumptions" that are the "thematic glue" holding together the core subject areas:

1. "each subject area of Black Studies is a vital aspect and area of the Black experience and, therefore, contributive to the understanding and appreciation of its wholeness";
2. "the truth of the Black experience is whole and thus, any partial and

compartmentalized approach to it can only yield a partial and incomplete image and understanding of it";

3. "effectively integrated into the pattern of the discipline as a whole, each subject area becomes a microcosm of the macrocosm, the Black experience, which not only enriches our knowledge of the Black experience, but also enhances the analytical process and products of the discipline itself";

4. "all the subject areas mesh and intersect not only at the point of their primary focus, i.e., Black people in the process of shaping reality in their own image and interest, but also in their self-conscious commitment and contribution to the definition and solution of the social and discipline problems which serve as the core challenges to Black Studies."[75]

But the challenges — the "social and discipline problems" — are serious and multi-dimensional. Karenga addresses them directly. His discussion of what he terms the "intellectual" challenge to Black Studies is pertinent.

First is the problem of definition, i.e., "the need of Black Studies to . . . establish in clear terms in a body of critical literature its academic and social missions." A central aspect of this problem for Karenga are the matters of focus and thrust:

> Whether Black Studies should be Afro-American centered or Pan-African. Usually, a Pan-African emphasis means a Continent centered program, but it may include Caribbean studies, the study of South American and Islander Blacks or any other Blacks as well. . . . Such a broadly based focus might satisfy some Pan-Africanists, but it still leaves fundamental questions unanswered. For example, which of these areas or peoples should get the most attention, and if it is to be equally divided, why? If Black Studies is still to link the campus to the community, how does it now define the community given its expanded focus?[76]

Karenga proposes a less "over-ambitious" scope that "begins where it is, in the U.S., among Afro-Americans, and then as it grows stronger, expands outward."[77]

A second problem of focus has to do with the debate regarding "values," particularly whether the value focus of Black Studies should be on "survival" or "development." Karenga opts for the latter: "Development is obviously the superior value, for not only does it stress the need for new competencies, but inherent in the concept of development, itself, is the assumption and insurance of survival."[78] Other problems include: the absence of a "standard rationale" for the existence of Black Studies, and, connected with this, theoretical and administrative thrusts toward "integration"; the absence of a standard curriculum; and, finally, the challenge of developing a definitive, substantial body of literature without which the future — even the worth — of the discipline will continue to be in doubt.[79]

Karenga's proposed correctives for these problems take us to the heart of the discussion regarding the move from Black Studies to Africology as a *discipline:*

> The thrust of Black Studies toward contribution of a body of literature which will help bring into being a new social science and at the same time contribute to the rescue and reconstruction of Black history and humanity, must have at least four characteristics. It must be holistic, critical, corrective and committed.[80]

What does each of these mean? For Karenga, a *holistic* approach is a "comprehensive inquiry into the core process and practices of Black life as well as an investigation into related internal and external factors which confront and affect us as a people."[81] A *critical* approach is

> concrete, rational and incisive. . . . Critical intellectual production moves beyond the insubstantiality of free flows of consciousness and pitiful calls for survival, digs beneath the surface and raises that which is absent in traditional literature, i.e., the rich variousness and potential of Black life and the subversive content of our history. Its search is for possibilities as well as achievements, for contradictions as well as tendencies that will lead us beyond the established state of things.[82]

An approach that is *corrective* moves beyond criticism to *reconstruction:* "*the most severe and effective criticism of a society is self-conscious practice which transforms it.*" Thus, "a corrective body of Black Studies literature must begin with a redefinition of the world in our own image according to our own needs."[83] Finally, Black Studies as a *partisan* enterprise

> must be unashamedly committed to a set of values contributive to its task — which in the final analysis — is both theoretical and practical. Committed intellectual work reflects the acceptance of one's role as an *unashamed partisan of one's people.* Moreover, it recognizes the fact that there is no pure research isolated and divorced from the urgencies of the day.[84]

Combining the arguments of Karenga with those of Molefi Asante (a legitimate combination in that both, in fact, are colleagues involved in some of the same organizations working to fulfill the Black Studies agenda), the following profile of Black Studies emerges. It is:

1. a multidimensional enterprise, centered on Africa and African peoples as the primary measure, with both theoretical and practical "missions" (i.e., knowledge production in service to social change) that cover seven key aspects of life;

2. guided by a conceptual framework that maps these aspects;
3. held together by a core of thematic principles;
4. grounded on a particular set of values thought to be indigenous to the lives of black people: the *Nguzo Saba* for Karenga, *Njia* for Asante;
5. holistic, critical, corrective, and committed; and
6. practiced by persons who are competent, clear, knowledgeable; who contribute new concepts and directions; and who know the value of other viewpoints while remaining *Afrocentric.*

Black Studies through the Criticist Frame

How has Black Studies in the Asante-Karenga mode fared as an enterprise devoted to the systematic development of conceptual schemes (among other things) needed for knowledge production and refinement? Apparently not sufficiently well if the implications of the call for the formation of a field and discipline of Africology are drawn out: the "discipline" is yet to be fully developed, the production of various works and the establishment of programs, departments, institutes, journals, and a national organization (The National Council for Black Studies) notwithstanding.

Others are in agreement. Again, Philip T. K. Daniel:

> When we look for constructs or postulates in Black Studies we find a collection of unordered attempts at theory building. Theories in Black Studies are like ships steaming ahead toward one destination, but at different longitudes. This obviously means that if they all keep their present course, only one, or perhaps none will reach the docking point. Thus, they will be in a perpetual circular motion until they run out of fuel.[85]

James Turner addresses this matter in his "Introduction" to *The Next Decade: Theoretical and Research Issues in Africana Studies,* a collection of essays from the Cornell University Africana Studies and Research Center's Tenth Anniversary Conference (1980). For Turner, Black Studies is a discipline of "reconstruction" by way of "a synthesis of what its criticisms imply, convergence with theories reviewed, and the philosophic methods of its pedagogical emphasis."[86] Further, Black Studies provides a unique "paradigm" for critical scholarship, and is fundamentally involved in "renaming the world." Still, Turner notes, the appropriate theory and methodology for this renaming continue to be matters of serious debate, one he thinks should continue. The question, however, is whether we have sufficiently completed the tasks necessary to provide the functions he identifies as common to all disciplines, thus to Black Studies:

> First, the intellectual parameters of the field must be relatively clearly established with rather apparent theoretical configuration. Second, the ideational and analytical "meanings" of the discipline—that is, what

characterizes what *we* do as different, and significantly, from what is done in other disciplines—must be delineated. In sum, a fairly commonly adhered-to definition of the raison d'être of the field must emerge, for example, what is the consequence of [an] "Afro-centric" perspective for the pursuit of truth.[87]

These issues are central to questions about the normative platform of Black Studies. Certainly, Black Studies has been particularly productive in this area, at the very least in setting out the programmatic-normative agenda for what the enterprise *ought* to be about, *whose* interests *ought* to be served, against what/whom to take *critical* stands, etc. As noted earlier, these concerns—the normative agenda—have been shepherded and nurtured most forcefully and consistently within the tradition of cultural nationalism, particularly along paths forged by Karenga and Asante. (This is not to disregard or deny the importance or influence of other "schools" of thought in Black Studies: e.g., Marxism-Leninism, Nkrumahism, and "integrationist"—i.e., non-racially centered—approaches, the latter being one that seeks to have studies of peoples of African descent "integrated" into prevailing disciplines.) Since Africology is an attempt, in part, to refine and continue this agenda, an assessment of Black Studies by way of the criticist frame might prepare the way for a consideration of Africology's normative possibilities.

A. The Historicity of Discursive Fields: From the beginning, Black Studies has been radically and consistently historicist. A major part of its program involves the critique of, and struggle against, institutionalizations of the articulation and deployment of disciplines as the supposed evolutionary flow of reason embodied in the history of Europe and America, subsequently in the discursive practices of persons of European descent. Black Studies emerged in the space opened by this historicist, relativizing critique, and in its cultural-nationalist orientations remains firmly wedded to this position.

B. Anti-foundationalism: From a critical, anti-foundationalist perspective, Black Studies does not fare well. A close reading of the Asante-Karenga agenda, for example, reveals that it involves a critique of, and opposition to, claims that "Eurocentric" styles of rationality[88] are, in fact, the telos of all of humankind, and that these styles—thus humankind's telos—spring from epistemologically originary foundations uncovered, as it were, in and by "European" thinkers who were said to be the originators of philosophy as the science of reason. But the move is then made to substitute an equally originary "African" foundation by way of reclaiming, rehabilitating narratives offering reassurance of our "Afrocentricity" through identification with forms of Africanness or Africanity supposedly preserved in their essence across all cultural spaces and times. The critical reconsiderations prompted by the criticist frame require that the discontinuities resulting from the spatial and temporal disruptions and from cultural and sociological differences (e.g., gendered experiences and class stratifications) be taken seriously.

Likewise for "ready-made syntheses" such as *the* "spirit" or "value system" of all African peoples (Njia; Nguzo Saba) or "African history" reclaimed and deliberately reconstructed in ways that attempt to satisfy our need to secure and reclaim originary "truths" established "at the beginning" which escape historical determination and discontinuities. As noted by Foucault, the consequences of such efforts for historiography are not insignficant:

> History, in its traditional form, undertook to "memorize" the *monuments* of the past, transform them into *documents,* and lend speech to those traces which, in themselves, are often not verbal, or which say in silence something other than what they actually say; in our time, history is that which transforms *documents* into *monuments.* In that area where, in the past, history deciphered the traces left by men, it now deploys a mass of elements that have to be grouped, made relevant, placed in relation to one another to form totalities. There was a time when archaeology, as a discipline devoted to silent monuments, inert traces, objects without context, and things left by the past, aspired to the condition of history, and attained meaning only through the restitution of a historical discourse; it might be said, to play on words a little, that in our time history aspires to the condition of archaeology, to the intrinsic description of the monument.[89]

From the context of the critique of historiography as the raising of monuments the theme and possibility of a "total" history begin to disappear and those of a "general" history emerge. The difference between the two is that a total history seeks to provide a *complete* description that "draws all phenomena around a single centre—a principle, a meaning, a spirit, a worldview, an overall shape." The aim is to "reconstitute the overall form" of a civilization or society in the identification of its material or spiritual principle, and, thereby, to fix "the significance common to all the phenomena of a period, the law that accounts for their cohesion." A general history, on the other hand, would "deploy the space of a dispersion," that is, would be sensitive to the possible *discontinuities* constitutive of a field of discourse.[90]

At issue in the distinction between these two approaches to history is the question whether the lived history of the civilization, society, or people under study can be properly thought to cohere around a material or spiritual principle, or set of norms, that fixes the significance common to all phenomena of the period. In the context of a consideration of Africology, the force of this question, when pursued through the criticist frame, opens us to a serious concern for *discontinuity* without the presumptions of unity involved in seeking the total history of "African peoples" across all times and spaces as is invoked, perhaps, in claims regarding the "cultural unity" of all African peoples, both on the continent and throughout the diaspora. We may be required, then, to reconsider our understandable commitment to historiography as a form of archaeology, in something of the old sense noted by Foucault: as an effort to raise *monuments* that glorify African pasts in correction to the disparaging lies and distortions of racist European and Euro-American historiography. While such efforts may be both laudatory and necessary to some extent, critical questions still must be faced.

Certainly we must question the veracity of our attempted reclamations and rehabilitations as "total history," given that they are executed from the platform of, and in service to, agendas constructed in the present. Further, our efforts are conditioned by anticipated, desired, or hoped-for futures the likes of which our ancestors did not live. Nor, for that matter, are the presents and anticipated futures the same in all their important particulars for *all* African peoples. The *similarities* of experiences of African peoples as a function of patterned and linked practices part and parcel of the global political economy of capitalism notwithstanding, it is also the case that, at the level of lived experience and its perpetuation as tradition, significant *differences* exist among us. Thus, we have to take much more seriously our characterization of our historiography as *reconstructive,* a project the meaningfulness and truthfulness of which are always controlled by the agenda by which it is shaped and deployed from the site of our prevailing historicity, our claims with regard to "cultural unity" notwithstanding.

We can invoke such unity among African peoples only by disregarding very important dissimilarities. But is the cost of that disregard too high for serious, self-critical scholarship that aspires to reasonableness and "truthfulness" with regard to the totalities that are involved? The unifying power of "African" ("black" or "*African*-American" "civilization") will have to be reconsidered: "unity" can no longer be presumed to be pre-given and automatically recovered with the deployment of "African," as though the term "gathers us all together" through the unifying power of its conveying of a trans-historical, trans-geographical racial *essence.*

C. The Discursive Field: In light of these considerations, we are left to review Black Studies as a discursive field. *What* we speak about on the plane of this field, *who* speaks *how,* using what *concepts,* for what *purposes* — all of these are determined by the *rules of discourse* at work in the constitution of the field. And if Foucault is right, these rules do not define "the dumb existence of a reality, nor the canonical use of a vocabulary" but, instead, involve "the ordering of objects."[91] The greater the historical distance from the "objects" we order, then it is *our* rules of ordering that are in force, not those of the objects we study.

We need only remember just how recent is our (re-)embracing of "black" and "African" as definitively constitutive of our identity for evidence of our need to take seriously the historicity of our rules of discourse. First, in regard to *what* we speak about: the terms "Africa," "African," "African peoples," etc., are, in part, backward-looking, second-order constructions that have emerged from historical encounters with Europe and America; in part forward-looking notions in the context of projects seeking the achievement of shared identities and shared historical endeavors. Second, as to the rules governing *who* speaks: those of us, in particular, involved in the reclaiming, rehabilitative efforts *we* take to be necessitated by the disruptive encounters with Europe. We have authorized ourselves to speak, and seek to justify our doing so persuasively: that is to say, by giving arguments that seek to link our praxis and its justification with the needs and interests of those in behalf of whom we speak. Third, with respect to *how* we speak: in part as persons who have come to identify ourselves—at identifiable historical moments that are both continuous and discontinuous with preceding periods—as "Africans" or persons of "African descent"; in part as "persuasive ideologues" not initially authorized by those in whose interest we claim to speak; often from organizational or institutional contexts not of our own making (e.g., historically and predominantly "white" institutions). Fourth, via *concepts* shot through with the experience of discontinuity brought on by violent disruptions (forced relocation and enslavement in the "New World"), concepts forged in a language often not the same as the language of those of whom we speak—whom we reconstruct *as* we speak—concepts (e.g., "Afrocentricity," "Nguzo Saba") created in service to contemporary needs and projects. For what *purpose*? Precisely to overcome *discontinuity* and the absence of unity; to promote *reconstructions* that we hope will lead to psychic wholeness and health, and to social and political empowerment, through which will come historical integrity.

But these are items on an agenda of the *present* that is conditioned by the lived experiences of disruption and marginalization. The rules of our discourse have thus been formed in the crucible of struggle: contemporary Black Studies emerged from the context of the contemporary Civil Rights and Black Power movements. The connection between the historicity and dimensions of those struggles and our African "origins" is anything but simple continuity.

Furthermore, there are serious questions with regard to the conceptual rigor and intellectual cogency of some of the normative positions of Black Studies. For example, consider the issue of the claimed "relativism" of all cultural norms. A rather stringently drawn—though not a necessary—consequence of a cultural relativist position is the radical claim that across cultures there is, necessarily, "fundamental" disagreement about normative matters with no possibilities of resolving the differences.[92]

However, it is important that we consider closely whether—and to what extent, if at all—it is ultimately in the best interest of Africology to push the relativist position to such an extent. To the degree that Africology is intended as a *discipline*, for which the most constitutive medium and form of praxis is discourse, then it cannot be the case that *inherently* its governing norms will be available only to persons of African descent, even though the discipline emerges out of, and works to be in service to, our life-worlds. Discourse is possible, and proceeds successfully, only if participants abide by shared governing rules. And, given the committed *social* imperatives conditioning Black Studies/Africology—for example, the requirement that the enterprise contribute to the rehabilitation of black folks and provide them normative guidance—the rules must be available to those to whom we wish to speak, in whose behalf we speak: in short, the rules of discourse must be *public*.

This is true, as well, for our discursive efforts addressed to others who, by virtue of race and/or ethnicity (or, even, class position), are not members of "our group" but to whom we feel compelled to speak. Our critiques of "Eurocentricism," for example, must be expressed in terms to which "others" of European descent have access *if* we would have them understand the limitations of their perspectives and practices and come to regard and treat us in ways that are more respectful of our integrity. Thus, "we" and "they" must share a norm-structured discursive context that transcends the bounds our own racial/ethnic life-world. And unless we wish to advocate a return to *apartheid* whereby we set social (and intellectual) boundaries according to social groupings determined by varying degrees of the presence or absence of melanin in the skin, then it must be accepted that persons not of African descent will have access to the terms of our discourse, thus to the projects that discourse articulates and to the norms that would guide our praxis.

At a deeper level, the basis for this sharing is provided by historical circumstances. When we have proper regard for the discontinuities conditioning our existence, we are compelled to realize that the "Africanity" of those of us of African descent in the "New World" is in no way purely "African": we are African *and* American (Caribbean, etc.). To that extent, we share important aspects of our being with peoples of European descent. Consequently, a stringently relativist cultural nationalism as a platform for Africology is inconsistent, even with our most quotidian praxis: ordinary speech expressed in "American" English and addressed to *both* black and non-black audiences.

More fundamentally, it is certainly inconsistent with intellectual praxis conducted in institutional settings and by way of disciplinary practices that are part and parcel of the modern academy with its "European" legacies. For these legacies provide much of the context within which, and the rules by which, Black Studies emerged and was shaped by efforts to make it a "discipline"—the importance and truth of the claims that it was to be a radically *different* discipline notwithstanding. Subsequently, if Africology is to involve practices of *systematic* knowledge development, acquisition, refinement, and distribution, and, as part of these efforts, is to contribute to the articulation and institutionalization of appropriate norms for peoples of African descent—if Africology is to be the disciplinary matrix that continuously constructs and is structured by the *logoi* of Africa and the African diaspora—then its structuring norms must satisfy rules that, among other things, promote such activities as critical and *self*-critical endeavors. Furthermore, since a discipline is an inherently *social* enterprise in which some degree of consensus is necessary, shared rules are required. Without them there can be no agreement, even among ourselves. The rules—the norms—for obtaining such agreement are not provided by melanin. And while particular rules may be "necessitated" by political demands having to do with the racial/ethnic, gender, class, and/or cultural realities of historical life-worlds, this necessity follows from particular *choices* attendant on recon-structions of histories and projections of preferred futures.

Still, the rules are not *necessarily* and *irrevocably* restricted to the cul-tural, historical life-worlds of particular racial/ethnic—or gender—groups. Norms can transcend particular groups such that they cover the intellectual and social life praxes of different groups in ways that make it possible to resolve what otherwise might seem to be fundamental disagreements. Norms, governing "ways of life" in general, systematic intellectual praxes in particular, are *strategies* serving *choices,* ultimately a choice about life "in general," in service to which research enterprises have their ground and being. Thus, the question whether those of us involved in the refinement of Black Studies into Africology will be concerned to shape it—at least in part—in conformity with norms whose range of universality, justifiability, objectivity, and truthfulness will extend, with consistency, beyond us to non-African peoples is a matter of choice. But it is a choice not only about *our* intellectual praxis, but about the world we would co-make and share with others *even as we do so with uncompromising commitment to ensuring, as best we can, "our" survival and "our" flourishing, now and in the foresee-able future.*

Thus, a crucial and complex question: How shall we shape our intel-lectual praxis to serve our best interests, and thereby provide us with nor-mative guidance, while, at the same time, we preserve norms that secure truthfulness and appropriate objectivity in larger socio-historical contexts within which our praxis is situated? The answer to this question cannot be provided by "us" alone. Even if we would have that sharing based on con-sensus regarding the rules of disciplinary discourse—for Africology as well —a consensus arrived at through *open, free,* and *democratic* discussion, we might question whether "others" will abide by these same rules. Still, as an enterprise of the modern academy that seeks to speak authoritatively to black folks and to others for and about black folks, the rules of discourse for Africology will have to satisfy institutionalized rules governing scholarly practices to a significant extent, even as we continue the legacy of Black Studies and refine institutional rules for disciplines to bring them into greater harmony with the agendas of our lives and our hoped-for futures.

As evidence of this need to "play by house rules," if you will, we need only to remind ourselves of the pressures on Black Studies programs and departments to justify themselves in terms of the substance, coherence, and, of course, the persuasiveness of the arguments in behalf of the enterprise (as well as in terms of the number of matriculating students and the productivity of program or departmental faculty). While the recognition that these matters are deeply grounded in cultural politics has been foundational to contemporary Black Studies, that recognition does not free us to do as we wish. We can change—have changed—the rules of discourse in the academy; however, as long as we consent to share in such institutional settings and to participate in national and international publics—whether academic or non-academic is irrelevant—through our disciplinary practices, our discourse cannot proceed by private rules.

But the same questions have to be faced when black folks are the focus of discussion. Some persons insist that the most appropriate values and norms for orienting Black Studies are to be found in a unique cultural system, said to be shared by all African and African-descended peoples worldwide, which orders ways of life generally, worldviews and belief systems in particular. "We are *all* African people!" was a frequent declaration heard during the years of the Black Power movement, when efforts to initiate Black Studies programs were most intense. At the heart of such declarations is the belief that "cultural unity" among African and African-descended peoples makes for a shared "Africanity."[93]

The rhetorical appeal and social impact of this orientation has a great deal to do, I think, with the emotional, psychological, and practical contributions it makes to the cultivation of identities crucial to our struggles against racial domination. But at what price to critical thought? Some Marxist-Leninists, and others equally critical, have reaped large harvests challenging the naiveté found in commitments of this kind when they tend to disregard important differences among African and African-descended peoples.[94]

"African" and "African-descended" are complex covering terms which have to be applied to individuals and populations with particular care. The unifying, grouping resourcefulness of these general concepts is complemented by disregard for differentiating details. In devising and using such notions appropriately, we intellectuals must be continuously self-critical and frequently seek to verify that living peoples we characterize as "African" and "African-descended" find it appropriate to identify themselves in these ways; that our reconstructions of their histories and prescriptions for their futures are justified. And we must worry about the character of our justifications, a critical matter for an enterprise that we seek to position as the arbiter of norms to govern research and scholarship with regard to African and African-descended peoples, and to guide them through daily life to increasingly liberating existences.

Norms and Africology

The concern for norms to structure the formulation of Africology as a discipline may be interpreted as anticipating (if not presupposing) norms that can be *distinguished* as "African" and *traced* across historical and cultural spaces and times — efforts in historical reconstruction and description. What this might mean for Africology as a discipline that completes these tasks and, further, that *prescribes* norms can be better determined by now recalling the questions posed for me to answer and by examining them in light of all that has been discussed.

First consider the proposition that there are *"fundamental, ontological axiomatic assumptions over time among peoples of African origin."* I am deeply suspicious of this complex proposition. I do not think such assumptions exist if we take "fundamental" as qualifying "assumptions" such that we think of them as being the same for *all* peoples of African origin throughout history ("over time"). Nor do I regard norms, in general, as "axiomatic," unless we speak analogously. A stringent foundationalist reading of this question might suggest (presume?) that the "fundamental assumptions" are somehow emergent at "the origin" and are preserved "over time," historical ruptures (colonization) and dispersals of peoples (relocation and enslavement in the New World) notwithstanding.

On the other hand, a less stringent, non-foundationalist reading might treat ontological assumptions as "fundamental" in the sense of providing a basis for the rationalization of norms, practices, and institutions in terms of a complex set of orienting beliefs to which norms, practices, and institutions are referred for their ultimate justification.[95] The "fundamental ontological assumptions" would then be "axiomatic": first, as assumptions that are not themselves justified (are not supported by further justifying arguments based on still other assumptions or principles); second, as "principles" on the basis of which (with reference to which) other matters are decided. The task would then be to determine what assumptions have functioned in these ways "over time" for various African peoples with no presumption that the assumptions have been the same for all throughout time — or that they have *not* been. Which is the case is an empirical matter and can be appropriately determined only by detailed, comprehensive investigations of all peoples of African origin and descent.

The results of these investigations, when compared, would then properly situate the task called for by the second suggested question: the *"discernment of the relationship between ontological assumptions and the ethical/moral precepts that are grounded in those assumptions."* (Note that the question presupposes what it seeks: namely, that there *is* a relation between ontological assumptions and ethical/moral precepts such that the latter are "grounded" in the former.) Determining whether this is the case for African and African-descended peoples requires a retreat from the heights of conceptual abstraction (speculative ontology) to the most hermeneutically appropriate comparative surveys of the structures and practices constitutive of the life-worlds of the various African peoples, including investigations of the micro-cells and macro-structures of daily life, to distinguish and record ontological assumptions and ethical/moral precepts, and to factor out the relations between them. Only on the basis of such interpretive-empirical inquiries can we speak appropriately of relations between ontological assumptions and ethical/moral precepts that are characteristic of African peoples.

Likewise with respect to the focus of the third question: the *"teleology of human conduct"* that *"emanates"* from responses to the first and second questions. Here, too, I argue strongly against a presumptive "universalist" response that presupposes (or requires), as a function of the agenda guiding the theorizing, that all African peoples necessarily share a distinctive *"teleology of human conduct"* that we theorists can appropriate and make a fundamental element of a normative platform for Africology and, through the discipline's prescriptive efforts, for the life-worlds and praxes of African peoples. Universally, all humans intent on surviving and "flourishing" work to secure food, clothing, shelter, pleasure, the reproduction of themselves, the stabilization of their struggle for existence, and, in the process, produce a culture.

African peoples are distinct in this regard in the ways we have done and continue to do so compared to other peoples. And, looked at from the perspective of the encounters of African peoples over the past four or five centuries with Europeans and people of European descent, and with others, we can find at least one manifestation of a "teleology of conduct" that has been shared by African peoples: to *survive* as *free* people. The continuity of this purposefulness across times and spaces, conditioning the very core of our being as living peoples, has been the subject of much song, writing, and discussion, narrated in a very powerful way, for example, in Vincent Harding's *There Is a River.*[96]

The continuous flowing of the "river" of black life and struggle throughout Africa and the African diaspora notwithstanding, however, it is equally clear that African peoples do not share quite the same notions regarding what constitutes "survival" and "freedom." Thus, though it is possible, in some cases, to speak in general terms about the purposeful conduct of African peoples, the range of that generality is necessarily conditioned by historical material, cultural, geographical, demographic, and exogenous factors, not all of which are shared by all African and African-descended peoples in the same way. Even among ourselves we are distinguished by the *variety* of our life-worlds.

Consequently, as with "ontological, axiomatic assumptions," so, too, with human purposefulness: what we *speak* of in universalist terms is *experienced* and *lived* in particularity. As a theoretical enterprise with practical intentions, Africology will have to take seriously the factual diversity of purposefulness among African peoples. Theoretical praxis provides no privileged site from which a particular "teleology of conduct" can be legislated. At best it can assist in critical reviews of conduct and its purposeful bases, and thereby assist the process of *deciding* what conduct might be most appropriate for a given set of purposes, relative to particular goals and objectives for a given people.

Similar considerations hold for the focus of the fourth question: "*the epistemology of human conduct as it emanates from 1 through 3.*" In light of considerations of the three previous questions, we are led to the conclusion that what we can know about human conduct — our theorizing about the knowledge we can have of human conduct — must be fully cognizant of the historicity of human conduct. But as theorists we also must be cognizant of the historicity of our theorizing. Here, too, there are no privileged epistemological positions.[97] The character of our knowledge of the conduct of African peoples is provisional and open to constant revision, and can only come *after* empirical investigations of particular peoples. And, when we take into account the horizontal and vertical groupings (by class, age, gender, division of labor, etc.) among the people of any given society of black folks and what these groupings require of an understanding of conduct (by which groups? to what ends?), we are compelled to appreciate how sophisticated a *sociology* of knowledge with historical depth we must have as a necessary prelude to developing an epistemology of the conduct of African peoples. Further, since the objects of our investigation — living peoples — are themselves *in development*, thus vary through time, so must our knowledge of their conduct. But, as we refine the character of our theorizing, that, too, will affect both how we know and what is known. Perhaps the strongest confirmation of this is the project to revise Black Studies into Africology in the context of which such questions are raised.

The issue to be addressed in the fifth question brings into sharp focus the methodological complexities discussed earlier that are relevant to the formulation of Africology as a discipline: "*criteria for the ascription of approbation and disapprobation.*" If, on the one hand, what is intended is that we assign Africology the task of identifying, cataloguing, and discussing critically the criteria for ascribing approval and disapproval that were or are used by particular African peoples, where the norms guiding the critique are drawn from the life-praxes of the people being investigated, then the fulfillment of this task poses no great difficulties. On the other hand, however, if we would have Africology follow Black Studies and authorize it to *set* the criteria, then more is demanded than can be delivered. In addition to the challenging question of the legitimacy of this authorization, there is the even more challenging question of how those of us involved in setting criteria would be able to implement them so as to impact on conduct in daily life.

These two challenges are equally compelling for the final question: the roles of the responses to the previous questions in *"the description, explanation, justification and prediction of human conduct."* Africology as an enterprise might appropriately describe, explain, justify, and predict human conduct, that of African peoples in particular, when construed through the "criticist frame." However, the results of these endeavors, no matter how well secured by the discipline's methodologies and the self-certainties of its practitioners, particularly when they are intended to be normatively binding, are but *provisional, second-order constructions* that are *recommended* to the members of these publics as *offerings*.

We may then *choose* to invoke — to prescribe — various norms that have, do, or should structure the life practices of whatever African peoples, and do so as an argued-for *recommendation* for present and future life-worlds. But we should do so with the awareness that our recommendation is drawn from *our* constructive readings of African peoples, readings for which we are prepared to take full responsibility, including our being open to the need to revise our formulations in light of responses from those in whose interests our recommendations are advanced, or those from whom our readings are taken. Any other posture sets the practitioners up for self-delusion and, ultimately, failure — or for authoritative, dogmatic arrogance.

The norms structuring the life-worlds of African peoples emerge from the choices we make as we take up the risks of negotiating the mined fields of human existence, in their particular configurations relative to us (though not exclusively so), on our way to places we have chosen, places our ancestors could never have imagined. Their values, then, can be no guarantee for us; some of them may, in fact, doom us. We must choose even those we would continue to observe.

And whom will this "we" comprise? Theory, no matter how well developed, cannot settle this by providing "axiomatic" justification for the theorists. We can never be more than provisional in our offerings. The question, I propose, is how to ground ourselves among those for whom and with whom we seek to work. Black Studies, in its nationalist modes, has been clear about this need. Let us not corrupt the initial insight by supposing we can "axiomatize" the response in a new venture we would term "Africology." Ours is the responsibility of *constantly* testing our notions by checking with our social base in the most open and democratic ways we can realize.

Here I have invoked a complex of norms for structuring the disciplinary praxis of Africology. We might refer to these collectively as a "criticist frame" that incorporates awareness of our historicity and of historical discontinuity and is supported by rules of discourse constitutive of democratic social-political praxis.[98] And as an enterprise devoted to the most complete understandings possible of Africans and peoples of African descent — understandings that will contribute to enhanced living — I would have

Africology continue the cultural-nationalist legacy of Black Studies of seeking to root itself in and devote itself to black life-worlds, but be guided by a critical appreciation of the complexities of these same life-worlds, thus of the complexity of competing normative agendas within them. I do not regard it as either appropriate or possible for Africology as a discipline to set the normative agenda for black life in general, nor for any particular African or African-descended people. What the enterprise might do—and do rather well—is offer a critical *mediation* of competing normative agendas relative to the goals and objectives of the particular people in question. Such a contribution requires the fulfillment of one of the definitive commitments of contemporary Black Studies to be in touch with and service to the communities that are the object of study; but, refined through the criticist frame, it also redefines the limits of this same commitment. The sincerity and intensity of our commitment must not degenerate into authoritarian dogmatism.

Nor into racism. As a socially and politically conditioned and conditioning intellectual enterprise of the modern academy, Africology, in its relations with non-black others, must manifest in its norms and practices the best world we would have for ourselves and our peoples that is shared with others, and on terms that, while doing so, also support critical scholarship of the highest levels of excellence possible as we have helped to define "excellence." This will require that the enterprise of Africology move beyond a restrictive cultural nationalism and be governed by refined norms for truth, objectivity, and justification that support the praxes of scholarship as, in the words of Molefi Asante, a "post-Eurocentric, transcultural" venture within which our understandings of our peoples bespeak their integrity.

It is a matter of perspective: the "frame" through which we structure and go about our work. The consequences, of course, are enormous. At stake is the safety of negotiating the mined field of life on the way to a chosen destination. Norms to govern theorizing about norms for social life are themselves part of social life, and are likewise conditioned by the choices of destination and route. No amount of theorizing can eliminate the risks involved in choosing, either in social life or in theorizing. Thus, we must not be pretentious about what is to come from an attempted refinement of Black Studies into a more mature and socially responsible "discipline" of *Africology*.

6

AGAINST THE GRAIN OF MODERNITY

The Politics of Difference and the Conservation of "Race"

For millions of people, in many nations throughout the world, these are very problematic and challenging times. While there is substantial agreement that contemporary history is flush with revolutionary opportunities for enriched existence for more human beings than has ever been the case in the history of the species, there are, as well, daunting challenges, some that threaten the very existence of the human species. By some accounts we are in the midst of more or less severe crises of one kind or another. Whatever the characterization — no consensus has been reached on any particular reading of the times as a full and adequate account — some of the challenges defy the societies in which they appear to be regarded as "advanced" and "enlightened." If we as a species are to survive and flourish, we must find ways to meet the challenges and resolve the problems that confront us while exploiting opportunities that might enhance our lives.

However, since much of what confronts us today is made more complex and challenging by its relative uniqueness, we often find ourselves without reservoirs of experience and knowledge that are directly and immediately applicable to the difficulties we face. We are compelled, then, to forge new strategies, as well as innovative goals and objectives, if we are to succeed in meeting the challenges. But in doing so we will have to confront all of the fear and trepidation, all of the risk, that such pioneering efforts embody because they provoke some of the deepest experiences of vulnerability and mortality. For in the midst of such anxieties often a comforting strategy is to turn to what seems to be the wisdom of sedimented experiences already at work either in what is done at present or in some reconstructed past. However, doing so may well be to succumb to the inertia of self-serving familiar and comforting rationalizations that are neither wise nor appropriate, and may in fact be part of the problem. Fear and trepidation have their roles in ensuring survival. Nonetheless, other experiences that are equally promoting of a deeply felt sense of ourselves are likewise vital to human well-being: namely, the joy and satisfaction that come with meeting challenges successfully and prevailing against the odds, and valued recognition of the additions to the store of socially accumulated knowledge that come from reflections on the experiences leading to success. For the best assurance humans have of confronting challenges successfully is the consolidation of critically mediated experiences through learning, which, in drawing on past experiences to anticipate possible and probable futures, reduces risks by eliminating the need to experience *every* possibility.

Among the compelling challenges to be faced today are vexing conceptual and practical difficulties that are consequences of our values, beliefs, commitments, and practices with respect to persons who share biological and/or cultural factors by which they are distinguished into groups that have come to be called "races" and "ethnies" (or "ethnic groups"). In the discussion that follows, I wish to explore the prospect of serious revisions to conceptual (philosophical) and practical legacies and strategies that would allow for a reconsideration of "race" and "ethnicity." In doing so I argue the need to conserve "race" and "ethnie" (and "ethnicity") as vital components of a philosophical anthropology, and of a social and political philosophy, more adequate in the present and near future to the exigencies of life in racially and ethnically complex societies.

The terms "race" and "ethnie"[1] (or "ethnic group") are associated with conceptions, beliefs, values, and practices and are used to make important distinctions among groups of peoples, and among persons, on the basis of physical features and cultural factors that are thought to be shared by persons in the group and which constitute the group as a distinct race and/or ethnie. In this discussion I shall use "race" to refer to a group of persons who share, more or less, biologically transmitted physical characteristics that, under the influence of endogenous cultural and geographical factors as well as exogenous social and political factors, contribute to the characterization of the group as a distinct, self-reproducing, encultured population. Thus, biologically transmitted physical factors, conditioned by and along with cultural processes and geographical factors, combine to constitute a "race." "Ethnie" I use to refer to those self-reproducing populations or groups relative to which the constitutive factors that are shared (more or less) by members of the group are for the most part cultural, and relative to whom physiological factors play a minor role in defining the group. Furthermore, I understand a "race" to be wider, more encompassing than an "ethnie" such that a particular "race" can have a number of "ethnies." (For example, the African race includes African-American, African-Brazilian, Lubo, Ashanti, and Afro-Cuban ethnies, among many others.)

Of course, the reality and nature of raciality (race-defining characteristics), especially, and ethnicity (the collection of factors that constitute an ethnie) are much contested. For some persons there are no such things as races, or ethnic groups, in the sense of groups of individuals who share unique physical as well as physiological, behavioral, and psychological characteristics.[2] Further, in some traditions of thought and praxis, raciality and ethnicity are regarded as having no place either in the formation of principles for rationally ordered social relations or in conceptualizing humans, even though different races and ethnies in some sense exist. For others, however, the existence of different races and ethnies is an obvious feature of social life. Racial and ethnic differences are thought to be *real* and, some persons argue, must be explicitly acknowledged in principles formulated to provide the bases for social order and for determining what is right and just in societies that have continuing histories of racial and ethnic oppression. Nonetheless, persons who do believe in the reality of raciality and ethnicity are often also committed to principles that regard all persons as *essentially* the same in the most important respects and that demand that all persons be regarded as equal, without regard to raciality or ethnicity. Consequently, all persons, on this view, must have equal access to opportunities, the protection of law, and enjoy equal rights and privileges by virtue of our *essential identity* as human beings.

Contentious social issues involving raciality or ethnicity in which such disparate views come into play place demands on social life that cause severe tensions and threaten national unity or even the stability and peace of entire regions. Is it possible to reduce the tensions and thereby substantially reduce the threats to social order by achieving and maintaining social order, harmony, and justice while allowing for the recognition—even the celebration and nurturing—of racial and/or ethnic differences? The two agendas—incorporating the recognition and respect for racial or ethnic differences into principles that provide the rationale for social order and justice; and in important respects regarding persons as essentially the same in devising and applying principles that will unify diverse peoples in a political community in which harmonious and just order prevails—present formidable conceptual and practical challenges.

Several conceptual difficulties arise. From the outset there is the problem of conceiving "race" and "ethnie" in ways that are both conceptually adequate (that is, that do not violate what might be taken to be appropriate rules of ordered classification) and accord with appropriate experiences with and of the persons classified by the terms. Yet this is rendered more difficult as racial and ethnic groups come and go over periods of time. Depending on environmental factors, and on cultural norms and practices affecting migration, communication, and interactions (including, especially, inter-breeding and inter-marrying), different groups of people may be more or less isolated from one another at different times and, thereby, be more or less involved in inter-group relations sufficient to alter the composition of the groups. Thus, human groupings are *historically* dynamic, *culturally* ordered, contingent *social* realities. This presents a particular challenge to efforts to delimit, define, and classify human groupings, a challenge that is both old and recurrent: how to name something that changes and by the naming provide a "handle" for dealing with it, intellectually and practically, in a way that is more or less stable, if not permanent, over time. But, as human groups can and do change in their composition over time, whatever the rate, what is it that the name is a "handle" on? Racial and ethnic classification and identification, as ventures involving efforts to relate *logically* ordered classificatory terms to *historically* dynamic social realities and have the names be appropriate objectively and subjectively, are no simple tasks.

The matter of the subjective adequacy of a name is especially important, for in this are the crucial matters of personal and group identities. A person's meaningful constitution of a sense of self is conditioned in very significant ways by the sense he or she has of his or her coming-to-be in and through a more or less determinate number of significant others, past and present, who are makers and carriers of cultural legacies that shape the key traditions and institutions through which the coming-to-be of the significant others and the person is realized. And, it is through these institutions and traditions that elements and configurations of identity are preserved and mediated (and sometimes revised) and thus become *shared*. This sense of oneself, as a person and as a member of a determinate group, a sense shared in like manner by others, is what constitutes, to a large extent, personal and group identities.

Furthermore, human groups, though historical, socially constructed realities, also have *natural* histories, and this makes for particularly thorny conceptual challenges. That is to say, humans are part of the natural world and are subject to many of the principles or laws that govern the processes that make for order in nature. To the extent that we take wisdom or true understanding to involve systematic knowledge of the rules or principles that govern the object of inquiry, then efforts to distinguish human groups are also efforts to understand and explain varieties of human groupings as in some sense "natural": as conditioned — though by no means strictly *determined* — by processes in the natural, but socially influenced world.

What is to be done with the two kinds of knowledge: of human groups as social realities and as natural realities? Must these remain distinct forms of understanding? Or, is there a single form of knowledge that is sufficiently comprehensive to combine them both, that is to say, that can reveal the processes that operate in both nature and society to produce human groupings and personalities, and distinguish the relative importance of each (nature on one hand, society and culture on the other) in the process of their being produced? Can we have a socially informed, natural history of races and ethnies?

Yet another conceptual challenge points the way to practical difficulties. Given human variety and the differences such variety entails — in beliefs, aspirations, values, social agendas, social-cultural formations, etc. —

on what terms (by which rules or *principles*) might different racial and ethnic groups live together in the same community, or in communities in close
proximity to each other, in ways that are sufficiently ordered so as to provide
social peace and mutual benefit in accord with shared notions of justice?
Should different groups live *together* in the same communities, or should
they live in geographically as well as politically distinct and more or less
separate social unities, whether these be neighborhoods, federated regions,
or nation-states? Can knowledge of processes that give rise to and condition
the formation of human groupings provide answers to these questions? Are
there any principles, inherent, perhaps, in the social-natural history of
human groups that we can recover and deploy to resolve conflictual racial
and ethnic relations? Or, must we *invent* the principles we need as bases for
forms of social order that can be sufficiently satisfying for enough persons in
all groups affected to ensure social stability with justice? How would such
invented principles have enough authority and legitimacy to play this important role? *Who* will do the inventing? *Who* will administer the principles? On
what terms and in the context of what kind of social formation?

These are some of the challenges emerging from relations between
and among races and ethnies to be faced in reconsidering raciality and
ethnicity. Certainly since the sixteenth century the play of raciality and ethnicity has a long and often horrid pedigree in Western history. For much of
the last few centuries, for example, many nations have been the scenes of
tensions and conflicts in which the meaning and significance, the appropriateness, of valuing raciality, ethnicity, or national identity in deciding important questions of individual life and social order and justice were highly
contested issues. In the United States in particular, there continue to be
court battles, intense public debates, demonstrations, social disturbances,
and serious disagreements in public and private institutions of various kinds
and on all levels of government over "affirmative action" (the pursuit of policies that use race, ethnicity, or gender as one criterion among others to
select, hire, promote, and otherwise reward persons in institutions and governmental agencies; to settle certain matters of political participation, such
as determining the boundaries of political districts, establishing voting
rights, or determining the makeup of representative political bodies, to cite
a few examples). And in many nations tensions and conflicts resulting from
racial and ethnic differences have been or are being exacerbated by significant demographic changes (differential rates of birth, longevity, and death
for different groups and the migratory flow of peoples, whether voluntary or
involuntary, into and out of various regions and nations) that are likely to
make the situation even more acute. In the April 1990 cover story of *Time*
magazine, the following observation was made regarding racial and ethnic
demographic developments in the United States: "Someday soon, surely
much sooner than most people who filled out their Census forms realize,
white Americans will become a minority group. Long before that day arrives,

the presumption that the 'typical' U.S. citizen is someone who traces his or her descent in a direct line to Europe will be part of the past." To say the least, such a development has the potential for decisive developments in the social, political, economic, and cultural dimensions of life in America, a nation that has been plagued for centuries by racial and ethnic problems.

The Politics of "Difference"

Such problems continue to be prominent and very challenging, even threatening, to aspects of much of contemporary history that affect virtually all of our lives. Much as W. E. B. Du Bois anticipated, the problem of the twentieth century has indeed been what he termed the "problem of the color line": the problem, in his words, of relations between "lighter" and "darker" races. However, the problem has not been limited to conflicts between light-skinned and dark-skinned groups or even limited to conflicts involving ethnic or national identities. In other instances, marginalized groups of persons have made gender or sexual preference, and cultural forms of life that have developed out of and in support of these preferences, the focus of claims for justice. "Difference," rather than similarity, has become a significant basis of political mobilization. But not for purposes of exclusion. Rather, "difference" is now a highly valued preference that many persons and groups would have accommodated and recognized as the basis for their participation in civic, political, and economic life.[3]

In previous eras, in many nations, struggles against injustices stemming from racism and perverted ethnocentrism[4] had as their goal the integration — in some case even the assimilation — of victimized groups into a nation's social, political, economic, and cultural life according to the terms of universal principles (that is, principles thought to be true and valid for all times and places, hence "universally"). Today this is often a much contested agenda. We are once again in an era in which "difference" has been made a virtue and has become the basis of organized political struggle in sometimes stringent competition with an ideal of equality that presumes essential sameness. What is common in many of these struggles is the attempt to revise social-political life, as well as intellectual domains and practices, so as to make "difference" a virtue. In the United States, for example, proponents argue the compelling social necessity of revisions since, some say, the universal principles that sanctioned the integration and assimilation of diverse peoples into a social formation that would be the basis of a new identity unrelated to old, supposedly archaic and divisive distinctions based on raciality and ethnicity, an identity based solely on individual character and achievement, were, in reality, principles that became a rationalizing mask for a long and continuing history of hierarchical domination and forced cultural homogenization principally at the hands of WASPs (white Anglo-Saxon Protestants), a particular ethnie of the "white" race. In addition, the "color line" has been a prevalent pretext for various "white" ethnics (many of whom have long histories of battles among themselves) to join forces against peoples of color in order to secure advantages for themselves and their progeny that are tied to privileges reserved for those with "white" skin. The celebration of universal principles has often turned out to be the rhetoric — rather than the realization — of liberal-democratic, socialist, or communist principles of universality and equality in the midst of the domination of political, economic, and cultural life by a particular race and/or ethnie(s).

Proponents of the politics of difference see one source of the problem in an inadequate notion of the person at the center of universal principles. They would counter this with a revised notion of the person as a basis for likewise revised principles of ordered social life. Central to such efforts are two basic beliefs. First, that a full appreciation of what it means to be human requires that proper note be taken of definitive characteristics of human groupings such as historically mediated biological/physical and cultural factors that are constitutive, in varying degrees, of the persons in the group. Second, the belief that the principles on which would be based the organization of socio-political life, and the organization and agendas for intellectual enterprises whose objects are living human beings, should also take explicit account of these constitutive differences.

Doing so, proponents say (myself included), can and ought to lead to the acknowledged and promoted substantial enrichment of collective life given the wealth of histories and cultures, the wealth of possible contributions, of various groups comprising our multidimensional local, national, international social worlds. Not doing so results not only in our collective impoverishment but also, particularly when there is active and invidious opposition to those who are "different," in distortions of the cultural, political, social, and economic aspects of societies shared by different races and ethnies. What results is the deformation and self-deformation of members of opposed groups, as well as the deformation of those doing the opposing.

For many persons advocating a politics of difference, then, the principles of political and social life must be rethought. Such rethinking is presently well under way in the very citadels of twentieth-century intellectual life. Heated debates are raging in public and private educational, research, and cultural institutions and agencies not only over the propriety of adhering to affirmative action policies and practices, and the principles — or interpretations of principles — used to support such policies and practices, but, particularly, over the use of racial, ethnic, gender, and cultural differences as substantive criteria in reaching judgments regarding matters that are particularly central to teaching, research, scholarship, and artistic creation and performance, among them norms of "truth," "objectivity," and of "practical reason" itself.

Too often these debates are distorted by simplistic name calling and pernicious characterizations, and by self-serving posturings as either the defenders or the avant-garde of the verities of order and civilization, old or new. Still, the issues involved are substantial and complex. For example, there are heated disputes over the relevance of raciality, gender, ethnicity, and cultural differences as criteria to guide revisions to curricula in educational institutions, particularly in those with students from a variety of racial and ethnic groups, but in which the programs of study have focused almost exclusively on the cultures and experiences of a limited range of peoples, generally the "white" race and some of its ethnies. Among the more controversial of these challenges have been efforts to critique and displace what is regarded by some as the hegemony of "Eurocentrism"[5]: the dominance of intellectual, social, and political life in institutions of cultural reproduction (schools, colleges, universities, and agencies that manage and/or play vital supporting roles in the mediation of culture such as museums and such governmental agencies as the National Endowments for the Arts and Humanities in the U.S.) by privileged valorizations of a complex of ideals, ideas, values, and legacies, and of behaviors, expectations, and practices that are "centered" in and on the experiences and legacies, the cultural norms and life agendas, of western European peoples (at least on the most "enlightened" and accomplished among them).

Critiques of this "Eurocentrism" in educational, research, and artistic institutions are often accompanied by arguments that promote revisions to curricula, research agenda and strategies, and artistic endeavors to modify —in some cases to replace—"Europe-centered" studies with others that are focused on, and take at least some (if not all) of their normative and interpretative orientations from, the histories and cultures of other, non-European races and ethnies as the makers and bearers of substantial cultural traditions and achievements. According to proponents, the revisions are required in order to have institutional endeavors reflect studied appreciations of the often unacknowledged and unappreciated achievements of non-European peoples (and, in important instances, of women of all groups). Of equal importance, the revisions are said to be needed to bring to light the likewise unacknowledged and underappreciated contributions to legacies that for centuries have been presented as the exclusive achievements of European peoples (males, mostly). It is these legacies that have been the celebrated and virtually exclusive focus of much research, teaching, scholarship, and artistic endeavors in institutions in many Western nations, though in many cases these nations (and institutions) are, in fact, quite diverse racially and ethnically.

In important instances the revisionary efforts have intended, and in some cases have resulted in, the development of new fields or subfields of study (e.g., African-American, Hispanic, Asian, and Women's Studies). And in other, sometimes related, instances they have led to quite substantial changes in the demographic make-up of some disciplines and fields (more women, more persons not of European descent) and, as an important consequence, to desired serious reconsiderations of and changes to the agendas, themes, subject matters, and curricula in traditional disciplines and fields. A fundamental concern of those promoting such revisions, thus a basic issue in the debates, is the appropriate form and content of education in nations of diverse peoples, especially when those nations have long and continuing legacies of invidious discrimination against and oppression of particular races and/or ethnies. For many persons involved in these debates, in a nation of diverse peoples the programs of teaching, research, scholarship, and artistic creativity and productivity in institutions of cultural mediation and reproduction must become democratically "multi-cultural."

At the center of this debate is a crucial issue that, in the American context, became the focus of national debate when it was taken up by E. D. Hirsch Jr. in his discussion of the need for nationally shared "cultural literacy," to be acquired through schooling, as the foundation of a democratic republic of diverse peoples. Hirsch's concern for cultural literacy stemmed from his belief that American education for the past half-century has been dominated by theories of education, stemming from Jean Jacques Rousseau and later taken up and applied by John Dewey, that were focused on encouraging the "natural development" of young children and not imposing adult ideas on them before they were capable of understanding them.[6] This approach gave rise to what Hirsch calls "'developmental,' content-neutral" curricula that, following Dewey, rejected education as the "piling up of information." Against this Hirsch offers his corrective "anthropological" theory of education

> that once again stresses the importance of specific information in early and late schooling . . . based on the anthropological observation that all human communities are founded upon specific shared information. . . . [A]n anthropological theory of education accepts the naturalness as well as the relativity of human cultures. . . . The anthropological view stresses the universal fact that a human group must have effective communications to function effectively, that effective communications require shared culture, and that shared culture requires transmission of specific information to children. . . . Like any other aspect of acculturation, literacy requires the early and continued transmission of specific information. Dewey was deeply mistaken to disdain "accumulating information in the form of symbols." . . . Only by accumulating shared symbols, and the shared information that the symbols represent, can we learn to communicate effectively with one another in our national community.[7]

While Hirsch's argument with Dewey is not immediately focused on raciality and ethnicity, certainly his concern is especially close to one of the crucial issues at the heart of the debate over "multi-culturalism": how to strike a balance among competing social needs. On one hand, the need to revise curricula so that they ensure both the cultural reproduction of different races and ethnies through the education of succeeding generations; and, on the other, the need to educate young people of various groups about the histories and cultures of peoples unlike themselves, thus democratizing education. In the process, however, there is the compelling need to ensure a *common* cultural literacy shared by all citizens in a democratic republic.

Revisionary projects have generated a storm of criticism, especially from prominent persons in educational and cultural institutions, government agencies, news media, and politics. Some of these critics have condemned the "multi-culturalists" for what they (the critics) regard as violations of fundamental principles of academic and political life: the "multi-culturalists," it is said, are really advancing a political agenda, disguised as curricular reform, which they deem "correct" and would impose on all others and in the process silence those who disagree with them. The "politically correct" programs of the "multi-culturalists" are both wrong and dangerous, say the critics. They are wrong because they involve the pronounced "trashing," or at least displacements that diminish the significance, of figures and legacies that, according to these critics, have, in fact, been key to the development of Western civilization (certain modern instances of which some among the critics regard as the highest forms of human achievement in recorded history, or at least since the Dark Ages). In contrast, the cultural developments and contributions of many of the peoples championed by the "multi-culturalists" are said to have no comparable records. It is thus inappropriate to make such cultures the center of study and learning. Their accomplishments merit no such consideration. Thus, one of the dangers of "multi-culturalism": unless the continued substitution of the celebrated study of the cultural legacies and persons of less accomplished peoples for the study of the truly great figures and traditions of the West is not halted, the nation—perhaps "Western civilization" itself—is threatened with a loss of position and status in the world, and with cultural decline that will eventuate in the West's being eclipsed by backwardness or, at worst, barbarity.

In less shrill and apocalyptic, but no less serious, tones speak those critics who worry about what they see as the dangers of discarding the achievements of the modern Enlightenment or "modernity"—particularly, making universal principles of impartial reason the basis of social order and justice—in the pursuit of a "multi-culturalism" that seems to value equally the ways of life of all cultures. In doing so, some critics argue, a debilitating and thereby dangerous relativism emerges, leaving us with no adequate standards by which to settle important questions that transcend particular racial or ethnic life-worlds or periods of history. If it is thought to be "politically incorrect" to seek such standards or to celebrate their realization, even if the realization is admittedly incomplete, in the cultural legacies undergirding modern liberal democracies especially—legacies of peoples who "just happen" to be ethnies of a particular race—because doing so leads to invidious comparisons with other races or ethnies, then we are denied the achievements of consolidated learning, critically fashioned into and invested in principles and practices of modern social order and knowledge acquisition, which "enlightened" peoples have to offer.

Yet another criticism raised by some opponents (and, it must be said, by some proponents) of "multi-culturalism" is that at least some proponents have abandoned long-established norms for research and scholarship and substituted rhetoric, propaganda, and political agendas for critical, public, peer-reviewed work in making the case against "Eurocentric" legacies and strategies. And some worry that the promotion of "difference" threatens the society with factional strife and disunity.

There are indeed very substantial issues involved in these controversies. In the American context in particular (though not in America alone), raciality and ethnicity are fundamentally, inextricably involved as well. At the center of these disputes is a concern that cuts to the very heart of traditional considerations in philosophy: the propriety of the efforts of those who seek to make raciality and ethnicity (or gender) central to the formulation and articulation — in some cases even the application — of methods and norms to govern quests for, and even to certify the achievement of, understanding, beauty, and truth in virtually all areas of knowledge and creativity, and to the formulation or application of norms and principles that provide the structure for just social order. How these issues are resolved will determine a great deal about the future of many nations.

Against the Grain of Modernity

There are many aspects to the challenge posed by advocating forms of political, social, cultural, and intellectual life in which the "play of differences" is normative and nurtured. My interest, primarily, is in what doing so requires of our basic conceptions of ourselves as individual persons, who are also members of races and/or ethnies, and as ordered associates in societies configured by political, economic, and social structures and practices at the core of which are beliefs and values regarding group-based differences that are not always in line with celebrated, supposedly universal, racially and ethnically blind principles, but that are operative in decisive ways nonetheless. Perhaps brief discussion of the legacy of modern universalist social principles will bring into sharper focus an argument in behalf of a reconsideration of raciality and ethnicity as vital elements of a revised philosophical anthropology and social and political philosophy.

Promoting the play of differences runs counter to some of the most basic social and political philosophies and practices that became the foundations of order in modern national communities. The historical processes that brought this about have been referred to as "the project of modernity," a partial, but nonetheless quite significant, historical realization of key proposals from the progressive, humanist agenda of the eighteenth-century European Enlightenments that were developed within normative horizons defined by what were taken to be the principles of "reason."

At the core of the modernity project is a complex set of commitments elaborated by key thinkers. The experiences of the individual person or "subject" — thus "subjectivity" — became the central focus of inquiry. In the works of modern (as opposed to "traditional" or dogmatic "religious") thinkers such as René Descartes, Immanual Kant, G. W. F. Hegel, and others, for example, subjectivity was elaborated by the concepts of "freedom" and "reflection" and came to carry four basic connotations: *individualism, the right to criticize, autonomy of action,* and *idealistic philosophy* as the ultimate form of self-understanding. Kant, especially, "installed reason in the supreme seat of judgment before which anything that made a claim to validity had to be justified."[8] And this "reason" was thought to be distinguished by a "rational content" that centered on the *individual* rational subject: *self*-consciousness, "authentic" *self*-realization, and *self*-determination in solidarity with others.[9]

The norms proposed for the project of modernity were likewise tied intimately to what were thought to be the norms of reason itself, norms that made authoritative values of *fallibilism* (the conviction that, in some areas of investigation, what is taken to be the right answer to a question is never assured absolutely since new evidence might require a change of view), *universalism* (the conviction that truth, where obtained, should hold without regard for time and/or place), and *subjectivism* (the conviction that the experiences of the single, autonomous individual are the only appropriate context for investigating and settling key questions regarding reasoning and living).[10] Furthermore, the thinkers of modernity took what would prove to be a decisive position on the question of the norms that would determine the basis and orientation of "modern" life: the norms would not be modeled on the values of past epochs; rather, modernity would "create its normativity out of itself" through the resources of reason.[11] It was these convictions that formed the rational and normative "contents" of the self-understanding of the thinkers who turned out to be the intellectual executors of the project of modernity.

The convictions were played out in a number of historical developments that served to validate the agenda of the program of reason centered on the individual subject: the Reformation, the Enlightenments, and the French and American revolutions especially. Each of these seemed to signal the triumph of a rising "modern" age over the past, a process in which historical development was taken to be increasingly ordered by the "objectification" of rationalized structures that, in turn, secularized culture and society. Cultural traditions lost authority when subjected to reflective treatment that dissolved what before had seemed their quasi-natural character; norms of action were universalized, and values generalized (the values of the executors of the project of modernity were declared the proper values for ensuring the future of human civilization). Together these processes enlarged the range of options for organized life compared to life in the tradition-ordered past. And social reproduction through education became focused on the formation of individualized, abstract ego identities unhinged from the intimate associations of traditional communities (family, tribe or ethnie, religious community, and so on)—thus on forcing the individuation of the growing child.[12]

Thus a diverse group of engaged thinkers situated in several European countries set an agenda by which all development—of the individual self, society, and exchanges with the natural world—subsequent to their coming on the scene, was to be under the aegis of "reason." In this the project of modernity became informed by a distinctive philosophy of history: that is to say, by the belief that the meaning and direction of human development across time, to the extent that it unfolded according to the dictates of reason, would, to paraphrase Hegel, result in "*progress* in the realization of reason and greater freedom." The essence of modernity was to be seen in the historical realization of enlightenment in the form, in Kant's words, of

> *man's emergence from his self-incurred immaturity. Immaturity* is the inability to use one's own understanding without the guidance of another. This immaturity is *self-incurred* if its cause is not lack of understanding, but lack of resolution and courage to use it without the guidance of another. The motto of enlightenment is therefore: *Sapere aude!* Have the courage to use your *own* understanding![13]

Yet, humanity's self-incurred immaturity (or, in other translations of Kant's text, self-incurred "tutelage") was intimately linked to social and political conditions and arrangements: appropriate conditions must be realized for the full exercise of reason and the realization of the benefits of doing so. As Kant goes on to say in the same essay:

> For enlightenment of this kind, all that is needed is *freedom*. And the freedom in question is the most innocuous form of all—freedom to make *public use* of one's reason in all matters. . . . By the public use of one's own reason I mean that use which anyone may make of it *as a man of learning* addressing the entire *reading public*. What I term the private use of reason is that which a person may make of it in a particular *civil* post or office with which he is entrusted.[14]

This linking of freedom with *public* versus *private* exercise of reason is a decisive feature of the project of modernity. For the Enlightenments were decidedly *political* projects: collections of convictions that set out the social, political, economic, and cultural conditions, and the agenda for realizing them in practice, thought to be most conducive to the realization of human "maturity." These collections of convictions, organized into history-making social, political, economic, and cultural projects, became known as "liberalism." Through a confluence of circumstances in the eighteenth century, in particular, liberalism became the dominant social, political, and economic philosophy driving the project of modernity, so much so that, by one account, the history of liberalism and the spread of Enlightenment in Western Europe (with the exception of England) and its spread to America "must be regarded as aspects of one and the same current of thought and practice."[15]

And for good reasons. The definitive conceptions of "man" and society that form the core of liberalism are central conceptions from the Enlightenments that became driving forces of the project of modernity: liberalism's individualism "asserts the moral primacy of the person against the claims of any social collectivity"; its universalism affirms "the moral unity of the human species" and accords "a secondary importance to specific historic associations and cultural forms"; the conviction of egalitarianism "confers on all men the same moral status and denies the relevance to legal or political order of differences in moral worth among human beings." And through the belief in meliorism, liberalism affirms "the corrigibility and improvability of all social institutions and political arrangements."[16] John Gray expressed it well: "Liberalism ... is the political theory of modernity."[17]

Here, then, is one of the major sources of conflict for proponents of the politics of difference: the clash with the principles of liberalism, its philosophical anthropology especially, that have served as the official political philosophy of modern nation-states, Western capitalist democracies in particular. A similar philosophical anthropology that draws from Enlightenment convictions has also informed social and political philosophies in socialist and communist nations, though without commitments to the primacy of individual and public freedom, political democracy, and market-regulated economic life thought essential by liberal thinkers. In either case, however, basic modern liberal convictions have required that one look beyond what has been regarded as "accidental" differences, including raciality, ethnicity, gender, and "national character," to the *essence* thought to be the definitive constitutive aspect of the human species shared by all humans that thus makes for the *essential* unity, oneness, and identity of all persons, all other differences notwithstanding: *reason*, a *capacity* or *capability* defined by unique laws or principles. By virtue of this essential sameness, all humans are thus *essentially* identical. When the principles of reason are understood and followed in the exercise of this capability in acts of reasoning, about certain matters especially, the result, supposedly, is universal and necessarily true knowledge that, applied to the social world, can and should become the foundation for unity, order, and justice. Thus, the contemporary tensions and social and political movements centering on matters having to do with raciality and ethnicity, when viewed against the backdrop of modern history, are for some a resurgence of disruptive and divisive anachronistic sentiments. It had been hoped that such socially threatening commitments had

reason as universal essence

been neutralized in modern political communities formed on the basis of universal principles.

However, as noted earlier, for others struggles involving raciality and ethnicity are an eruption in public spaces of long simmering tensions barely contained under a façade of harmony, unity, and order, though not always with justice. In many respects, it is thought, tensions and struggles over raciality and ethnicity have a great deal to do with inadequacies and failures involving the principles undergirding modern societies, and with substantially failed or inappropriate practices that have been rationalized by them. In some cases the failure results from distorted applications of the principles, that is to say, with inappropriate restrictions of the range of persons of various groups covered by the principles, as in cases involving the flagrant contradiction of the universalism of the principles when their application is restricted to privileged groups on the basis of racial or ethnic distinctions.

In other cases the inadequacy — some would say the failure — of the universalist principles of modern liberalism is not just that they have not been fully applied, but that the conception of the human being as an autonomous *individual* that serves as the normative anchor of the principles is insufficient since this conception deliberately excludes such aspects of the person as race and ethnicity (and gender). This notion of the human being is thought to be inadequate to the task of providing a foundational conception for diverse societies: it cannot encompass the concrete being of the person who is intimately and inextricably related to others by substantive factors, among them raciality and/or ethnicity, that are themselves *essential* (not "accidental") aspects of who we are.

However, for opponents of the project that would have fundamental principles give freer rein to the play of differences, the emphasis on *particularity* over universality (that is, emphasis on difference rather than sameness) threatens the always tenuous historic achievements of modern social, political, economic, and cultural life organized on the basis of practices and commitments tied to cognitive and political norms that are regarded as the foundation of true knowledge and of unity, order, justice, and, especially, of individual freedom in social and political life — all secured by the authority and universality of *reason*. By this account, it is through the proper exercise of reason that the principles have been delineated as the inherent and self-evident rules or laws of nature and social life, that is, of *reality*. For without the guiding presumption that the real world, single and whole, is governed by a single set of unified principles, the achievement and perpetuation of systematic, true knowledge in the forms of science and philosophy become exposed to the acidic effects of the solvent of relativism. And the freedom, peace, and prosperity made possible by political stability won through the organization of social life on the basis of universal principles of liberalism are jeopardized by possibilities of confusion or social chaos that may result from the politics of difference.

As is painfully evident in developments in the former Yugoslavia and the former Soviet Union, such possibilities are real. Whether they are *probable* in any given case depends, however, on a number of factors, all of them relative to individual national situations. It is not *necessary* that such consequences follow from a greater emphasis on racial and/or ethnic differences. Recognizing and nurturing such differences while preserving and enhancing social and intellectual life without sacrificing political unity in the process is what I regard as the profound challenge to be faced in determining and realizing appropriate valorizations of raciality and ethnicity in the context of a revised notion of democracy. Such a revision should preserve some of our modern commitments to the individual, but would incorporate respect for cultural pluralism — of racial and/or ethnic group-based cultures — as a necessary (though not necessarily sufficient) constitutive, formative context for the development and nurturance of the individual.

However, this rethinking would need to cut against the grain of the modern Enlightenments in conserving the notions of race and ethnicity and situating them in a revised philosophical anthropology to undergird revised ideals for social and political life. As noted, it was the social and political philosophy of liberalism and its universalist principles and associated notions of the human individual that provided the normative foundations and intellectual scaffolding for the transformations that gave rise to modern nation-states. While modern liberal philosophy was supposedly irrelevant to raciality and ethnicity, a much closer look discloses serious tensions between ideals and reality at the heart of the project of modernity that, under the pressures of national formation and reformation in various countries, exacerbated by the developmental forces of capitalism, transformed ambivalences toward "different" non-Europeans into outright contradictions of enlightened thought in the declarations that such peoples were in various ways "inferior." Perverted ethnocentrism and racism (as well as sexism and class biases) were, in fact, nurtured by rationalizations that drew on core aspects of Enlightenment philosophies even as much of this thought became the intellectual midwife of modernity.

It is, in part, for these reasons that the project of modernity has become the focus of contemporary criticism. Plagued by a dialectic of conflicting tensions inherent in the notion and historical realizations of "reason," the Enlightenments gave rise to an in some ways false universalism that blocks the appreciation of racial and ethnic differences among groups of peoples and contributed to deceptions that masked various forms of domination that were rationalized using these same differences. One result of the perpetuation of what some regard as a fraudulent universalism has been the creation of conditions that have been the nurturing soil for the growth of the politics of difference: the failure to find norms to accommodate the reality of a pluralism of authentic cultural life-worlds and substantive legacies of diverse racial and ethnic groups. Likewise, other developments in the

realms of culture, society, socialization, and individual psychic development
are transforming the historical conditions in many societies contrary to the
norms and agenda of the Enlightenments. Consequently, by some accounts
the project of modernity, as a fulfillment of an agenda for social reconstruction bringing freedom and progress, is, at the very least, incomplete.
However, a significant number of critics have concluded that "pure reason,"
in and of itself, is unable to supply norms that will secure universality and
guarantee continuous historical progress in the form of individual autonomy,
material well-being, and social peace and stability. For these critics the project of modernity *cannot* be fulfilled. We are, they say, in a new historical era
that is *beyond* modernity, an era of "post-modernity."

That, I think, is to go too far. Such declarations fall far short of providing guidance in confronting the challenges at hand. So too in taking up the
seemingly intractable problems of raciality and ethnicity. To a very great
extent, what is at issue is the question of the appropriate principles, or
appropriate interpretations of principles, for determining justice and fair-
ness; for setting norms, determining agendas, and devising and choosing the
best strategies by which to realize the agendas for public and private life;
and, as well, questions regarding appropriate principles and norms to structure quests for knowledge. It is not "beyond" modernity that we will find our
way. Rather, I think we would be wise to take up once again the quest for
critical understanding that ushered in modernity and carry it through, but
this time conserving raciality and ethnicity in reconceptualizing the ordering of social life as a means of providing understandings more appropriate
for ordering social formations with a diversity of racial/ethnic cultural
groups. How might a reconsideration of raciality and ethnicity contribute to
such a reconceptualization?

The Conservation of "Race"

I find the effort of W. E. B. Du Bois in his 1897 essay "The Conservation of
Races" to be an important example of how one might work at such a reconsideration. This essay has long been a source of strategic insight and understanding for me, in particular because Du Bois, mindful of advances in biology and other sciences in the late nineteenth century that discredited the
notion of races as unique and fixed groupings determined by biologically
transmitted characteristics, sought to rethink "race" in support of a project
that would "conserve" races in the context of democratic pluralism. His was
an approach that anticipated present discussions of multi-culturalism (and
anticipated, as well, earlier discussions of cultural pluralism):

> Although the wonderful developments of human history teach that the
> grosser physical differences of color, hair and bone go but a short way
> toward explaining the different roles which groups of men have played

in Human Progress, yet there are differences — subtle, delicate and elusive, though they may be — which have silently but definitely separated men into groups. While these subtle forces have generally followed the natural cleavage of common blood, descent and physical peculiarities, they have at other times swept across and ignored these. At all times, however, they have divided human beings into races, which, while they perhaps transcend scientific definition, nevertheless, are clearly defined to the eye of the Historian and Sociologist.

If this be true, then the history of the world is the history, not of individuals, but of groups, not of nations, but of races, and he who ignores or seeks to override the race idea in human history ignores and overrides the central thought of all history. What, then, is a race? It is a vast family of human beings, generally of common blood and language, always of common history, traditions and impulses, who are both voluntarily and involuntarily striving together for the accomplishment of certain more or less vividly conceived ideals of life.[18]

As noted, Anthony Appiah regards Du Bois's argument in support of the concept of "race" as incomplete and, in the end, as foundering on a tension between conflicting purposes Du Bois would have the definition serve: "The tension in Du Bois' definition of race reflects the fact that, for the purposes of European historiography . . . it was [cultural features] that mattered; but for the purposes of American social and political life, it was [shared physical features of a geographical population]."[19] Having isolated and analyzed each of the elements in Du Bois's definition, Appiah concludes that the concept of "race" is illusory: "The truth is that there are no races: there is nothing in the world that can do all we ask 'race' to do for us."[20] Culture is the "reality" that is missed by the notion of "race": "Talk of 'race' is particularly distressing for those of us who take culture seriously. . . . What exists 'out there' in the world — communities of meaning, shading variously into each other in the rich structure of the social world — is the province not of biology but of hermeneutic understanding."[21]

I think there is a great deal more to be had in Du Bois's offering than Appiah has recognized. On my reading, Du Bois was working at a definition of "race" in which culture was to play the leading role.

We find upon the world's stage today eight distinctly differentiated races, in the sense in which History tells us the word must be used. They are, the Slavs of eastern Europe, the Teutons of middle Europe, the English of Great Britain and America, the Romance nations of Southern and Western Europe, the Negroes of Africa and America, the Semitic people of Western Asia and Northern Africa, the Hindoos of Central Asia and the Mongolians of Eastern Asia. There are, of course, other minor race groups, as the American Indians, the Esquimaux and the South Sea Islanders; these larger races, too, are far from homoge-neous; the Slav includes the Czech, the Magyar, the Pole and the Russian; the Teuton includes the German, the Scandinavian and the Dutch; the English include the Scotch, the Irish and the conglomerate American. Under Romance nations the widely-differing Frenchman, Italian, Sicilian and Spaniard are comprehended. The term Negro is, perhaps, the most indefinite of all, combining the Mulattoes and Zamboes of America and the Egyptians, Bantus and Bushmen of Africa. Among the Hindoos are traces of widely differing nations, while the great Chinese, Tartar, Corean and Japanese families fall under the one designation — Mongolian.

The question now is: What is the real distinction between these nations? Is it the physical differences of blood, color and cranial mea-surements? Certainly we must all acknowledge that physical differ-ences play a great part, and that, with wide exceptions and qualifica-tions, these eight great races of today follow the cleavage of physical race distinctions. . . . But *while race differences have followed mainly physical race lines, yet no mere physical distinctions would really define or explain the deeper differences—the cohesiveness and conti-nuity of these groups. The deeper differences are spiritual, psychical, differences—undoubtedly based on the physical, but infinitely tran-scending them. . . .* The whole process which has brought about these race differentiations has been a growth, and the great characteristic of this growth has been the differentiation of spiritual and mental differ-ences between great races of mankind and the integration of physical differences.[22]

While there is wide disagreement about the appropriateness of Du Bois's (or any such) classification, in his case "race" was intended to identi-fy what Appiah calls "communities of meaning" and was thus intended to guide efforts in hermeneutical understanding. Most importantly for Du Bois, he was concerned that these "communities of meaning," constituting and constituted by distinct racial (and, we might add, ethnic) populations, be "conserved" and nurtured as the most basic unit of social life in and through which each race developed its own cultural "message" manifested in various forms of achievement. It was Du Bois's belief that life in general was enriched by the wide, inter-racial sharing of the "messages" of the var-ious races. Of particular importance to Du Bois were the prospects of culti-vating, refining, and sharing the "messages" of what he termed the Negro race:

The question is, then: How shall this message be delivered; how shall these various ideals be realized? The answer is plain: By the develop-ment of these race groups, not as individuals, but as races. . . . For the

development of Negro genius, of Negro literature and art, of Negro
spirit, only Negroes bound and welded together, Negroes inspired by
one vast ideal, can work out in its fullness the great message we have
for humanity. [23]

"The Conservation of Races" was in fact prepared and delivered as the second of the Occasional Papers of the then newly formed American Negro
Academy, which was devoted to encouraging intellectual activity among
black folks and to defending them against racist attacks.[24]

Du Bois's reconsideration of "race," then, is not simply an effort in taxonomy. Rather, it is part of a decidedly *political* project that involves prescribing norms for the social construction of reality and identity, for self-
appropriation and world making. In his words, "the history of the world is
the history, not of individuals, but of groups, not of nations, but of races."
Peoples of African descent, of the African "race," can share their message
with the world only through organized *group* efforts *while taking themselves
to be* a particular group. Thus, "race," as used by Du Bois, is meant to have
"the unit of classification . . . be the unit of identification" in the context of a
project to mobilize and galvanize persons whose oppression was rationalized by invidious oppositions inscribed in the notion of "race."[25] Crucial to
this mobilization, for Du Bois, would be a shared sense of *identity* forged, in
part, out of a concept of "race" that involved, as Appiah says, a "rotation of
the axis" defining the "scale of values" invested in the concept. Du Bois was
involved in an effort to make room in the "space of values" for a positive valorization and appreciation of the cultural achievements of peoples of African
descent (and of other groups):

> Manifestly some of the great races of today—particularly the Negro
> race—have not as yet given to civilization the full spiritual message
> which they are capable of giving. I will not say that the Negro race has
> as yet given no message to the world, for it is still a mooted question
> among scientists as to just how far Egyptian civilization was Negro in
> its origin; if it was not wholly Negro, it was certainly very closely allied.
> Be that as it may, however the fact still remains that the full, complete
> Negro message of the whole Negro race has not as yet been given to
> the world.[26]

However, in defining "race" Du Bois was sufficiently insightful not to
regard the relationship between physical characteristics, on one side, and
mental and cultural ("spiritual") factors on the other, as necessary such that
the former determined the latter. More subtle still, Du Bois, as I read him,
did not define "race" in an essentialist fashion, as a term for identifying natural kinds, by connecting the elements in the definition (physical characteristics, geography, cultural elements) conjunctively, making each element
severally necessary and all together jointly sufficient.[27] Du Bois's "race" is

best read as a *cluster* concept in which the elements are connected in an indefinitely long *dis*junctive definition such that "each property is severally sufficient and the possession of at least one of the properties is necessary."[28] Reading Du Bois's effort as though he attempted to define a natural kind disregards his explicit concern to situate a discussion of race squarely within an understanding conditioned by attention to history and sociology, and to the work of Charles Darwin:

> So far as purely physical characteristics are concerned, the differences between men do not explain all the differences of their history. It declares, as Darwin himself said, that great as is the physical unlikeness of the various races of men their likenesses are greater, and upon this rests the whole scientific doctrine of Human Brotherhood.[29]

In his turning to what he termed "real history," Du Bois was not unmindful of the deeply troubling tensions involved in the effort to forge an identity in racial terms in the context of a nation-state that called for its own socially constructed identity as "American":

> Here, then, is the dilemma, and it is a puzzling one, I admit. No Negro who has given earnest thought to the situation of his people in America has failed, at some time in life, to find himself at these cross-roads; has failed to ask himself at some time: What, after all, am I? Am I an American or am I a Negro? Can I be both? Or is it my duty to cease to be a Negro as soon as possible and be an American? If I strive as a Negro, am I not perpetuating the very cleft that threatens and separates Black and White America? Is not my only possible practical aim the subduction of all that is Negro in me to the American? Does my black blood place upon me any more obligation to assert my nationality than German, or Irish or Italian blood would?[30]

The oscillating questioning that this dilemma gave rise to was, in Du Bois's judgment, having devastating effects on persons of African descent in America, even as the re-valorization of race generated its own tensions:

> It is such incessant self-questioning and the hesitation that arises from it, that is making the present period a time of vacillation and contradiction for the American Negro; combined race action is stifled, race responsibility is shirked, race enterprises languish, and the best blood, the best talent, the best energy of the Negro people cannot be marshalled to do the bidding of the race. They stand back to make room for every rascal and demagogue who chooses to cloak his selfish deviltry under the veil of race pride.

Du Bois posed his own series of related questions:

> Is this right? Is it rational? Is it good policy? Have we in America a dis-

tinct mission as a race—a distinct sphere of action and an opportunity for race development, or is self-obliteration the highest end to which Negro blood dare aspire?[31]

The import of these questions is such that the appropriate answers given cannot be determined simply by an evaluation of the persuasiveness of answers judged by criteria of logical rigor. Rather, it is the end in view that is at issue, in this case the historical development and well-being of a relatively distinct group of people who suffer oppression at the hands of persons of another group. That development and well-being require a strategically crucial form of self-understanding.

> If we carefully consider what race prejudice really is, we find it, historically, to be nothing but the friction between different groups of people; it is the difference in aim, in feeling, in ideals of two different races; if, now, this difference exists touching territory, laws, language, or even religion, it is manifest that these people cannot live in the same territory without fatal collision; but if, on the other hand, there is substantial agreement in laws, language and religion; if there is a satisfactory adjustment of economic life, then there is no reason why, in the same country and on the same street, two or three great national ideals might not thrive and develop, that man [*sic*] of different races might not strive together for their race ideals as well, perhaps even better, than in isolation. Here, it seems to me, is the reading of the riddle that puzzles so many of us. We are Americans, not only by birth and by citizenship, but by our political ideals, our language, our religion. Farther than that, our Americanism does not go. At that point, we are Negroes, members of a vast historic race that from the very dawn of creation has slept, but half awakening in the dark forests of its African fatherland.[32]

This development and well-being also require concerted and coordinated efforts *on the part of black people themselves:*

> As a race we must strive by race organization, by race solidarity, by race unity to the realization of that broader humanity which freely recognizes differences in men, but sternly deprecates inequality in their opportunities of development.

> For the accomplishment of these ends we need race organizations: Negro colleges, Negro newspapers, Negro business organizations, a Negro school of literature and art, and an intellectual clearing house, for all these products of the Negro mind, which we may call a Negro Academy. Not only is all this necessary for positive advance, it is absolutely imperative for negative defense. Let us not deceive ourselves at our situation in this country. Weighted with a heritage of

moral iniquity from our past history, hard pressed in the economic world by foreign immigrants and native prejudice, hated here, despised there and pitied everywhere; our one haven of refuge is ourselves, and but one means of advance, our own belief in our great destiny, our own implicit trust in our ability and worth.[33]

Thus must the race be mobilized and organized. The unit of focus, for Du Bois, if one is to understand human history and attempt to structure the making of the future through organized effort, is the racial group, the "vast family" of related individuals. Individuals are necessary, but they are neither sufficient nor self-sufficing, the political philosophy of modern Enlightenment liberalism notwithstanding. Whether or not an individual can enjoy a relatively unrestricted and flourishing life is tied to the well-being of the group; the well-being of the group requires concerted action predicated on self-valorization within the context of a shared identity without succumbing to chauvinism. Further, the racial and/or ethnic life-world provides the resources and nurturing required for the development, even, of individual talent and accomplishment such that distinctive contributions can be made to human civilization. Thus must the race of African peoples — all races — be "conserved." For many persons — and I place myself in this group — the continued existence of discernable race- and ethnic-based communities of meaning is highly desirable *even if, in the very next instant, racism and perverted, invidious ethnocentrism in every form and manifestation would disappear forever.*

They will not. As was Du Bois, I remain convinced that both struggles against racism and invidious ethnocentrism, as well as struggles on the part of persons of various races and ethnicities to preserve, enhance, and share their "messages" with all humans, require the conservation of races. As we struggle to realize social justice with harmony in America, given this nation's history of race relations, we are unable to do away with the notion of "race," the difficulties of definition notwithstanding. The challenge is to find ways to conserve a sense of raciality that is both socially useful and consistent with democratic justice. Du Bois, in my judgment, has been one of the foremost thinkers in modern history to have wrestled with this seemingly intractable problem. Examining the issues through his writings provides, I think, a worthy context for the effort to achieve understanding to guide praxis as we struggle to find a consensus that will help us find our way through the politics of difference.

7

LIFE-WORLDS, MODERNITY, AND
PHILOSOPHICAL PRAXIS

Race, Ethnicity, and Critical
Social Theory

The "Modernity" Debate

Currently, many intense efforts to characterize and assess contemporary
historical developments as a total configuration center on whether we are in
a "modern" or "post-modern" period. At the center of the philosophical wing
of the debate are some of the most recent endeavors of Jürgen Habermas.[1]
For him "modernity" is the name for a partial, but nonetheless quite significant, historical realization of key proposals from the progressive, humanist
agenda of the European Enlightenment—the "project of modernity"—
developed "within the horizon of Reason." Some of these developments and
commitments are to be defended, even while critically refined and extended along with the "rehabilitation" of reason, against what he views as the
naive—at worst self-contradictory—"Nietzscheanism" of critics of the project of modernity: Adorno, Foucault, Heidegger, and Derrida, among others.
    On the side of the critics are those who argue, among other things, that
a dialectic of Enlightenment is at the heart of the modernity project and
includes a false universalism that blocks an appropriation and appreciation
of substantive differences (for example, race and ethnicity, or gender), thus
has contributed to totalitarian deceptions that mask various forms of domination. This has led the project to shipwreck on the shoals of (a) the reality
of a pluralism of agendas emerging from the life-worlds of diverse groups of
persons who have exerted themselves politically and broken through rea-
son-rationalized domination with force sufficient to threaten social restruc-
turing, and (b) social-structural developments (affecting the realms of culture, society, and socialization and individual psychic development) that
transform the historical conditions of society in ways contrary to the agenda
of modernity. "Reason," the critics conclude, is unable to secure universality
or guarantee continuous historical progress in the form of material well-
being, social peace and stability, and individual autonomy. At the very least,
the project of modernity, as a fulfillment of the agenda of the Enlightenment,

is incomplete; for some the project *cannot* be fulfilled. Historically, then, we are *beyond* modernity.

In this essay I join this wide-ranging debate by bringing into the discussion concerns from what Habermas has labeled a defensive, "particularist" cultural subgroup: i.e., challenges to aspects of the project of modernity, especially its universalist philosophical anthropology, from the tradition of black nationalism, one legacy contributing to a resurgence of what has recently been called the "politics of difference." My concern is with the social, cultural, and personal significance of life-worlds and practices that are conditioned, to a significant degree, by self-understandings partially shaped by matters having to do with raciality and/or ethnicity, and their importance for Habermas's proposal to rehabilitate reason as "communicative reason" as part of his project to develop a revised critical social theory.

The question motivating the discussion is whether a revised agenda for philosophical praxis along lines proposed by Habermas can contribute to the effort to chart a passage between anarchic pluralism and totalitarian universalism to a diverse but unified social world, locally and/or internationally, one that achieves and secures appropriate degrees of tolerance for diverse life-worlds that is grounded in a consensus that provides practical universality. The discussion will include a review of the core of thought shaping the Enlightenments' agendas, its philosophical anthropology in particular, as the script for the project of modernity, a review conducted against the historical backdrop of the politics of race and ethnicity in the American context, an ongoing and unfinished attempted revolutionary instantiation of Western modernity. I propose something of a middle passage, one that participates in the critique of some aspects of Enlightenment projects of modernity while redeeming and refining others, in arguing that the philosophical anthropology of the Enlightenment remains inadequate to the practical tasks of overcoming racism and invidious ethnocentrism while conceiving and realizing a just society. Hence, the Enlightenment-inspired project should be revised, and this revision ought to involve a reworking, as well, of the notion of "universality" that will serve as a key norm of likewise revised notions of "reason" and "reasonableness." Much of the promise of Habermas's effort is to be found here, that is, in its suggestiveness for just such a critical reworking of the theoretical underpinnings of social "modernization."

The Project of Modernity

A set of philosophical articulations forms the intellectual core of the agenda of the project of modernity and, for Habermas, was first problematized and connected to rationality by Hegel.[2] The central notion is "subjectivity," which, he offers, Hegel elucidated by means of the concepts of "freedom" and "reflection" with subjectivity carrying four basic connotations: *individ-*

ualism, the right to criticize, autonomy of action, and *idealistic philosophy* as the ultimate self-understanding of modernity, particularly in the philosophies of Descartes and Kant. It was Kant who "installed reason in the supreme seat of judgment before which anything that made a claim to validity had to be justified."[3] Within the context of this notion of reason (what Habermas calls the "horizon of Western reason") the "rational content" of the modernity project was constituted by self-consciousness, authentic self-realization, and self-determination in solidarity: rationality was thus "subject-centered."[4] Further, on the normative side a decisive position assumed by the thinkers of modernity was that the criteria by which the modern age would set its orientation could not be taken from the models of another epoch; rather, modernity would "create its normativity out of itself" through the resources of reason.[5] Thus, the "normative content" of the project of modernity was centered on fallibilism, universalism, and subjectivism.[6] For Habermas, these rational and normative "contents" were constitutive of the self-understanding of the intellectual executors of the project of modernity.

The contents were also internally connected with the processes of modern historical development. The Reformation, Enlightenment, and French revolution were the key historical events that validated the agenda of subject-centered reason and signaled the triumph of the "modern" age over the past. With the playing out of this agenda, historical development became increasingly subject to processes that involved the "objectification of rational structures" that, as described by Weber, Mead, and Durkheim, contributed to the rationalization, hence the secularization, of culture and society. These processes were characterized by:

- "the reflective treatment of traditions" by virtue of which they "lost their quasinatural status";
- "the universalization of norms of action and the generalization of values, which set communicative action free from narrowly restricted contexts and enlarge the field of options";
- "patterns of socialization that are oriented to the formation of abstract ego-identities and force the individuation of the growing child."[7]

Once the project of modernity was well under way, all subsequent development—of self, society, and nature via exchanges with humans—was expected to be brought under the aegis of reason. In this respect the modernity project was informed by a particular philosophy of history: historical development, when guided by reason, would be characterized, in Hegel's view, by steady, progressive orderings of individual and social life and, as a result, by the realization of more and more freedom and autonomy for human beings. Thus as a combination of efforts to bring about practical realizations of Enlightenment in the form of new societies, the project of modernity was a distinctive, even revolutionary, *political* venture, in the widest and most substantive senses, and came to be guided by a distinctive social, political, and economic philosophy — "liberalism" — the definitive features of which include the following:

- individualism — "asserts the moral primacy of the person against the claims of any social collectivity";
- universalism — "affirming the moral unity of the human species and according a secondary importance to specific historic associations and cultural forms";
- egalitarianism — "confers on all men the same moral status and denies the relevance to legal or political order of differences in moral worth among human beings"; and
- meliorism — "affirmation of the corrigibility and improvability of all social institutions and political arrangements."[8]

Race, Ethnicity, and the Politics of Difference

This broadly stroked characterization of the modernity project must be tempered by allowances for important differences in the formation of the project's agenda, and in its deployment, in response to the specific problems and historical conditions prevailing in different national contexts (continental Europe and France, England, Scotland, and North America).[9] What is true of each context, however, though with varying degrees of success and different consequences, is that the project of modernity brought about revolutionary social, cultural, political, and economic transformations during the seventeenth and eighteenth centuries.

This is certainly true in the case of the United States of America, which originated as a grand experiment to realize the formation of a nation-state according to principles drawn from Scottish and French currents (among others) of European Enlightenments, and from British and other European traditions. According to John Gray, the dominant influence on American liberals was the Scottish social philosophers — Adam Smith in particular — who, more than French or American thinkers, aspired to develop "a science of society in which liberal ideals are given a foundation in a theory of human nature and social order."[10] In his reading of the *Federalist Papers* Gray finds that the carriers of Enlightenment liberalism in America differed from the French *philosophes* and agreed with the Scottish Enlightenment thinkers in stressing human imperfectability. In this regard American liberalism shared a commitment of central importance to classical liberals: "that individual liberty and popular democracy are contingently but not necessarily related."[11]

This important distinction between the philosophical anthropology of individualism and the political tenets of universal law and popular democracy would prove decisive in the unfolding of the United States of America as a nation-state. The reason-derived universalist and egalitarian aspirations of the project of modernity notwithstanding, the liberals seeking to found a nation-state, as were many Enlightenment thinkers, were particularly aware of the realities of human diversities and of their possible social and political consequences. Not all persons, as members of particular groups, were *initially* at their best. Some (or their progeny) might be improved; others, by virtue of their "nature," could not be. The egalitarian and universalist elements of liberalism had to be tempered by the reality of human diversities, thus by the need to put into play, in some circumstances, the meliorist element of the liberal conviction. These were the grounds on which a circumscribed, dehumanizing, dominated subworld was constructed and institutionalized, into which Africans were herded and confined as slaves and denied the rights to "life, liberty, and the pursuit of happiness" otherwise available to males of European descent of the appropriate class.

The enslavement of Africans was a crucible for the liberal modernity project in America that was won through revolutionary battle and enshrined in the Constitution, Bill of Rights, and the Declaration of Independence. The political philosophy that gave primacy to the *individual*, supposedly without regard to "race, creed, or national origin" since "all men are created *equal*," and to the rule of law with *universal* binding force, had also to rationalize social distinctions, ultimately group-based in terms of race (ethnicity, or gender), curb its own egalitarianism, and seriously distort the nation's subsequent historical development. Thus, while America became paradigmatic as a project of modern Enlightenment with its capitalist, so-called free enterprise economic order, its representative democracy structured by a host of rights, and its protected realm of civic privacy — all three resting on a (partially) universalized and privileged Enlightenment notion of Man — it was also equally paradigmatic of the self-contradictory tensions inscribed in the core of Enlightenment thought and practice: the universalist implications of the commitment to the "unity of mankind" in the philosophical anthropology undergirding the political philosophy of modernity anchored in ideas of reason, on one side; the attempt to manage human diversity and imperfectibility by elaborating a hierarchy defined, in significant part, in terms of the purity, corruption, or level of development of reason (or even the presence or absence of the ability to reason) in particular groups of persons, on the other. As the nation was unfolding, the compromise in behalf of solidarity among the colonies — increasingly regionalized by conflicting emerging political economies of neo-feudal agricultural capitalism based on slave labor in the South, and mercantile capitalism in the North and East — required a retreat from the enlightened norms of modernity. The deal was done with reason's sanction; but, in the process, reason was made the whore of political expediency. (Or, as we might now say, after Foucault: the nexus of power and knowledge, in which the latter served the former, was demonstrated with brutal frankness.)

But, the terms in which the deal was cut had been worked out much earlier. During the Greek Enlightenment Aristotle had worked out a scheme in which the recognition of human diversity in terms of hierarchical ordering was in accord with reason: groups of persons differed as a function of their *natures*, which determined their *end* or *telos*, the most that they were capable of being when fully developed. In his words: "The nature of a thing is its end. For what each thing is when fully developed, we call its nature, whether we are speaking of a man, a horse, or a family. Besides, the final cause and end of a thing is the best."[12] The roles filled by persons of different groups demonstrated the practical truth of this "explanation" in Athens. Thus, it was "rational" to order social relations such that hierarchy brought the range of natures into functional relationships that were appropriate to those on each level: husband to wife; father to children; master to slave; Greek to barbarian:

> But is there any one thus intended by nature to be a slave, and for whom such a condition is expedient and right, or rather is not all slavery a violation of nature?
>
> There is no difficulty in answering this question, on grounds both of reason and of fact. For that some should rule and others be ruled is a thing not only necessary, but expedient; from the hour of their birth, some are marked out for subjection, others for rule.[13]

> For in all things which form a composite whole and which are made up of parts, whether continuous or discrete, a distinction between the ruling and the subject element comes to light. Such a duality exists in living creatures, but not in them only; it originates in the constitution of the universe.[14]

When Europeans encountered Africans, these valorizations were readily deployed in the rationalization of racial/ethnic differences into relations of superordination and subordination. Hegel, *the* philosopher of modernity, was quite explicit about the matter:

> The peculiarly African character is difficult to comprehend, for the very reason that in reference to it, we must quite give up the principle which naturally accompanies all our ideas — the category of Universality. In Negro life the characteristic point is the fact that consciousness has not yet attained to the realization of any substantial objective existence — as for example, God, or Law — in which the interest of man's volition is involved and in which he realizes his own being. This distinction between himself as an individual and the universality of his essential being, the African in the uniform, undeveloped oneness of his existence has not yet attained; so that the Knowledge of an absolute Being, an Other and a Higher than his individual self, is entirely wanting. The Negro, as already observed, exhibits the natural man in his completely wild and untamed state. We

Aristotle

Hegel

must lay aside all thought of reverence and morality—all that we call feeling—if we would rightly comprehend him; there is nothing harmonious with humanity to be found in this type of character.[15]

This orientation rode the ships with the Europeans migrating to this land and was literally made to order for the situation of compromise faced by the thinkers in America who had to square slavery with the heritage of the American revolution. Liberalism was reason prepared, by both classical and modern Enlightenments, to handle diversity through reason-privileged hierarchy that restricted egalitarianism to equality among equals. Africans had their differences fixed ontologically through reasoning strategies initially articulated by Aristotle, historically and culturally by Hegel, spiritually and biologically by the Bible, to mention just a few participants in this grand conspiracy.

"Race" became a primary vehicle for this fixation and was later secured by the imprimatur of *science*, the rising authority figure of modern reason in its exact, empirical forms. It was through scientific accounts of "race" that the executors of the project of modernity sought to take morphological, cultural, social, and historical distinctions among groups of peoples and erect them into a reason-certified hierarchy that had its proper place in the social and political arrangements of liberalism. These scientific efforts are worth reviewing, in particular for what they reveal of the failure to conscript scientific reason in the ploy to justify the institutionalization of racial exclusion and domination in the midst of the realization of the liberal project of modernity. This failure would help to confirm the original tenets of liberal modernity's philosophical anthropology, namely, that beneath the differences all peoples were *essentially* the same. The recovery of this commitment would fuel the flames of struggle against oppression.

The career of "race" does not begin in science but predates it and emerges from a general need to account for the unfamiliar or, simply, to classify objects of experience, thus to organize the life-world. How—or why—it was that "race" came to play important classifying, organizing roles is not clear.[16] The nineteenth-century development of the use of "race" to distinguish groups biologically was antedated by others in preceding centuries that apparently generated a more compelling need for classificatory ordering in the social world and, subsequently, the use of "race" as such a device. First, there were the tensions within Europe arising from encounters among different groups of peoples, particularly "barbarians"—whether defined culturally or, more narrowly, religiously. (And it should be noted that within European thought, and elsewhere, the color black was associated with evil and death, with "sin" in the Christian context. The valorizing power inherent in this was ready to hand when Europe encountered Africa.) A more basic impetus, intensified by these tensions, came from the need to account for human origins in general, for human diversity in particular.

cf
Smedley
&
the
Irish

Finally, there were the quite decisive European voyages to the land that would come to be named "America"and to Africa, and the development of capitalism and the slave trade.[17]

The authority of "race" as an organizing, classificatory concept was strengthened during the unfolding of the project of modernity, in the eighteenth century in particular, when "evidence from geology, zoology, anatomy and other fields of scientific enquiry was assembled to support a claim that racial classification would help explain many human differences."[18] "Race" contributed to a form of "typological" thinking — a mode of conceptualization that was at the center of the agenda of emerging scientific praxis at the time — that facilitated the classification of human groups. In the modern period the science of "race" began in comparative morphology with its stress on pure "types" as classificatory vehicles.

A major contributor to this unfolding agenda of classificatory thought was the botanist Linnaeus.[19] Other persons were particularly significant contributors to the development of such thought as it related to theories of racial types. According to Banton and Harwood, Johan Friedrich Blumenbach provided the first systematic racial classification in his *Generis humani varietate nativa liber* (*On the Natural Variety of Mankind*, 1775). This was followed by the work of James Cowles Prichard (*Generis humani varietate*, 1808).[20] Georges Cuvier, a French anatomist, put forth a physical-cause theory of races in 1800 in arguing that physical nature determined culture. He classified humans into three major groups along an implied descending scale: whites, yellows, and blacks. As Banton and Harwood interpreted his work, central to his thinking was the notion of "type" more than that of "race": "Underlying the variety of the natural world was a limited number of pure types and if their nature could be grasped it was possible to interpret the diverse forms which could temporarily appear as a result of hybrid mating."[21] Other important contributions include S. G. Morton's publication of a volume on the skulls of American Indians (1839) and one on Egyptian skulls (1845). His work was extended and made popular by J. C. Nott and G. R. Gliddon in their *Types of Mankind* (1854). Charles Hamilton Smith (*The Natural History of the Human Species*, 1848) developed Cuvier's line of argument in Britain. By Smith's reckoning, according to Banton and Harwood, "The Negro's lowly place in the human order was a consequence of the small volume of his brain."[22] Smith's former student, Robert Knox (*The Races of Men*, 1850), argued likewise. Finally, there was Count Joseph Arthur de Gobineau's four-volume *Essay on the Inequality of Human Races* (1854) in which he argued that, in the words of Banton and Harwood, "the major world civilizations . . . were the creations of different races and . . . race-mixing was leading to the inevitable deterioration of humanity."[23]

Two significant achievements resulted from these efforts. First, drawing on the rising authority of modern science as the realization and guardian of systematic, certain knowledge, "race" was legitimated as a gathering concept for morphological features that were thought to distinguish varieties of *homo sapiens* supposedly related to one another through the logic of a *natural* hierarchy of groups. Second was the legitimation of the view that the behavior of a group and its members was determined by their place in this hierarchy.[24] Consequently, science-authorized and legitimated notions about raciality, when combined with social projects involving the distinguishing and, ultimately, the control of "racially" different persons and groups—as in the case of the enslavement of Africans—took root and grew to become part of modern common sense. Race had become an "obvious" factor of social life.

But these scientific accounts of race were unstable: insights gained through attempts to secure racial distinctions scientifically in support of political projects of subordination and oppression subverted the projects themselves. The situation was both assisted and complicated by the work of Darwin and Mendel. Social Darwinism emerged as an effort by some (notably Herbert Spencer and Ludwig Gumplowicz) to apply Darwin's principles regarding heredity and natural selection to human groups and endeavors and thereby to provide firmer grounding for scientific studies of races (something Darwin did not do). Such moves were particularly useful in justifying the dominance of certain groups over others (British over Irish; Europeans over Africans). On the other hand, however, the insights set forth by Charles Darwin in his *The Origin of Species*, when combined with Mendel's successful working out of the mathematically calculable regularities of trait inheritance by studying particular plants, shifted the terrain of scientific investigations from a focus on morphology and the stability of "pure types" to a gene-based focus on individual characteristics and the effects on them of processes of change, thus shifted the focus of scientific studies to the analysis of variety. The effects of this shift would be revolutionary:

> A racial type was defined by a number of features which are supposed to go together. . . . The racial theorists of the nineteenth century assumed there was a natural law which said that such traits were invariably associated and were transmitted to the next generation as part of a package deal. Gregor Mendel's research showed that this was not necessarily the case. . . . [It] also showed that trait variation *within* a population was just as significant as trait variations *between* populations . . . traits do not form part of a package but can be shuffled like a pack of playing cards.[25]

And, since environmental impacts that condition natural selection are important factors in the "shuffling" of traits, in addition to the roles played by heredity and the interplay between dominant and recessive traits, the notion of "pure" racial types with fixed essential characteristics was displaced: biologically (i.e., genetically), one can only speak of "clines."[26]

Biological approaches to races thus increasingly focused on studying diversities within — as well as among — groups, and, of particular interest, on studying how groups evolve over time and in various environments. Complementing these efforts were new approaches to studies of races in several of the social sciences: while racial groups were taken to be made up of persons many of whom share to some degree relatively distinctive biological features (though not sufficient to constitute the groups as pure types), shared socio-cultural characteristics were thought to be most important in making the groups distinct. This approach to understanding racial groups is significantly different from that typical of many nineteenth-century theorists of racial types who thought that the social and cultural "character" of each race or nation was determined by its distinctive biological makeup.

Revolutionary changes in natural and social sciences thus influenced the development of new, transformed approaches to raciality. For many contemporary scientists the old, nineteenth-century notion of "race" had become useless as a classificatory concept, hence it certainly did not support in any truly scientific way the political agendas of racists. The conceptual terrain for many contemporary approaches to raciality continues to be provided, in large part, by notions of evolution, which were significantly conditioned by the precursive work of Mendel and Darwin. In the space opened by the concept of "evolution," it became possible at least to work at synthesizing insights drawn from both the natural sciences (genetics, biochemistry) and the social sciences (anthropology, sociology, psychology, ethology) for a fuller understanding of "geographical races"[27]: studies of *organic* evolution focus on changes in the gene pool of a group or groups; studies of *super-organic* evolution are concerned with changes in the "behavior repertoire" of a group or groups — that is, with their socio-cultural development.[28] And it is a legitimate question — though one difficult to answer — to what extent, if at all, super-organic evolution is a function of organic evolution or, to add even more complexity, to what extent, if at all, the two forms of evolution are mutually influential. The question of the relations between both forms of development continues to be a major challenge.

But what is a "race" in the framework of organic evolution and the global social context of the late twentieth century? Certainly not a group of persons who are genetically homogeneous. That is only likely in the few places where groups might be found that have remained completely isolated from other groups, with no inter-group sexual reproductions. Among other things, the logics of the capitalist world system have drawn virtually all peoples into the "global village" and facilitated much breeding among the old racial groups. But capitalism notwithstanding, "raciation" — i.e., the development of the distinctive gene pools (and cultural repertoires) of various groups which determine the relative frequencies of characteristics shared by their members, but certainly not by them alone — has also been a function, in part, of chance. Consequently:

Since populations' genetic compositions vary over time, race classifications can never be permanent; today's classification may be obsolete in 100 generations. More importantly, modern race classifications attempt to avoid being arbitrary by putting populations *of presumed common evolutionary descent* into the same racial group. Common descent, however, is inferred from similarity in gene frequencies, and here the problem lies. For . . . a population's gene frequencies are determined not only by its ancestry but also by the processes of natural selection and genetic drift. This means that two populations could, in principle, be historically unrelated but genetically quite similar if they had been independently subject to similar evolutionary forces. To place them in the same racial group would, as a step in the study of evolution, be quite misleading. In the absence of historical evidence of descent, therefore, it is difficult to avoid the conclusion that classifying races is merely a convenient but biologically arbitrary way of breaking down the variety of gene frequency data into a manageable number of categories.[29]

When we classify a group as a race on biological terms, at best we refer to generally shared characteristics derived from a "pool" of genes. Social, cultural, and geographical factors, in addition to those of natural selection, all impact on this pool, thus on raciation: sometimes to sustain the pool's relative configuration (for example, by isolating the group — culturally or physically — from outbreeding); sometimes to modify it (as when "mulattos" were produced in the Americas in significant part through slave masters of European descent appropriating African women for their — the "masters'" — sexual pleasure). It is possible to study, with some success, the evolution of a particular group over time (a case of *specific* evolution). The prospects for success are more limited, however, when the focal concern is *general* evolution — that is, the grouping of all of the world's peoples in ordered categories "with the largest and most heterogeneous societies in the top category and the smallest and most homogeneous in the bottom."[30] In either case (that is, the study of general or specific evolution) the concern is with super-organic evolution: changes in behavior repertoires. And such changes are not tied to the genetic specificities of races.

But not all persons (or groups) think so. Though evolutionary — as opposed to typological — thinking, in some form, is at present the dominant intellectual framework for systematic reconstructions and explanations of human natural and social history, it, too, has been enlisted in the service of those who would have "science" pass absolution on their political agendas: i.e., to legitimate the empowerment of certain groups, certain races, over others. Even shorn of the more crude outfittings of social Darwinism's "survival of the fittest" (those with power, or seeking power, over others being the "fittest," of course), scientific studies of race are still offered as orderings of human groups along an *ascending* scale with a particular group's placement on the scale being a function of the level of their supposed development (or lack thereof) toward human perfectibility: from "primitive" to "civilized"; from "undeveloped" or "underdeveloped" to "developed" or "advanced."

Such arguments find fertile soil for nourishment and growth now that "evolution" (organic and super-organic, often without distinction), frequently conceived of as linear development along a single path which *all* races have to traverse, is now a basic feature of "common sense" (except among creationists, perhaps) as we still face political problems emerging from conflicts among racial groups. Raciality continues to function as a critical yardstick for the rank-ordering of particular groups both "scientifically" and socio-politically, efforts of the latter kind with support from those of the former. At bottom, then, "race"—sometimes explicitly, quite often implicitly—continues to be a major fulcrum of struggles over the distribution and exercise of power.

Certainly one of the more prominent contemporary struggles has centered on the validity of measurements of the "intelligence" of persons from different racial groups that purport to demonstrate the comparative intelligence of the groups. This struggle is propelled by the social weight given to "intelligence" as an important basis for achievement and rewards in a meritocratic social order. At its center is the question of the dominant roles played by either the genes or the environment in determining intelligence (and, by extension, in determining raciation). But at basis we have in this struggle only a return of "reason" in disguise as the critical measure of humanity.

After this review of scientific accounts of race, what are we to conclude? Certainly, that raciality is *not* wholly and completely fixed by biological factors, but only partially so. Biological factors do not *determine* raciality, but in complex interactions with environmental, cultural, and social factors and processes they provide certain boundary conditions and possibilities that affect raciation in terms of the development of distinctive gene pools from which are derived physical and biologically conditioned characteristics shared in certain frequencies by members of various groups. Further, the resources provided by concepts of "evolution" do not make for scientifically secure access to race-determining biological, cultural, and social developmental complexes that fix each race's rank-ordered position on an ascending "great chain of being." Racial categories are seldom simply taxonomic, meant to catalog groups in some socially disinterested way; rather, they tend to be motivated by social and political concerns and always rest on the shifting sands of biological heterogeneity.[31] The biological aspects of raciality are conscripted into projects of cultural, political, and social construction.[32]

A review of the career of the concept of "ethnicity," which became paradigmatic among North American social scientists for conceptualizing groupings of different humans during the 1920s–1930s after successful challenges to prevailing biologistic approaches to races that evolved after slavery to "explain" the supposed racial inferiority of people of African descent—and, thereby, the supposed superiority of the "white race"—reveals a legacy similar to that for "race," in part because the terms have often been used as synonyms. With good reason, apparently, for the etymology of "ethnicity" reveals that the root term involved a physiological association that has been retained in English: the word "ethnic" derives, via Latin, from the Greek *ethnikos*, the adjective form of *ethnos*, a nation or race.[33] Later there were shifts from a biological (physiological) context of meaning to one that included cultural characteristics and political structures, though the shifts have been neither consistent nor unidirectional.[34]

First, prior to the 1930s, the focus on ethnicity was an insurgent approach that challenged the biologistic view of race, an attack that was led by "progressive" scholars, activists, and policymakers for whom what has come to be called the "Chicago school" of sociology (prominent social scientists at the University of Chicago) was a decisive institutional site. In this intellectual and social context "race" was regarded as a social category and but one of a number of determinants of ethnicity or ethnic group identity. Second, during the decades spanning the 1930s through the mid-1960s, the ethnic paradigm served as the liberal/progressive "common sense" regarding raciality, a period in which assimilationism and cultural pluralism emerged as themes of discourses devoted to the articulation of strategies to guide the development of America into an "integrated" social whole in which racial/ethnic differences were "melted" away by the rationalist heat of egalitarian principles. This agenda, and the theorizing of ethnicity that was its intellectual articulation, were formed to meet the problems resulting from the flood of immigrants to the U.S. from various European countries and the consequent conflicts from what were called "culture contacts." Hence the emphasis on—and the intellectual acceptance of the inevitability and desirability of—"integration": the assimilation of various European ethnies into a new "American" national identity.[35]

But the victory of the ethnicity paradigm in service to assimilation was to prove hollow, in significant part because the paradigm and agenda were rooted in a framework structured so tightly around European experiences and concerns that there was a serious failure to appreciate the extent to which inequalities conditioned by biologically informed geographical raciations differed from inequalities that could be understood appropriately through the concepts of an "ethnicity" localized to groups of various lines of European descent. Thus, in the post-1965 period, when the Black Power movement ushered in an agenda decisively distinct from the assimilationism of the Civil Rights movement—and, in doing so, excited persons comprising other groups to likewise seek social justice in distributive terms referenced to their racial or ethnic identity, not just to their being Americans—ethnicity as paradigm for assimilation was sharply challenged. The responses of some proponents of its continued dominance defined the paradigm's

[handwritten margin note: ethnic a means of assimilating "new" white folk from Europe / 30s-60s]

third agenda of deployment: as a defense of "conservative" egalitarianism against the "radical" assault of proponents of "group rights"—blacks, women, and "ethnics," as they were called, who refused to surrender their cultural traditions and identities, their life-worlds, to the homogenizing processes of America's "melting pot." And, once again, the defenders invoke the charge that the ethnics and other proponents of "difference" are being "unreasonable."

We are thus in the midst of a period of social turbulence described my Michael Novak as "the rise of the unmeltables": that is, a time in which there are increasing numbers and intensities of social and political developments in each case motivated, in part, by the quest for a "new ethnicity"—"new" relative to the long dominance of the paradigm of assimilation—in which those involved use cultural as well as biological characteristics to identify themselves as constituting or being a part of particular ethnic or racial groups, and who formulate and promote their claims for social justice using these identifiers.[36] I agree with Novak, an astute observer of these developments, that the heightened articulation and awareness of ethnicity (he terms it "cultural awareness"), when politicized, is a major factor in global affairs, "perhaps even one of the major sources of political energy in our era."[37] Novak identifies a number of important aspects of conditions affecting the new quest for ethnicity that are worth noting:

- it is "post-tribal," that is to say, it arises in an era when virtually every cultural group has been obliged to become aware of many others;
- it arises in an era of advanced technology that, paradoxically, liberates energies for more intense self-consciousness while simultaneously binding many cultures together in standardized technical infrastructures;
- it arises during a period of intense centripetal and homogenizing forces; and
- in some cases it involves a rebellion against forces of technical power, thus manifests a certain rebellion against the supposed moral superiority of modernity.[38]

But why this resurgence of political movements, the central mobilizing terms of which involve valorizations of factors of difference, of particularity, such as raciality and ethnicity? Because, I think, the existential concerns and actions of specific groupings of peoples to realize their particular(istic) interests, when pulled into the bounds of the theoretical and practical legacies of the project of modernity, have generally been poorly accommodated, if not eclipsed or eliminated, by the twin pressures of reductionist moves to individualism and flights into abstract universalism derivative of an overemphasis on subject-centered reason. The historical, cultural, social lifeworld is the foundation and context of human lived experiences, of our very being. And in the particular case of people of African descent in America,

the projects of enslavement and subordination, facilitated by the hierarchiz-
ing, differentiating racial categories elaborated by some Enlightenment
thinkers, helped to ensure the development and perpetuation of distinctive
New World African life-worlds evidenced in our arts, musics, religions, literatures, forms of social life, and, most prevalently, in the very nature of our
various forms of vernacular speech. In addition, it is well beyond dispute
today that reason is never "pure," never without specific historical and cultural clothing appropriate to the particular projects of particular persons of
particular groups situated in particular ways in a particular social order, the
reason-certified egalitarian and universalist promises of liberal modernity
notwithstanding. Consequently, those who would oppose efforts to promote
racial and ethnic identities and communities, who would oppose efforts to
seek distributive and retributive justice on terms that include ethnic and
racial qualifiers, can no longer be confident that they are justified and legitimated in doing so because they have reason on their side. We are now in the
midst of a historical conjucture that is highly charged by efforts to reorga-
nize many multi-ethnic, multi-racial societies—in some cases to make them
more democratic—in which "group thinking" is a decisive feature of social
and political life. Particularity has become a principal (and principled) basis
of struggle. Neither liberalism nor the critical theoretical tradition of
Marxism is a sufficient mediator.

In light of all this, how might the challenges of raciality and ethnicity
be met successfully, both theoretically and practically, in the U.S. in particular? Are there insights that, when combined with critical social thought, will
assist us in the practical realization of a social order structured, in part, by
valorizations of raciality and ethnicity as substantive aspects of a democratic pluralism in which "difference" is prized over forced homogenization, or
over the hegemony of one group and its values and practices over all others
while disguising this dominance in the dress of liberal democracy, or that of
party totalitarianism that invokes its legitimacy by repeating its mantras—
"the proletariat," "the workers," "the people"—though always backing its
stay in power and the enforcement of its agenda with willing use of brutal
force?

In posing the questions in these terms it is obvious that the terrain on
which theoretical and practical projects might be formed to accommodate
"the politics of differences" cannot be that of the political philosophy of
modernity (i.e., liberalism) alone. Nor can it be that of the revised, radicalized, but equally modern political project of Marx-inspired social transformation. I find the philosophical anthropology of the liberal Enlightenment
historically progressive but, at the same time, impoverished. The same is
true of Marxism, since its core philosophical anthropology draws from the
same well of resources. For while raciality and ethnicity cannot be given
"scientific" grounding in biological terms alone, this does *not* mean that

these notions are completely void of positive, distinguishing social value, racism and invidious ethnocentrism notwithstanding. For me, raciality and ethnicity (and gender) are constitutive of the personal and social being of persons, thus are not secondary, unessential matters: they make up the historically mediated structural features of human life-worlds and inform lived experience. Further, they have both absolute (i.e., in themselves) and relative (i.e., in relation to other racial, ethnic, gender groups) value *to the extent that, and for as long as, persons take them to be constitutive of who they are*. It is here that the philosophical anthropology of the Enlightenment comes up short. A theory of society that sets itself the task of understanding, scripting, and producing revolutionary social transformation while disregarding these basic "social facts" is, in my judgment, seriously deficient.

In searching for new terrain and terms on and through which to fashion new theoretical and practical agendas, I am committed to two basic beliefs. First, that a full appreciation of what it means to be human requires that we take proper note of human groupings the definitive characteristics of which (combining historically mediated physical, psychological, and cultural factors) are constitutive, in varying degrees, of the persons in the group. Second, that the principles on which we would base both the organization of socio-political life, and those intellectual enterprises whose objects are living human beings, must take explicit account of these constitutive differences.

One of the most demanding provocations of the "politics of differences" is the challenge to our basic conceptions of ourselves as individual persons and as associates in socio-political structures and traditions of practices bequeathed by both liberal and radical (Marxian) traditions of modernity: namely, the requirement to look beyond what is often regarded as "accidental" differences, including raciality and ethnicity, to the "substantial core" or *essence* which, ontologically, has been thought of as being the definitive constitutive aspect of the human species, thus one shared by all humans. For a long time now that "essence" has been identified as *reason*. Knowing and exercising this "essence" has been thought central to securing universal truth and validity in epistemological matters as a foundation for stable and just unity and order in socio-political life.

Philosophical Praxis: Critical Social Theory as "Cosmopolitan Liberalism"?

For opponents of the project to give freer rein to the play of differences the emphasis on *particularity* subverts these quests and, in practical terms, threatens the always tenuous achievements of cognitive and political normativity thought to be secured by the universality of reason: the achievement and perpetuation of secure knowledge (in science and philosophy, for example) become endangered by the effects of "relativism"; and the freedom,

"Fear of "relativism""

peace, and prosperity of political stability won — or to be won — through liberal or revolutionary politics threatened by possibilities of drift, chaos, or, at worst, anarchy.[39]

Such possibilities are real. Whether they are *probable* depends on a number of factors. But it is neither logically, socially, or historically *necessary* that such consequences follow from a greater play of differences. Achieving that increased play while preserving and enhancing social and intellectual life is precisely what I see as the challenge to be met in an appropriate valorization of raciality and ethnicity.

To this end I join others in calling for a serious revision of the traditions flowing out of the modern Enlightenments, traditions that too often have been a cloak for the hegemony of the complex metaphysics, ontology, and philosophical anthropology of a "white mythology" that "reassembles and reflects the culture of the West: the white man takes his own mythology, Indo-European mythology, his own *logos*, that is, the *mythos* of his idiom, for the universal form of that he must still wish to call Reason."[40] This notion of reason, articulated most forcefully by philosophers of the classical and modern Enlightenments, must be revised if it is to offer us guidance. In the words of Michael Novak:

> No one would deny that there is a perfectly straightforward sense in which all human beings are members of the same human family; every human being is bound by imperatives of reasoning, justification, and communication across cultural and other boundaries; and each human being is entitled to claims of fundamental human dignity. Still, it is also widely grasped today that reason itself operates in pluralistic modes. It would be regarded as "cultural imperialism" to suggest that only one form of reasoning is valid in all matters. It would be regarded as naïve to believe that the content of human experiencing, imagining, understanding, judging, and deciding were everywhere the same. . . . It seems important for a liberal civilization today to thread its way philosophically between the Scylla of relativity and the Charybdis of too narrow a conception of universal reason.[41]

This challenge confronts philosophy directly. One of the central endeavors of Western philosophy continues to be that of attempting to provide the definitive characterization of what it is to be human (of what it is to be "man"). And, in general, the terms in which the characterizations have been and are articulated are void of any explicit references to raciality and ethnicity. Certainly the achievements of modernity inspired by the Enlightenments have been a triumphant partial realization of precisely this mode of characterizing humans. And it is a realization that has made possible substantive progressive achievements in human history, won against some forces that, had they triumphed instead, would have given us a world not much to the liking of many of us, myself included.

value of Enlightenment

But the victory has not been without substantial costs. At the very least, in focusing on what is shared in pursuit of unity and universality, the unique, the dissimilar, the individual, the particular is disregarded. And in doing so a tension is created at the core of Enlightenment philosophy's view of man: between its specification of the shared and universal in the characterization of the human species that makes us all "the same," and its emphasis on the free, rational *individual*. This tension, we noted, was handled, to some extent, by elaborating hierarchical categories for sorting different persons and groups. Further, the aspirations of universalist philosophy notwithstanding, where *generally* race, ethnicity, gender, etc., were irrelevant to the formulations of key notions, the full truth of the matter discloses the invidious ethnocentrism and racism, sexism, and class biases at the very heart of the enterprise: whether invoked in the Greek-barbarian distinction, the enslavement of non-Greeks and constraining of women when fifth- and fourth-century B.C. Greece was at its zenith, or in the continued oppression of women and the enslavement and oppression of African and other peoples during and after the modern Enlightenments.

Of course, one might argue that where we find racism, ethnocentrism, class bias, or sexism in philosophizing it is because particular thinkers fail to live up to the terms of humanism called for by the universalist notions of humans as rational beings—for some, created in the image of God—who are rightly worthy of respect, and that a correction of such situations requires only that the guilty parties come to be governed by the logic of these notions. Consequently, no revision of the central notions regarding "man" is required.

I disagree. While substantive in many ways in contributing to our sense of ourselves, thus to the organization of our individual and collective lives, the privileged notions are also insufficient in ways that can be corrected only by revising them to include space for an appreciation of group-based particularities. It is necessary to extend the privileged notions to groups of persons previously excluded from coverage (e.g., women, Africans and people of African descent, other peoples of color). We must rethink "man" if some of the challenges to practical life are to be overcome.

But philosophers have seldom taken up such a project, having been much too preoccupied with the search for the invariant structures of experience and the invariant operations of human understanding.[42] As important as this quest has been—and it has resulted in significant achievements in thought that have contributed, as well, to our practical life in very positive ways—it is not sufficient. Moreover, when it is allowed to dominate our efforts to give philosophical grounding to our collective and individual lives, we sow the seeds that are harvested as the strife of renewed ethnicity and raciation as millions are unable to locate themselves in satisfying ways, or find social justice, in the terms and practices of social ordering predicated on the stifling universalisms of the old liberalism and moribund attempted instantiations of dictatorial Marxism.

As in previous Enlightenments, philosophers can make substantial contributions to the project suggested by Novak. But we can do so only after adopting a more critical appreciation of difference, in appropriate cases difference conceived in terms of raciality and/or ethnicity, that preserves the progressive achievements of the old Enlightenments while contributing to our moving beyond them toward a new pluralist consensus. In promoting this development I do not seek refuge in Romanticism. Instead, what I desire is a new form of "liberalism," what Novak terms a *cosmopolitan* rather than *universalist* liberalism, which should rest on two pillars: "a firm commitment to the laborious but rewarding enterprise of full, mutual, intellectual understanding; and a respect for differences of nuance and subtlety, particularly in the area of those diversifying 'lived values' that have lain until now, in all cultures, so largely unarticulated."[43] The elaboration of this new liberalism in its possible social-political realizations would be an important contribution from philosophers, something we have not yet worked out as fully as we might.

This elaboration must include insights gained from explorations of the "other side" of raciality and ethnicity: namely, the lived experiences of persons within racial/ethnic groups for whom raciality or ethnicity is a fundamental and *positive* element of their identity, thus of their life-world, in ways that are far from detrimental to the social whole. A new liberalism that truly contributes to enlightenment and emancipation must appreciate such endeavors and appropriate the integrity of those who see themselves through the prisms of raciality and ethnicity, and who change their definitions of themselves. Certainly, the socially invidious and thereby divisive forms and consequences of "race thinking" or "ethnic thinking" ought to be eliminated, to whatever extent possible. But we should not err, yet again, in thinking that "race thinking" or "ethnic thinking" must be completely eliminated on the way to an emancipated and just society, something that is both unlikely and unnecessary.

Such thinking has informed the tradition of critical social theory and left it divided on the issues of raciality and ethnicity, sometimes against itself: the Frankfurt School thought "race" to be without scientific basis as an explanatory notion; "official" Marxism in its classical form treated raciality and ethnicity as factors of conflict secondary to the primary contradiction of class struggle which would be of no significance under socialism; later "official" Marxism of 1928–1957 allowed that race — in the case of African-Americans in particular — was the basis of a black *nation*, that is, a group whose members shared a common history and culture. A revised critical theory of society that would help shape a cosmopolitan liberalism — one that would contribute to the learning and social evolution that secure democratic emancipation in racial and ethnic diversity—would be of no small consequence socially and politically.

But would such a project require that we become "post-modern" and retreat from the progressive achievements of ancient and modern Western Enlightenments won through both liberal and Marxian traditions and practices? Perhaps, depending on how one proceeds. It also opens us to challenging possibilities for social learning that may provide us with bases for enhanced living, for realizing futures which we otherwise might not live because of our failure to learn and evolve. Here we rejoin Habermas, better prepared to appreciate the significance of what he offers as he takes up the philosophical challenge to elaborate a critical social theory that preserves the progressive achievements of the liberal and critical-Marxist projects of modernity while rehabilitating as "communicative reason" the reason of modernity of which I have been critical, and which he criticizes as "subject-centered" reason.

And how is this "communicative reason" different from "subject-centered reason"? Habermas offers the following distinctions:

> "Rationality" refers in the first instance to the disposition of speaking and acting subjects to acquire and use fallible knowledge. . . . Subject-centered reason finds its criteria in standards of truth and success that govern the relationships of knowing and purposively acting subjects to the world of possible objects or states of affairs. By contrast, as soon as we conceive of knowledge as communicatively mediated, rationality is assessed in terms of the capacity of responsible participants in interaction to orient themselves in relation to validity claims geared to intersubjective recognition. Communicative reason finds its criteria in the argumentative procedures for directly or indirectly redeeming claims to propositional truth, normative rightness, subjective truthfulness, and aesthetic harmony. . . . This communicative rationality recalls older ideas of logos, inasmuch as it brings along with it the connotations of a noncoercively unifying, consensus-building force of a discourse in which the participants overcome their at first subjectively biased views in favor of a rationally motivated agreement. Communicative reason is expressed in a decentered understanding of the world.[44]

Habermas *wants* a form of understanding in which "the paradigm of knowledge of objects has to be replaced by the paradigm of mutual understanding between subjects capable of speech and action," a form of reasoning that, at the same time, remains aware of the contexts of its own emergence and position, aware that even its most basic universalist concepts "have a temporal core"; but he must also take care to ensure that communicative reason does not resurrect "the purism of pure reason."[45]

He must tackle other worries as well. On the one hand, "whether the concepts of communicative action and of the transcending force of univer-salistic validity claims do not reestablish an idealism that is incompatible with the naturalistic insights of historical materialism," the idealism of "a pure, nonsituated reason" that reintroduces the chasm between the tran-scendental and the empirical.[46] The protection against idealism, for Habermas, is gained in the recognition of the fact that "the symbolic repro-duction of the life-world and its material reproduction are internally inter-dependent," and the recognition that the life-world provides the resources that nourish networks of communicative action and is "the *medium* by which concrete forms of life are reproduced."[47] In Habermas's rejoinder to these worries are to be found the challenges to be met in articulating a rehabilitated notion of reason that preserves universality while also pre-serving the particularity of historically situated life-worlds:

> There is no pure reason that might don linguistic clothing only in the second place. Reason is by its very nature incarnated in contexts of communicative action and in structures of the life-world. . . . The tran-scendent moment of *universal* validity bursts every provinciality asun-der; the obligatory moment of accepted validity claims renders them carriers of a *context-bound* everyday practice. Inasmuch as commu-nicative agents reciprocally raise validity claims with their speech acts, they are relying on the potential of assailable grounds. Hence, a moment of *unconditionality* is built into *factual* processes of mutual understanding — the validity laid claim to is distinguished from the social currency of a de facto established practice and yet serves it as the foundation of an existing consensus. The validity claimed for propositions and norms transcends spaces and times, *"blots out" space and time*; but the claim is always raised *here and now*, in specific con-texts, and is either accepted or rejected with factual consequences for action.[48]

We must wonder whether this is sufficient to support a theory of com-municative reason and action as the means toward a socially realized rest-ing place between the universal and the particular, a theory that will finally allow us to escape the "opposing impulses" that Habermas sees as having dominated the history of philosophy since Plato and Democritus.[49] Certainly, Habermas's efforts to elaborate such a theory are promising and, taken as a whole, represent one of the most consistent and comprehensive attempts in recent social theorizing.

For me, much of that promise is provided by his appreciation of the life-world as the locus of cultural tradition, socially integrated groups, and identity formation and socialization, each dimension of which he sees as having its own processes of reproduction and standards for evaluating them, and his incorporation of the insights gained through that appreciation into his social theory. For it is through the notion of a life-world that we can come

179

to appreciate in our theorizing the constitution of social groups — their cultural traditions, the identities of their members, and the forms of solidarity by which they achieve their social integration — appropriately characterized, in some cases, in terms of their raciality or ethnicity. And we can do so without abandoning completely modernity's quest for reason-sanctioned universality. For Habermas, at least, rationality is still to be found grounding communication, the life blood of the life-world:

> The rational potential of speech is interwoven with the *resources* of any particular given life-world. . . . As a resource from which interaction participants support utterances capable of reaching consensus, the life-world constitutes an equivalent for what the philosophy of the subject had ascribed to consciousness in general as synthetic accomplishments. Now, of course, the generative accomplishments are related not to the form but to the content of possible mutual understanding. To this extent, *concrete* forms of life replace transcendental consciousness in its function of creating unity. In culturally embodied self-understandings, intuitively present group solidarities, and the competencies of socialized individuals that are brought into play as know-how, the reason expressed in communicative action is mediated with the traditions, social practices, and body-centered complexes of experience that coalesce into *particular* totalities.[50]

We must note, however, that even as we understand the form of "transcendence" involved in the redeemed validity claims of historically situated speech during which consensus is reached to be different from the ahistorical "transcendental" of subject-centered reason, "transcendence" still trades off of "transcendental" in securing universality for reason. Moreover, the universality achieved through reason-redeemed validity claims is still *formal*: the notion points us to *conditions of validity* for redeeming validity claims, not *which* claims are — or are not — valid. I do not think it quite as easy, nor in crucial cases even appropriate, as Habermas might make it appear, to have the only "force" operating in unconstrained dialogue be "the force of reason," where "force" is the universalistic binding power of redeemed claims that hold without regard to what he takes to be "particularistic" claims emerging from contexts of interests that are significantly linked to raciality or ethnicity.

But Habermas is fully aware of the limitations of what he offers as a critical theory that is free from the dialectic of impulses mentioned earlier that has dominated philosophy: └ of universal & particular

> I have attempted to free historical materialism from its philosophical ballast. . . . A theory developed in this way can no longer start by examining concrete ideals immanent in traditional forms of life. It must orient itself to the range of learning processes that is opened up at a

given time by a historically attained level of learning. It must refrain from critically evaluating and normatively ordering totalities, forms of life and cultures, and life-contexts and epochs *as a whole*. . . . Coming at the end of a complicated study of the main features of a theory of communicative action, this suggestion cannot count even as a "promissory note." It is less a promise than a conjecture.[51]

Again, the promise is in the theoretical—and if informed by it, the practical—spaces opened by the theory offered, up to now, as a conjecture. And, coming from one who deliberately seeks to further the progressive achievements of modernity in its liberal and Marxian moments, that is no insignificant offering. For African peoples have always been a force of difference for both traditions. Neither the full nature and extent of our oppression, nor our historical-cultural being as African and African-descended peoples, has been comprehended adequately by the concepts and logics involved in Marxian and liberal analyses and programs for the projects of modernity in societies in Europe and Euro-America.

In part this is a function of the subtle, but pervasive, racism mediated in the liberal and Marxian voices that narrated periods of the histories of particular European peoples as though, on one hand, they were the histories of *all* peoples, and, on the other, as though Hegel had in fact provided the definitive word on Africans: a people without history because a people not yet sufficiently developed as to be makers of history. In part it was a function of the failure to deal with the heterogeneity of the populations of European centers of the rise of capitalism,[52] in part a failure to deal with racism as an indigenous element of European history and culture.[53] These failures were both institutionalized and compounded in the construction of the false universality that infected key concepts and strategies of the analyses and practices of liberalism and Marxism.

Could the articulation of a critical social theory leading to the formation of organizations and strategic implementations that promote social transformation take place in a context conditioned by the exploration of difference, by an explicit valorization of differences? There is the danger that we could well founder on our differences and become a confusion of particularistic "interest groups" without transcending unifying principles that bind us into a real, living community. Instead of consensus, we could resurrect the Tower of Babel.[54]

This is indeed a real danger. But it cannot be removed theoretically. It is a danger that is concomitant to existential realities that should not be bleached out, as it were, by ahistorical, universalist categories intended to secure us against possible fragmentation. The new society must be won in the struggle to realize it. The excursion through "difference" involves, potentially, more than a concern on the part of women, peoples of Amer-Indian, African, Hispanic, Asian descents, gays, etc., to tell our own stories

we need some unifying principles even as we value particularity

theory & practice

181

and, in doing so, to re-affirm ourselves. The important point is *why* the histories and cultures — the modalities of being, the life-worlds — are meaningful and important, *why* they have an integrity worth preserving and struggling for while subjecting them to progressive refinement.

The issue, then, in its theoretical, practical, and *existential* realness, is whether there is sufficient commonalty in our sufferings and our hopes — the modes and sources of our oppressions and in the requirements for a social order that would be void of them — as well as in our joys and accomplishments, to allow our coming together and forging a concrete universal, a unity in diversity. If so, then we must move from theory to praxis in terms of moving from universality via conceptual strategies to universality in the form of democratically based shared unity as an existential project. The stress is on "project," that is, on constant practical efforts that are likewise constantly reconciled by the renewed recognition that no amount of "knowing" or "critical thought" secures the laws, meaningfulness, and trajectory of human history. Rather, it is a constant "doing" that is constituted in the very micro-cells of daily existence, and is structured by the powerfully binding and constituting forces of raciality, ethnicity, nationality, gender, and sexuality as mediated and mediating elements of cultural historicity.

is he saying that just as meaning arises within various life-worlds, communicative/reasoned meaning must be struggled for between life-worlds?

yes

I love this graph lots here

8

THE FUTURE OF "PHILOSOPHY" IN AMERICA

Introduction

Academic philosophy in America is undergoing a significant transition. However, if projections of its future are to be more than idle and irresponsible speculation, an account must first be taken of philosophy's contemporary situation and of recent and mediate-distance historical developments that have contributed to the development of modernity in Europe and North America, thereby, to the development of the present.

For some persons the contemporary situation is marked by the displacement of once dominant analytic philosophy by, among other things, "de-disciplinizing" considerations by some philosophers of issues in other disciplines, by questionings of grounding assumptions of basic fields in the discipline, and by attempts to create new fields. Central to these developments have been challenges to key notions of "reason" and "rationality" with implications for equally important notions of "truth" and of "philosophy" itself, as well as for conceptions of "morality," "humanism," and "human development."

The challenges have been extended to the sometimes latent, sometimes explicit, philosophical anthropologies and philosophies of history that undergirded the thought and practices of various European and American philosophers and became part of Western modernity's "official nationalism" (and official racism and ethnocentrism), which regarded particular intellectual activities and traditions, practiced by particular persons (and not others) of particular groups, as central to Western European and American histories that were thought by many to be "the universal future for the rest of the world."[1] Often a constitutive element in such thinking and associated practices, which were decisive in the making of modern Europe and North America, was the belief that the peoples of Western Europe, the "white 'race'," were the avant-garde of human civilization, if not the only civilized humans. "Race" became a decisive normed factor in relations between lighter and darker peoples, the purported universalism of modern norms notwithstanding.

Challenges to this self-serving and perverting "Eurocentricity" have intensified in recent decades as various peoples, with notable success, have struggled to free themselves from Western European and Euro-American hegemony in part by attempted deconstructions and reconstructions of narratives of American and European histories and philosophies of "man" that have been the intellectual carriers of the hegemony. Consequently, we are experiencing another historical period in America of increased tensions and struggles in which raciality and ethnicity are central as particular groups of persons that have been victims of invidious discrimination by Americans of European descent respond to the incomplete realization of ideals and promises of modernity sanctioned by the American revolution.

These developments are having their effect on academics of philosophy. One result is that philosophy, by one account, is now "a discipline in crisis" marked by serious debates and self-questionings that involve fundamental disagreements about its purpose and identity and by the proliferation of agendas and "styles of reasoning."[2] Several questions are central: "Who should be acknowledged as a philosopher?" "What counts as genuine philosophical activity?" "What counts as a product of such activity?" According to Rajchman, those debating these questions form two opposing camps: those who have an "essentialist" view of philosophy and regard it as a *natural* kind of activity that is continuous throughout history (or, I might add, by some accounts throughout the history of certain peoples or civilizations); and those who view philosophy as a *social institution*, thus a cultural creation, whose history is part of the history of culture at large (or that of particular cultures).[3]

I wish to add my voice to those in the second camp, for I am persuaded that questionings of the traditions and legacies constitutive of the philosophy profession must include an interrogation that discloses the function of race, that is to say, discloses instances in which philosophical thought and disciplinary practices have been conditioned by judgments and/or norms tied to valuations of raciality. Drawing on and extending previous work, I offer a sketch of an interpretative strategy for a critical examination of ways in which norms and beliefs with regard to raciality have been related implicitly and/or explicitly to modern philosophical praxis. I take it to be the case that there have been such relations, varied and complex, and that they have affected, and continue to affect, the discipline of philosophy in important instances and in non-trivial ways.

Such an examination can be focused by a number of questions: Why was it that philosophers, as participants in an enterprise devoted, supposedly, to the guardianship of knowledge at its best, including critical personal and social self-understandings, and to the guardianship of notions of justice and the good life, could be so silent with regard to — and even participate in — the enslavement and oppression of peoples of African descent, among others? Why has it been the case that histories of American philosophy have been void of articulations by African-Americans, and anthologies of American philosophy, with the exception of *Philosophy Born of Struggle* edited by Leonard Harris,[4] have failed to include the writings of Africans-become-Americans? Was it because the enterprise has been an accomplice to racism through institutionalized core agendas and strategies, and through the norms, institutions, media, organizations, and canons that have shaped the traditions through which we philosophers form our understandings and identities, through which we forge and perpetuate our practices?

These questions cannot be answered completely, nor the present situation of philosophy understood fully, "philosophically": that is to say, simply by searching for possible inadequacies or failures in logical reasoning on the part of individual philosophers of European descent, anthologists and historians of American philosophy among them. There is more to philosophizing than cogent and rigorous argument. And this dramatizes most poignantly an important aspect of the plight of contemporary philosophy: the illnesses of the discipline cannot be diagnosed simply by using what have often been regarded as its most essential tools and agenda, namely, description, analysis, and prescription in the form of critical, logically rigorous arguments divorced from and unaffected by considerations of factors such as raciality. Rather, contemporary philosophy in America must also be understood as a complex *social institution* in a particular, yet equally complex, historical-cultural *situation* that is part and parcel of the historical situation of America and "the West." Injustices having to do with "race" continue to infect our nation and, thereby, our discipline. The future prospects of philosophy, to the extent that matters having to do with race are involved, are tied to developments beyond the scope of the discipline. If the enterprise of philosophy is to try to meet self-imposed responsibilities for clarifying the real possibilities for realizing reasonableness in a just and harmonious social order, then we philosophers will have to accommodate critically revised considerations of raciality (and of gender and ethnicity) into our understandings of the constitutive features of our traditions, our work, and our practices. And these developments will have to be accompanied by further changes in the racial, ethnic, and gender demographic compositions of professional philosophers, and by consequent changes in disciplinary norms and practices conditioned by considerations of ideals, norms, and practices from the life-worlds of participants of different racial, ethnic, and gender groupings of persons. To this end a rethinking of raciality in the context of philosophy is in order.

Modernity, Philosophy, and Race: An Interpretative Strategy

Locally, nationally, and internationally we are living through yet another historical period in which arguments, practices, and social movements of various sizes and complexities involve characterizations and valuations of raciality (and ethnicity, gender, class, and national identity) as central issues of contention that condition our lives in decisive ways. Not the least of the effects are substantial challenges to long-prevailing notions of "justice," "reason" and "reasonableness," and "true knowledge" as arguments are advanced that definitions of, and norms regarding and derived from, each of these notions are merely the conventions of particular groups of persons that have come to have hegemony while rationalized as "self-evident" truth. For many, the tasks of defining and deriving norms have been thought consistent with the essential mission of philosophy in the West: identifying or defining norms for "man" and "the good life," specifying the nature of reason and understanding, and orchestrating the fullest possible reason-guided realization of "human" potentialities in ways that would secure "the good life."

This mission is under severe challenge. Likewise the promise that philosophers would provide epistemologically secure knowledge — about knowledge, human nature, ethics, and social and political life — which would be normatively compelling for ordering social life. Thus, it is appropriate to ask whether contemporary philosophers are sufficiently enabled by disciplinary resources to play significant and positive roles in meeting the challenges posed by the resurgence of valuations of raciality and ethnicity as bases for norms regarding truth and justice by contributing, both theoretically and practically, to the achievement of social peace and harmony with justice.

I am convinced that an answer to this question requires that a critical inventory be taken of the resources of the discipline and of the real possibilities for such a contribution. This is especially true relative to matters having to do with raciality, a subject under-theorized in the discipline. For in some of its modes and moments, through some of its key figures, philosophy has been — and continues to be — a significant contributor to historical processes that have now led to the absence of social peace and harmony with justice on matters involving raciality and ethnicity. When we look, for example, at that long period in Western history in which our distinctively modern communities were first formed (the seventeenth and eighteenth centuries in particular), *philosophes*, among whom were many we recognize as "philosophers," were decisively involved in constructing and institutionalizing Enlightenment: complex sets of ideas, beliefs, and commitments, and of intellectual, social, and political ventures, that were decisive aspects of "the project of modernity," which resulted in the formation of modern nation-states.[5]

It was during this same period that modern racism (distinguished from older manifestations of ethnocentrism) was constructed as a set of invidious beliefs about, and invidious practices directed at, persons divided into "racial" groups on the basis of physical and cultural characteristics. The construction rested on two basic and linked assumptions: first, "that a correlation exists between physical characteristics and moral qualities" such that the latter are determined by the former; and, second, given a presumed *natural* division of human beings into distinct races on the basis of physical characteristics and moral qualities, that "mankind is divisible into superior and inferior stocks."[6] The belief that moral and cultural matters could be explained by biological factors was part and parcel of important instances of Enlightenment thought structuring the project of modernity, including the thought of particular philosophers, among them Hume, Kant, and Hegel.

Let me put the matter in the form of a charge: modern philosophy, in important instances, is implicated in the formation and legitimation of modern racism. But just how deeply? Was it simply a matter of the shortcomings of individual *philosophes* and not of what we have come to regard as the enterprise of philosophy? Or, was racism implicated in the very formation of the enterprise itself, for example in the articulations of some *philosophes* who took "reason" or "rationality" to be a definitive criterion of humanity, or of a human being of a particular kind among persons of a particular group compared to persons in other groups (say, men compared to women, Greeks to barbarians, "whites" to "blacks")?

The charge has been put even more sharply by Christian Delacampagne.[7] He contends that the relation between what he calls "European reason" and racism is not a chance linkage but goes deeper, both historically and epistemologically: historically, back, for example, to Aristotle's rank-ordered characterizations of types of persons and, from him, through the medieval church to the modern Enlightenment, rank-ordered characterizations of different peoples by virtue of their "national character" or, later, their "race"; epistemologically, in the use of "reason" in typologies of characterization used to *order* the natural, and thereby the social, worlds. And Martin Bernal's *Black Athena: The Afroasiatic Roots of Classical Civilization*[8] has become a significant addition to arguments long advanced (and long ignored or rejected) by several generations of scholars of African descent who continue to argue that the intellectual sources of Western philosophy are not to be found in ancient Greece, but in traditions of thought of the high African civilization of ancient Kemet (Egypt). For these scholars (George G. M. James,[9] W. E. B. Du Bois,[10] Chiekh Anta Diop,[11] St. Clair Drake,[12] Molefi Kete Asante,[13] Maulana Karenga and Jacob H. Carruthers,[14] and Henry Olela,[15] among others), it was modern European racism directed at African peoples in support of their enslavement and exploitation and the exploitation of the African continent, that required the construction of notions of the superiority of the white race to an inferior black race, and, consequently, required the destruction of the history of the linkage of achievements on the part of peoples of Europe (supposedly the geographical origin of "white" peoples) to achievements by African peoples. Within the cauldron of this racism particular scholars of European descent, during the seventeenth, eighteenth, and nineteenth centuries especially, constructed histories of philosophy that set the origins and informing legacies of philosophy and civilized human development in fifth- and fourth-century B.C. Greece. In the process Kemet was displaced as the source of much of what is now regarded as having originated with European civilizations, and African peoples were ejected from the forms of regard reserved for those thought civilized.

In that grand experiment in modern nation-building that involved the design and construction of a United States of America, very similar strategies were articulated and deployed by the Founding Fathers and other key persons who became America's foremost "public philosophers," and as such were intimately involved in the institutionalization of the enslavement of Africans.[16] Later, however, after the revolution of the late 1700s and early 1800s and the curtailment of the radical impulses of the Enlightenment, philosophers in America, especially after becoming academic "professionals," contrary to the public involvements of the Puritan thinkers and the *philosophes* (and much later the pragmatists), retreated, for the most part, from concern with social life, and so retreated from the problems of the enslavement of Africans and the institutionalization of racism against persons of African descent as well as against persons of other racial and/or ethnic groups.

The impact of these developments on the enterprise of philosophy has been decisive. As noted, even today virtually all of the texts that collectively form the canons of American and Western philosophy are all but mute with respect to the subjects of the historical origins of Western philosophy in African thought or to the European enslavement of Africans and, through and beyond slavery, the institutionalization of European racism against black folks. Nor, for example, do these canonizations tend to give consideration to reflections, speeches, and writings of Africans and African-Americans, or to anything that might come from African and African-American traditions, as instances of philosophizing, hence as worthy of study in the discipline. Thus, in the normal day-to-day activities through which the philosophy profession manifests and reproduces itself—teaching, research, scholarship; reproduction of the professoriate through the training of graduate students; extra-curricular professional activities—legacies are perpetuated that, while they may no longer *explicitly* exclude people of African descent, until rather recently left the clear impression that such persons were not welcome. Relative to this the insights of Maurice Mandelbaum are especially pertinent:

> In all societies the political and economic conditions tend to determine the classes of people who have the time and the social positions which make it possible to engage in philosophic thought in full awareness of the traditions of that thought. Furthermore, at different times the social structure seems to determine what groups of people, in what occupations, form the groups in which one finds concerted efforts to

social location of philosophers

deal with philosophical problems. . . . If this fact had no influence upon the history of philosophy it would be as surprising as if the fact that mediaeval philosophers were churchmen had no impact upon how they thought and wrote.[17]

An investigation of the social configuration and reproduction of the profession would illuminate aspects of the circumscribed and selective social formation of social memory at work in the socializing processes of the discipline, and in the legitimation and institutionalization of its traditions (in part in the form of canons and histories), as these contribute to national social and intellectual life. For philosophers, principally through disciplinary operations within institutions of higher education, both participate in and contribute to the maintenance — sometimes to critique-guided transformation — of intellectual and social life through strategies of legitimation that include the mediation of sedimented memories in the form of selected traditions. The how and why of this participation and contribution are in need of review.

An interrogation of the kind I have in mind would involve several related inquires. First, a history of philosophy that seeks to narrate what key historical figures and traditions have had to do with the very complex history of relations of super-ordinated Europeans to sub-ordinated Africans, relations rationalized by strategies and according to agendas that together constitute endeavors in "philosophy." Of course, an extended investigation along this line would probe changes in the historiography of philosophy that substituted ancient Greece for ancient Kemet as the wellspring of Western philosophy. A second line of inquiry would take the form of a history of ideas that, within the boundaries of the first inquiry, would explore the "Chain of Being" as a particular "unit-idea" that, according to Arthur O. Lovejoy, was a decisive organizing and foundational element in systematic knowledge in the modern period (though its legacy is much older).[18] The "Chain of Being" was a scheme within which racial distinctions were made and races rank-ordered relative to one another.

This history of ideas would be followed by, and linked to, an *archaeo-logical* inquiry that would seek, on one hand, to probe the epistemological field — the *épistème* — constituted by the "network of analogies" that were "common to a whole series of scientific 'representations' or 'products' dispersed throughout the natural history, economics, and philosophy" in the seventeenth and eighteenth centuries.[19] If Foucault is correct, the *épistème* was part of what he terms the *"positive unconscious"* of knowledge that eludes awareness but still informs philosophical discourse. This "positive unconscious" provides what Foucault identifies as the *rules of formation* by which the proper objects of study in a discipline are defined, concepts formed and employed in discourse, and theories built and strategies devised that set the themes and theories which guide the processes of inquiry and discourse; and the *rules of discourse* that determine *who* speaks and with what authority.[20] Especially relevant is Foucault's examination of the table of classification and associated strategies ordering the epistemological fields — and providing the very form of *order* — during periods when European encounters with Africa and Africans took the forms that have subsequently been termed "racist."

Finally, these three inquires would be supplemented by a review of philosophy that takes the form of *a sociology of knowledge*. In this case the task would be, again within the boundaries of a span of history that includes the modern and contemporary, to situate philosophy as a knowledge-producing enterprise within a sociologically informed understanding through which it is examined as a norm-structured, complex, socially and politically conditioned *institution*. The objective would be to account for social causality in philosophy in terms of the dialectic of the social construction of norms that inform disciplinary roles, structures, intellectual agendas, and practices through which, in turn, knowledge and norms are constituted, legitimated, and mediated as part of traditions of socially distributed knowledge of various kinds (sub-specialities, styles, genres, etc.) carried by certain persons.

The combination of these interpretative inquires I would characterize, borrowing from Richard Rorty, as a "historico-metaphilosophical reflection on philosophy" in the form of a "historical narrative which places the works of . . . philosophers [and the discipline of philosophy] within the historical development of . . . culture,"[21] in this case a cultural context that has been significantly conditioned by concerns regarding raciality. What follows is a brief rehearsal of the interrogation I have proposed employing the interpretative strategy just sketched out.

Africans and Philosophy in Western History

The enslavement of Africans in the New World created profound dilemmas for the revolutionary projects of forming decidedly modern nation-states. In what would become the United States of America, the dilemma would be particularly acute since the political philosophy providing the justification for the nation-building project centered the weight of moral significance on the *individual* without, supposedly, attending to otherwise irrelevant characteristics such as race, creed, or national origin since, it was claimed in the founding documents, "all men are created *equal*" and must be subject to the rule of law applied equally to all. America, then, was to be a paradigmatic Enlightenment achievement in which, drawing on the resources of reason, normativity would be created and perpetuated by self-correcting adherence to norms regarding fallibility, subjectivity, and universality.[22] However, racial slavery required substantial intellectual — as well as practical — efforts to ameliorate the bold contradicting of grounding principles while maintaining and legitimating the peculiar institution. The political philosophy of modernity was compromised by even more compelling commitments to notions regarding different races and other social collectivities. The new, unstable compound of thought was then used to rationalize invidious practices and beliefs directed at various groups characterized on the basis of social and physiological distinctions by race (the enslavement of Africans), gender (restricting the rights of women), and socio-economic class (restricting participation in political life to property-owners), and to curb the egalitarianism the political philosophy of Liberalism encouraged. With the sanction of reason, a compromise was reached that allowed the continuation of racial slavery in order to gain agreement among the colonies-becoming-states on terms for national unification: that is, it was a "reasonable" thing to do in order to secure unity, particularly in the face of conflict leading to war with Britain. A major consequence was the serious distortion of the nation's subsequent historical development.

The terms and strategy by which the formulation of the compromise was made possible were hardly new, thanks to Aristotle, who had accounted for particular forms of human diversity using a scheme of hierarchical ordering that he thought met criteria of reasonableness: persons differ *by nature*, as confirmed by the functionally beneficial ways in which different types of persons (free males, women, slaves) filled different types of roles in Athens.[23] Similar approaches were used by Europeans to justify regarding racial and ethnic differences as grounds for super-ordination and sub-ordination when they encountered Africans during the seventeenth century while searching for new lands and riches.[24] Hegel, as noted earlier, was quite explicit in declaring African peoples not to have reached a level of development at which they would even live historically.[25]

Such orientations were significant components of the mind-sets of many Europeans migrating to the Americas and was literally made-to-order for the subsequent situation of compromise faced by the thinkers who had to confront America's racial dilemma. As noted by one historian: "From the time of the American Revolution the words *reason*, *humanity*, and *nature* appeared frequently in proslavery literature and became epistemological tools in religion and philosophy. They also developed into authorities for morality. Although few proslavery writers dwelt on them extensively, almost all at some point affirmed the compatibility of slavery with reason, nature, and humanity."[26] Their position accorded well with and was reinforced by America's troubled, unstable compound political philosophy that was forged around a concept of reason that had been legitimated by both classical and modern Enlightenments to characterize racial and cultural diversity in terms of a reason-privileged hierarchy of racial types. Accordingly, Africans had their non-white differences accounted for in historical terms by Hegel as due to a lack of development; theologically by argumentative strategies effected through interpretations of particular passages in the Bible that focused on the marked (by "burnt" skin), deficient spirit and capacity of the race;[27] ontologically through strategies, reminiscent of Aristotle, employed, among others, by Hume[28] and Kant, that focused on their racial "nature" or "character":

> The Negroes of Africa have by nature no feeling that rises above the trifling. Mr. Hume challenges anyone to cite a single example in which a Negro has shown talents, and asserts that among the hundreds of thousands of blacks who are transported elsewhere from their countries, although many of them have even been set free, still not a single one was ever found who presented anything great in art or science or any other praiseworthy quality, even though among the whites some continually rise aloft from the lowest rabble, and through superior gifts earn respect in the world. So fundamental is the difference between these two races of man, and it appears to be as great in regard to mental capacities as in color. The religion of fetishes so widespread among them is perhaps a sort of idolatry that sinks as deeply into the trifling as appears to be possible to human nature. A bird feather, a cow's horn, a conch shell, or any other common object, as soon as it becomes consecrated by a few words, is an object of veneration and of invocation in swearing oaths. The blacks are very vain but in the Negro's way, and so talkative that they must be driven apart from each other with thrashing.[29]

Race and the "Chain of Being": History of a Unit-Idea

Here the work of Lovejoy is of central importance. As he shows in *The Great Chain of Being*, a crucial "unit-idea" that was an organizing element of systematic knowledge in the modern period was that of a "Scale of Being" which we find at work in the thought of many modern philosophers, for example that of Thomas Jefferson:

> The opinion, that they [blacks] are inferior in the faculties of reason and imagination, must be hazarded with great diffidence. To justify a general conclusion, requires many observations, even where the subject may be submitted to the Anatomical knife, to Optical glasses, to analysis by fire, or by solvents. How much more then where it is a faculty, not a substance, we are examining; where it eludes the research of all the senses; where the conditions of its existence are various and variously combined; where the effects of those which are present or absent bid defiance to calculation; let me add too, as a circumstance of great tenderness, where our conclusion would degrade a whole race of men from the rank in the scale of beings which their Creator may perhaps have given them. . . . I advance it therefore as a suspicion only, that the blacks, whether originally a distinct race, or made distinct by time and circumstances, are inferior to the whites in the endowments both of body and mind.[30]

The idea of a "scale of being" originates with Plato (in the *Timaeus*), to whom Lovejoy attributes the contribution of two closely related conceptions to the general stock of Western philosophical ideas in response to two questions, which conceptions were to play a decisive role in the development and history of the idea of a scale of being. In response to the question "Why is there any World of Becoming, in addition to the eternal World of Ideas, or, indeed, to the one supreme Idea?" Plato reasoned that "a timeless and incorporeal One became the logical ground as well as the dynamic source of the existence of a temporal and material and extremely multiple and variegated universe." The One was a Self-Transcending Fecundity. And to the question "What principle determines the number of kinds of being that make up the sensible and temporal world?" the response was that it was the principle of *plenitude*: for Plato, with respect to living things or animals, there must *necessarily* be "complete translation of all the ideal possibilities into actuality."[31] Thus, from the One, Many: "The universe is a *plenum formarum* in which the range of conceivable diversity of *kinds* of living things is exhaustively exemplified . . . no genuine potentiality of being can remain unfulfilled . . . the extent and abundance of the creation must be as great as the possibility of existence and commensurate with the productive capacity of a 'perfect' and inexhaustible Source, and . . . the world is the better, the more it contains."[32]

To this unit-idea, according to Lovejoy, Aristotle added the conception of *continuity* as a principle operative in natural history and suggested the idea of arranging animals in a single graded natural scale according to their degree of "perfection," since any division of creatures with reference to some one determinate attribute manifestly gave rise to *a* linear series of classes (though, Lovejoy notes, Aristotle did *not* hold that all organisms could be so arranged and made no attempt to frame a single and exclusive scheme of classification).[33]

> There were in the Aristotelian metaphysics and cosmology certain far less concrete conceptions which could be so applied as to permit an arrangement of all things in a single order of excellence. . . . This vague notion of an ontological scale was to be combined with the more intelligent conceptions of zoological and psychological hierarchies which Aristotle had suggested; and in this way what I shall call the principle of unilinear gradation was added to the assumptions of the fullness and the qualitative continuity of the series of forms of natural existence.[34]

Plotinus contributed to this developing notion of a "scale" by adding further support to the belief that difference in kind is necessarily "equivalent to difference of excellence, to diversity of rank in a hierarchy."[35] Thus neo-Platonism prepared the way for medieval thinkers, Augustine and Aquinas in particular, to add "the thesis of the inherent and supreme value of variety and existence as such" in service to agendas formed in the context of the theology and cosmology of medieval Christendom.[36]

But a major conflict among opposing motives emerged: accounting for goodness and evil while remaining consistent with a conception of God, the principle of plenitude (of Many from the One), and the principle of Sufficient Reason (the *necessity* that there be both One and Many). If the Many come from the One necessarily, and the One is good and, thus, cannot be the source of evil, must not the Many be of equal value? Or, at the very least, how could any of God's creations *be* by necessity yet not be good in their own right? Further, what did the principle of Sufficient Reason demand in fulfillment of the principle of Plenitude? An infinite number of beings with no "gaps" in the chain of being? How to reconcile the necessity that there be an infinite number of beings in a finite, temporal world with the equally necessary principle of Sufficient Reason?

By the eighteenth century two conflicting positions were taken on these questions. For some, notions of plenitude, continuity, and sufficient reason led to arguments against equalitarian movements: variety by means of inequality was evidence of Infinite Wisdom, and the social microcosm should reflect in its organization the principles ordering the macrocosm. Demands for social equality were thus "contrary to nature." For others, including Voltaire, Leibniz, and Pope, the whole of creation was perfect and therefore good: "The limitations of each species of creature, which define its place in the scale, are indispensable to that infinite differentiation of things in which the 'fullness' of the universe consists, and are therefore necessary to the realization of the greatest of goods."[37] But in the latter, more optimistic view was a paradox: "*the desirability of a thing's existence bears no relation to its excellence.*"[38]

This conflict was played out between Romanticism and the Enlightenment: between diversitarianism and universalism. For Lovejoy, the dominant tendency of the Enlightenment had been devotion to the simplification and standardization of life and thought by way of the confirmation of a principle thought to be universal, immutable, uncomplicated, and uniform for every rational being. From the 1500s to the 1700s, efforts were made to correct and improve beliefs, institutions, and art guided by the assumption that in every phase of activity man should conform to such a standard as nearly as possible. "Nature" was most often the conceptual vehicle carrying the connotation of universality and uniformity of content and was drawn out and expressed in ethical applications such as the "law of nature" invoked in moral and political philosophy.[39]

Romanticism reversed the values of the Enlightenment by substituting "diversitarianism for uniformatarianism as the ruling preconception in most of the normative provinces of thought." Against the prevailing ideas of the Enlightenment, Romanticism, drawing out implications of the principle of plenitude, was characterized by the belief that not only are there diverse excellences in all areas of life, but that diversity itself is of the essence of excellence. One consequence of this posture was "the cultivation of individual, national, and racial peculiarities." This development, in turn, led to a revision of the notion of universality from "uniform" to "expansive' universality.[40]

However, a latent danger in Romanticism emerged: a revolt against universal standardization of life became a revolt against the whole conception of standards. Consequently, Romanticism

> lent itself all too easily to the service of man's egoism, and especially — in the political and social sphere — of the kind of collective vanity which is nationalism or racialism. The belief in the sanctity of one's idiosyncrasy — especially if it be a group idiosyncrasy, and therefore sustained and intensified by mutual flattery — is rapidly converted into a belief in its superiority. . . . A type of national culture valued at first because it was one's own, and because the conservation of differentness was recognized as a good for humanity as a whole, came in time to be conceived of as a thing which one had a mission to impose upon others, or to diffuse over as large a part of the surface of the planet as possible.[41]

This was the context in which the notion of "race" was taken up by natural philosophers and other *philosophes* in the modern period. How — or why — it was that the word and concept of "race" came to be used to classify human groups is not entirely clear.[42] But, a number of contributing factors do stand out. First were the tensions within Europe arising from encounters among groups of peoples who differed culturally or, more narrowly, religiously. Second, a more basic impetus, intensified by these tensions, came from the need to account for human origins in general, for human diversity in particular. Natural philosophy gave way to the development of various modern natural and social sciences, including anthropology, as endeavors to meet this need. Third were the quite decisive European voyages to America and Africa, and the development of capitalism and the slave trade.[43] These developments, combined with the rise of European nation-states and concomitant nationalisms, particularly where the states were involved in efforts to fashion an empire through colonialism, "gave powerful impetus to the natural tendency of nationalism to become chauvinism. And chauvinism, perverting to its uses the new sciences, could become and, where conditions were propitious, did become racism. The interaction between colonialism and this nationalism provided the necessary *milieu* for the emergence and development of racism."[44]

The authority of "race" as an organizing, classificatory concept within the scheme of a "Chain of Being" was strengthened during the unfolding of the project of modernity, in the eighteenth century in particular, when "evidence from geology, zoology, anatomy and other fields of scientific enquiry was assembled to support a claim that racial classification would help explain many human differences."[45] Use of conceptions of raciality contributed to "typological" thinking—regarding individuals as instances of determining *types*, a mode of conceptualization that was at the center of the agenda of natural philosophy—which facilitated the classification of human groups.

Two significant achievements resulted from these efforts. First, drawing on the rising authority of natural sciences as the realization and guardian of systematic, certain knowledge, race was legitimated as a gathering concept for morphological features that were thought to distinguish natural varieties of *homo sapiens* supposedly related to one another through the logic of an equally natural hierarchy of groups in terms of capacity for, and development and display of, species-determining factors (i.e., language, religion, art, and thought of certain kinds that mark "civilization"). Thanks to the preparatory efforts of some proponents of the idea of a "Chain of Being," "fact and value became combined in the concept of race."[46] Second, the view was legitimated that the behavior of a group and its members was determined by their place in this hierarchy.[47]

Thus, notions of raciality that were authorized and legitimized by natural philosophers and scientists, when combined with social projects involving the distinguishing and, ultimately, the control of "racially" different persons and groups—as in the case of the enslavement of Africans—took root and grew to become part of modern common sense, particularly as racial apartheid was institutionalized in Great Britain and the Americas. Such notions became part of the "positive unconscious" that undergirded virtually all knowledge forms, those that dealt with "man" especially, as history unfolded into the contemporary period. *The* problem of modern North America, to paraphrase W. E. B. Du Bois, was indeed the problem of the "color line": the problem of relations between darker and lighter races. To be a North American, to be in North America, meant that one had to learn to negotiate the social landscape guided by a compass whose ordered and ordering points were, in significant part, matters having to do with "race." Philosophers were not immune; nor, therefore, were the practices and traditions that were constitutive of philosophy.

An "Archaeology" of Race in the Epistème of Modern Philosophy

Academic philosophy in America has centered on the thought of particular male persons of European descent with, until very recently, systematic exclusions of traditions of thoughts of people of African descent, and of others. The exclusions have often been justified by arguments that presume philosophy to be an enterprise that "operates independently of its material circumstances" and is "composed of various claims advanced and defended on the basis of intrinsic philosophical considerations, above all, on the basis of the net persuasiveness of the arguments put forward."[48] It is my contention that the legitimacy and adequacy of such "justifications" do not rest on transcendental, universal logical rules that the arguments supposedly satisfy, but on tradition-mediated conventionalized norms shared by persons in the discipline (though certainly not all persons) for whom, despite many differences among them otherwise, the inferiority of African peoples was assumed, whether the assumption was made explicit (as with Hegel, Hume, and Kant) or not. Further, such an assumption was and is not "extra-philosophical." Rather, it was at the core of widely shared commitments that conditioned Enlightenment discourses generally, "philosophical" discourse in particular, as the project of modernity unfolded.

The locus of these commitments is to be found, in part, in the unit-idea of the Chain of Being. However, this locus can be explored further by way of the archaeological strategies of Michel Foucault, which probe *epistemological figures* and, among them, the network of analogies transcending traditional relational proximities (i.e., how various things in the world are thought to be related) that he finds "common to a whole series of scientific 'representations' or 'products' dispersed throughout the natural history, economics, and philosophy" of the seventeenth and eighteenth centuries.[49] Racial classifications emerged in the context of and in service to these enterprises (natural philosophy, history, and economics) in which the notion of the "Chain" or "Scale" of Being was ready to hand and facilitated the ordering strategies of classification. The ordering strategies — that is to say, efforts to determine, by articulation of "discoveries," the *order* in nature — were devised in service to what Foucault terms fundamental ordering "codes" in the cultures of key Enlightenment thinkers.

Such codes are fundamental to every culture and are found in the language, schemas of perception, exchanges, values, hierarchy of practices, and in techniques and recipes for practices. They "establish for every man, from the very first, the empirical orders with which he will be dealing and within which he will be at home."[50] Emerging out of and, in turn, constitutive of ordered experiences of an ordered world, the codes become first order to the second-order reflections of scientific theories and philosophical interpretations formulated to "explain why order exists, what universal law it obeys, what principle can account for it . . . why this particular order has been established and not some other."[51] The "codes" establish a classificatory "table" that "enables thought to operate upon the entities of our world, to put them in order, to divide them into classes, to group them according to names that designate their similarities and their differences."[52]

The sign and symbol systems of a culture, particularly those manifested in its language, are primary vehicles of its codes.[53] Language especially is the sign system par excellence in which are contained the encoded shared objectivations of everyday life. Further, in and through language "semantic fields" or "zones" of meaning are constructed and ordered by vocabulary, grammar, and syntax, fields or zones that distinguish and configure racial and gender orderings, for example. Within these fields biographical and historical experiences are selectively objectified, retained, and accumulated into a "social stock of knowledge" that is made available to individuals in the culture and mediated to succeeding generations. However, the distribution of the social stock of knowledge is governed by socially and politically weighted rules of selectivity. That is, different individuals and different types of individuals come to possess different portions of the social stock of knowledge. African slaves were not to know (were claimed incapable of knowing though, in contradiction, great steps were taken to prevent their coming to know) what European and American slavemasters knew. Nor, within institutionalized traditions of Western philosophy, could everyone be a "philosopher."

The fundamental codes of European cultures, and the social stock of knowledge to which they gave rise, must be investigated to locate the commitments that have been the basis for restricting legitimate "philosophical" thought to certain males of European descent. A Foucault-inspired archaeology would interrogate the theories of representation and language, of natural orders, and of wealth and value that reigned as systematic thought in the period of the project of modernity. It was during this period that African peoples were appropriated into the project as the beasts of burden in the production of wealth, freeing self-selected others for the task of providing intellectual guidance to the making of modernity. Such an investigation would provide a "deep level" account of European racism and show how this racism was continued in philosophy as part of the organizing *epistème* or epistemological field, with its rules of formation and rules of discourse, that conditioned the formation of norms constitutive of philosophical practices.

In Winthrop Jordan's *The White Man's Burden*, we find a ready example. Jordan offers several areas of commitment (values, beliefs) that became key to the formation of racism on the part of persons from England toward Africans. First, "the most arresting characteristic of the newly discovered African was his color."[54] However, the "arresting" experience of Africans' color was not simply phenomenological, that is to say, simply a reaction to a color gradient different from that of English people. Rather, the color "black" was already loaded with invidious meanings:

> In England perhaps more than in southern Europe, the concept of blackness was loaded with intense meaning. Long before they found that some men were black, Englishmen found in the idea of blackness a way of expressing some of their most ingrained values. No other color except white conveyed so much emotional impact. As described by the *Oxford English Dictionary*, the meaning of *black* before the sixteenth century included, "Deeply stained with dirt; soiled, dirty, foul. . . . Having dark or deadly purposes, malignant; pertaining to or involving death, deadly; baneful, disastrous, sinister. . . . Foul, iniquitous, atro-

cious, horrible, wicked. . . . Indicating disgrace, censure, liability to punishment, etc." Black was an emotionally partisan color, the hand-maid and symbol of baseness and evil, a sign of danger and repulsion.

Embedded in the concept of blackness was its direct opposite — whiteness. . . . It was important, if incalculably so, that English discovery of black Africans came at a time when the accepted English standard of ideal beauty was a fair complexion of rose and white. Negroes seemed the very picture of perverse negation.[55]

In addition to notable English people's efforts to valorize Africans' skin color negatively in the process of "explaining" the causes of the blackness, Jordan notes that they also made use of prevailing cultural codes to account for African differences and to order those differences by way of equally negative valorizations: African religions were termed "defective"; much of their behavior "savage"; their sexuality "libidinous."[56]

Sexuality continues to be one of the most emotionally charged areas of thought and action (though not of open discussion) with regard to relations between African and European peoples, relations between black males and white females especially.[57] In the earliest encounters between English and African, codes regarding sexuality provided the means for handling questions of Africans' place in the Chain of Being. According to Jordan, it happened to be the case that the English became acquainted with Africans and anthropoid apes "at the same time and in the same place." Facilitated by a long tradition of thought that designated Africa as the source of beasts and devils of various kinds, "it was virtually inevitable that Englishmen should discern similarity between the manlike beasts and the beastlike men of Africa." The place of Africans in the Chain of Being was fixed by linking them sexually to apes: "The notion that Negroes stemmed from beasts in a literal sense was not widely believed. . . . Far more common and persistent was the notion that there sometimes occurred 'a beastly copulation or conjuncture' between apes and Negroes, and especially that apes were inclined wantonly to attack Negro women."[58] The classification of Africans as "beast-like" was thus sufficient to authorize their enslavement.

The "New" Englanders brought these values to the land they renamed "America" and institutionalized them as part of the official nationalism that included the legalization of the enslavement of Africans. An immediate and direct effect on the developing traditions of thought that we now include in histories of American philosophy was that the codes and normed practices concerning Africans made it unnecessary — literally impossible — to consider Africans and their descendants as having thoughts of a kind that would qualify as "philosophy."[59] Not beasts but Civilized Men (of European descent), really the most civilized among Men (of European descent), in societies with sufficient wealth to provision a few to enjoy the luxury of free, leisured contemplation, think "philosophically." As was shown through passages quoting Kant and Hegel, rank-ordering valorizations of race were constitutive of the thought of major figures in Western philosophy and employed in explicit efforts to exclude Africans from discourses about modern, self-making, rational Man. The exclusions both justified, and were in turn justified by, the codes and norms that underwrote the enslavement of Africans. Enslavement, combined with official and informal apartheid in colonies-become-states in early North America, served to order the terms and spaces of social relations between Africans and Europeans such that as philosophy became an institutionalized academic enterprise it evolved conditioned by presumptions of the superiority of "the white race" relative to an "inferior black race," even where race was never mentioned. There were, however, important exceptions as courageous, philosophically minded, activist men and women pressed for the social realization of the universalist promises of the best of the European and American Enlightenments for African peoples. Among these were Frances Wright,[60] William Tory Harris and Denton Harris of the St. Louis Hegelians,[61] Francis Lieber,[62] many abolitionists,[63] and others. Still, the processes of exclusion at work as academic philosophy developed made mentioning race unnecessary. Silently but powerfully, the epistemological fields of philosophy, the rules and authorities of philosophical discourse, were infected by socially constructed and socially distributed valorizations of race.

If this sketch of the history of philosophy in America is accurate, what bearing does it have on considerations of the future of philosophy? While a full response must await a more thorough critical review than that presented, it is possible to indicate something of what might be called for should the fuller examination substantiate the interpretation so far given.

Certainly, at this critical moment in our nation's history we are in need of a clarified and shared understanding of raciality that will be appropriate to conditions of social justice and harmony in a nation comprised of people of different racial and ethnic groups. (The recent distorted debates between Congress and the President, and the appeals to the public from both sides, regarding the presence or absence of "quotas," explicitly or by implication, in proposed legislation are indicative of the urgent need for a rethinking of raciality in the context of considerations of justice.) And such an understanding will require that we rework the individualist philosophical anthropology undergirding the liberal political philosophy of the modern Enlightenment while avoiding the pitfalls of extremist particularism of a distorted Romanticism that overly privileges racial or ethnic identities. However, philosophers must first attend to injustices and inadequacies in the discipline that rest on invidious valorizations of raciality before we can, with legitimacy and authority, contribute to a rethinking of raciality and justice in ways that can withstand close scrutiny. Deeply infected by the virus of racism, philosophy has significant ways to go before it can be declared no longer a carrier.

Philosophy from the Point of View of a Sociology of Knowledge

More than house cleaning will be required. Renovations are in order, as well, in legacies and strategies of thought and in the sociological composition of the discipline. And these developments must be guided by the results of explorations of the ways in which norms functioned to socially structure organized philosophical praxis and of the ways in which the social configurations of a knowledge-producing enterprise have a crucial bearing on what passes for knowledge.[64] Without disregarding norms for philosophical thought, which are intended to ensure that it be governed only by the persuasiveness of arguments as judged by their logical properties alone, it is beyond question that both the norms and the subject matter of philosophical discourse are determined by *who* participates in the discursive communities of philosophers *as they have been socialized into the traditions and practices of the communities.* Fundamentally, epistemological criteria for determining what constitutes "proper" practices and terms of discussion in philosophy are grounded socially, not transcendentally. Perhaps better put, "transcendental" grounding is but a name for shared norms in communities of philosophers, the nurturing soil of which are institutionalized traditions within the cultural life-worlds of particular mortal humans. What transcultural, natural, species-specific epistemological structures there are that are shared by all human beings simply provide the boundary conditions for the activities constitutive of "philosophizing." They do not, however, determine either the agenda, the strategies, or the consequences of philosophizing and in no way provide absolute epistemological validity for the philosophical claims of anyone or any tradition. The development and use of language is universal among organized human groups, but not the same language in terms of grammar, syntax, etc. Likewise philosophizing. No group of people, no race, is the paragon of humanity by virtue of philosophizing, nor is any race the "less developed" relative to some supposed absolute standard manifested in a singular philosophy posing as absolute knowledge. Rather, though academic philosophers like to understand themselves in terms of a definition of the enterprise "by reference to what it is like when it is flourishing," philosophy "is inherently grounded in its own practice" and "philosophical practice is inherently pluralistic. All philosophical ideals are local."[65]

This way of expressing the matter is drawn from A. J. Mandt's insightful examination of a recent decade-long dispute between "analysts" and "pluralists" in the American Philosophical Association. His description and analysis are pertinent to a critique of philosophy with respect to matters involving raciality, and with regard to considerations of the future of the discipline. Several additional points in his discussion are worth noting on the way to a conclusion.

"Philosophy," Mandt observes, refers to the writing of a particular person, to a tradition or genre of writings, or, again, to the totality of a highly selective history of writings. In these cases the term refers to "a province within the republic of letters, an intellectual domain governed by the laws of logic and rationality." However, the term also refers to a "community" of persons governed by laws of rhetoric and politics. In short, "philosophy" references both "a rational enterprise and a community of practice."[66] But the two are intimately related: community norms provide the context of sanction for what counts as "rational" and for determining who is an "appropriate" participant in the community.[67] Consequently, philosophy is a fragmented discipline, one divided into traditional branches which are further subdivided into numerous active sub-specialities. Further:

- "Each . . . specialization forms a community of discourse in its own right, often centered in a few leading graduate departments, with recognized journals of record for communicating work to others, and, typically in the past few years, a philosophical society devoted to advancing the work of the community";
- "Within each . . . subcommunity, there are norms that define the limits of significant and intelligible discourse, and permit detailed, critical judgments of merit. . . . Within each sub-community, the local criteria of merit are usually clear, consistent, and generally understood. Even when they are not, implicit standards sufficiently definite to demarcate the community from others exist";
- "These norms emerge from the community and are subject to periodic revisions";
- It is within subcommunities of discourse and according to prevailing norms that it is determined that "certain works are canonical";
- "Each philosophical sub-community exists in some sort of relation to other, neighboring communities. . . . The norms governing discourse in the two communities will partly overlap, and where they do not, members of one community are likely to regard the disjunct norms of its neighbor-collaborator as valid within that community, although not within their own. They will often have an account of why this is properly so, an account rooted in the different interests and purposes of the two communities."[68]

Contemporary philosophy is thus a structured "web" of communities of discourse, "partly overlapping and partly discontinuous with one another":

The totality forms a "great community" that is highly organized even though its constituent parts are largely autonomous. The great community has norms that define its limits, but these norms are equivocal and conventional. They are interpreted differently in various sub-communities. . . . Although in each locality norms operate productively as conventions that shape philosophical activity, their extension to the larger community makes them the basis for *merely* conventional justifications.[69]

Mandt's description and analysis make for a persuasive discussion of the process by which conventions of discourse that are valid in a "local community" (i.e., a sub-specialty in philosophy) became merely conventional — hence without sometimes supposed deductive justification — when extended inappropriately beyond the range of the subject matters, texts, and practices of the subcommunity yet were used by philosophers who remained "convinced that they possess rationally warranted normative criteria when in fact they have slipped imperceptibly into what amounts to an arbitrary or biased point of view."[70] The norms of a particular community of discourse in philosophy may become conventionalized, that is to say, they may be taken up by other communities. However, there are "no general rules or principles of custom" governing when the processes of conventionalization operate.[71]

A community tends to listen only to familiar voices speaking in their familiar idioms. Yet a member of the family can win a hearing for peculiar notions on occasion. Attempting it too often can alienate one from the community, but the insider has a margin for innovations denied to an outsider, no matter how insightful or brilliant. These sorts of structures, involving personal associations, shared experiences and styles of discourse, a common history and agreed purposes reveal more about the life of the philosophical community and its development than do any of the formal definitions that seek to represent the nature of philosophy.[72]

Mandt's investigation of a recent struggle in the profession, one which has had major effects on the discipline (as a domain of intellectual activity and as a social institution), assists the effort to make the case that peoples of African descent have been systematically excluded from philosophy except for discursive and social placements predicated on invidious race-focused norms that, until most recently, have not been the focus of systematic critical reflection directed at the enterprise of philosophy, the claim that critical self-knowledge is the hallmark of the philosopher notwithstanding. Confronting and accepting the implications of Mandt's examination for an understanding of the relation of race to philosophizing might compel more of us to accept a much more modest agenda for philosophizing, one that no longer is motivated by an aspiration for absolute knowledge accompanied by the self-serving but pernicious presumption that philosophers, or some especially privileged and/or gifted group of philosophers, of a particular race, are alone capable of achieving such knowledge. Doing so might also allow more of us in the profession to see the need for racial and ethnic pluralism as a necessary (though not sufficient) condition for intellectual diversity reflective of the diverse cultural life-worlds in our nation that, at the same time, still have enough in common, with more to come, without attempting to assimilate all to a complete identity, to support social justice with peace and harmony. Certainly this would open the way to more widespread appreciation of the philosophical contributions of peoples of African descent, and of other peoples not generally studied in the profession. Further, and of particular importance, should a critical review and reconstruction of the history of Western philosophy involve a restoration of the legacies of achievements of ancient Egyptians (the people of Kemet) as a major resource for Greek civilization, we philosophers may well be called on to revise our professional identities with regard to the intellectual traditions and figures in terms of which we define ourselves and that we mediate to our students and colleagues. Were we to do so, perhaps we might be able to speak to others in our nation about the prospects for resolving problems involving raciality and ethnicity in just ways that are demonstrated by our own profession life and in our philosophizing. And we may do so while meeting one of our major responsibilities: namely, contributing to social reproduction through our teaching of subsequent generations of young men and women of various races and ethnicities.

NOTES

Introduction: On Race and Philosophy

This is a revised version of a draft essay, portions of which were presented at the New School for Social Research, New York, as part of the Hannah Arendt/Reiner Schürmann Memorial Symposium in Political Philosophy, October 19, 1994, and subsequently published, in revised form, in the New School's *Graduate Faculty Philosophy Journal* (vol. 18, no. 2, 1995, pp. 175–199). Portions of the first draft were prepared and read as the second of two public lectures at Hamilton College (Clinton, New York) delivered as the Truax Visiting Professor of Philosophy on November 9 and 16, 1994. Previous versions were also presented as lectures at Bucknell University, Oklahoma State University, and Furman University.

1 David R. Rodiger, "Introduction: From the Social Construction of Race to the Abolition of Whiteness," *Towards the Abolition of Whiteness* (London/New York: Verso, 1994).

2 (New York: Alfred A. Knopf, 1962), pp. 660–662.

3 Howard Brotz, ed., *African-American Social and Political Thought 1850–1920* (New Brunswick, New Jersey: Transaction Publishers, 1992, pp. 483–492), pp. 483–484.

4 W. E. B. Du Bois, *The Autobiography of W. E. B. Du Bois: A Soliloquy on Viewing My Life from the Last Decade of Its First Century* (New York: International Publishers, 1968), p. 148.

5 Du Bois, "The Conservation of Races," in Brotz, ed., *African-American Social and Political Thought 1850–1920*, p. 484.

6 For a particularly focused discussion of the difficult problem of articulating such a political philosophy, see John Rawls, *Political Liberalism* (New York: Columbia University Press, 1993).

7 Du Bois, "The Conservation of Races," in Brotz, ed., *African-American Social and Political Thought*, p. 486.

8 Du Bois, *The Autobiography of W. E. B. Du Bois*, p. 62.

9 Floya Anthias and Nira Yuval-Davis, "The concept of 'race' and the racialization of social divisions," *Racialized boundaries: Race, nation, gender, colour and class and the anti-racist struggle* (New York: Routledge, 1993), pp. 2, 15.

10 For an engaging reconstruction and critical discussion of the historical emergence and recent forms of political struggles over identity see Charles Taylor, "The Politics of Recognition," in Amy Gutmann, ed., *Multiculturalism: Examining the Politics of Recognition* (Princeton: Princeton University Press, 1994).

11 Nathan Glazer and Daniel P. Moynihan, "Introduction," in Glazer and Moynihan, ed., *Ethnicity: Theory and Experience* (Cambridge,: Harvard University Press, 1975), p. 7.

12 "Talk of 'race' is particularly distressing for those of us who take culture seriously. For, where race works — in places where 'gross differences' of morphology are correlated with 'subtle differences' of temperament, belief, and intention — it works as an attempt at metonym for culture, and it does so only at the price of biologizing what *is* culture, ideology. . . . What exists 'out there' in the world — communities of meaning, shading variously into each other in the rich structure

of the social world—is the province not of biology but of the human sciences." Kwame Anthony Appiah, *In My Father's House: Africa in the Philosophy of Culture* (New York: Oxford University Press, 1992), p. 45.

13 K. L. Little, "U.N.E.S.C.O. on Race," *Man*, No. 31 (1951), p. 17, as quoted by Pat Shipman, *The Evolution of Racism: Human Differences and the Use and Abuse of Science* (New York: Simon and Schuster, 1994), p. 166. The characterization of proposals to substitute another term for the troublesome "race" as "lexical surgery" Shipman (p. 166) attributes to Stanley M. Garn, "Race," *Man*, No. 200 (1951), p. 115.

14 Pat Shipman, "Facing Racial Differences—Together," *The Chronicle of Higher Education*, August 3, 1994: B1–3.

15 See Peter L. Berger and Thomas Luckmann, *The Social Construction of Reality* (New York: Doubleday, 1966).

16 Du Bois, "The Conservation of Races," in Brotz, ed., *African-American Social and Political Thought*, p. 484.

17 A. J. Mandt, "The Inevitability of Pluralism: Philosophical Practice and Philosophical Excellence," in Avner Cohen and Marcelo Dascal, ed., *The Institution of Philosophy: A Discipline in Crisis* (La Salle, Illinois: Open Court, 1989), p. 91.

18 For this sketch I rely heavily on Peter Berger and Thomas Luckmann's *The Social Construction of Reality*.

19 In our historical accounts of philosophizing, we philosophers have tended to provide narrations that legitimate us as those, and only those, capable of fulfilling such crucial functions as being the producers and guardians of the knowledges vital to surviving and living well. Of course, we have had competitors. Centuries ago we won out over the women "witches" with the assistance of priests and preachers, but later had to strike a deal with our former allies to share the job. . . . For nearly 3,000 years of Western history, a powerful minority of persons among various peoples among the variety of still changing populations, collectivities, and geo-political configurations we call "Europe" have convinced themselves (and others) that they alone—or they primarily—have the most well-developed capacity for knowing than anyone else, than non-Europeans especially, and that they thus have produced or can produce the knowledges needed to provide the ordering necessary for survival and well-being of their natal or adopted communities—some even claim for the entire world, a few even claim for the known and unknown universe ("true for all possible worlds," as some philosophers require of our justifications). But this is a story of racism at work in fields of the intellect in which rationalizations of white supremacy have been constructed. I will say more about these matters in essays that follow. For the moment I'm supposed to be pursuing the third path, between racist and anti-racist endeavors.

20 A number of thinkers have wrestled with this problem. For example, Will Kymlicka, in his *Liberalism, Community and Culture* (Oxford: Oxford University Press, 1989), makes a valiant effort to revise political liberalism to accommodate the "cultural rights" of certain kinds of groups.

1   Black Folk and the Struggle in "Philosophy"

Originally published in *Endarch: A Journal of Social Theory* (Department of Political Science, Atlanta University), Vol. 1, No. 3 (Winter 1976), pp. 24–36. Revised for this collection.

1 Cf. John Bracey Jr. et al., *Black Nationalism in America* (New York: Bobbs-Merrill, 1970).

2   William Barrett, *Irrational Man* (Garden City, New York: Doubleday, 1962), pp. 4–5.

3   (New York: William Morrow & Co., 1967).

4   Cruse, *The Crisis of the Negro Intellectual*, p. 364.

5   Vincent Harding, "The Vocation of the Black Scholar," *Education and Black Struggle: Notes from the Colonized World*, edited by The Institute of the Black World, *Harvard Educational Review*, Monograph No. 2, 1974 (pp. 3–29), p. 6.

6. *Ibid.*, p. 8.

7   Svetozar Stojanović, *Between Ideals and Reality: A Critique of Socialism and its Future*, trans. by Gerson S. Sher (New York: Oxford University Press, 1973), p. 12.

8   Max Horkheimer, "The Social Function of Philosophy," *Critical Theory* (New York: Herder and Herder, 1972), p. 268.

9   Horkheimer, "The Social Function of Philosophy," p. 270.

10 Herbert Marcuse, "A Note on Dialectic," *Reason and Revolution* (Boston: Beacon Press, 1968), p. ix.

2   Philosophy, African-Americans, and the Unfinished American Revolution

1   Herbert W. Schneider, *A History of American Philosophy*, 2d ed. (New York: Columbia University Press, 1963). The remainder of the discussion in this section is adapted from my "The Deafening Silence of the Guiding Light: American Philosophy and the Problems of the Color Line," *Quest: Philosophical Discussions* (Department of Philosophy, The University of Zambia, Lusaka), Vol. 1, No. 1 (June 1987), pp. 39–50.

2   Elizabeth Flower and Murray G. Murphey, *History of Philosophy in America* (New York: Capricorn Books, 1977).

3   Writing of the American Enlightenment of the 1700s, Schneider notes: "Never in America were philosophical thinking and social action more closely joined. Though much of the philosophizing was ad hoc, finding universal solutions for particular problems, it will not do to dismiss the thought of the Enlightenment as mere rationalization. For the conspicuous fact about American life then was that not only were the eyes and hopes of the world centered on America but also American men of affairs themselves were genuinely concerned with the wider, if not the universal, implications of their interests and deeds. . . . Never was history made more consciously and conscientiously, and seldom since the days of classic Greece has philosophy enjoyed greater opportunity to exercise public responsibility. " Schneider, *A History of American Philosophy*, p. 29.

4   Schneider, "Academic Awakening," pp. 375–388.

5   See Robert H. Brisbane, *The Black Vanguard: Origins of the Negro Social Revolution, 1900–1960* (Valley Forge, Pennsylvania: Judson Press, 1970), pp. 27ff.

6   For discussions of African-American philosophy see the collection of essays in Leonard Harris, ed., *Philosophy Born of Struggle: Anthology of Afro-American Philosophy from 1917* (Dubuque, Iowa: Kendall/Hunt, 1983).

7   This discussion is adapted from my "Making History: America's Future and African-Americans," an edited version of which was published as "The Future of Black People in the United States" in *Sojourners*, Vol. 10, No. 5 (May 1981), pp. 12–16.

8   Derrick Bell, *And We Are Not Saved: The Elusive Quest for Racial Justice* (New York: Basic Books, 1987).

9   For an insightful characterization and analysis of this group, and of its situation and prospects, see William J. Wilson, *The Truly Disadvantaged: The Inner City, The Underclass, and Public Policy* (Chicago: University of Chicago Press, 1987).

10 For an important example of discussions along the lines suggested here, see Mihailo Marković, *Democratic Socialism: Theory and Practice* (Sussex/New York: Harvester Press/St. Martin's Press, 1982).

11 I was asked to consider this question in contributing to a panel on "Foundations of a New Black Movement: Theoretical and Practical Dimensions" at the Ninth Annual Black Studies Conference, Olive-Harvey College, Chicago, 19 April 1986. What follows is drawn from what I offered during the panel's presentations.

12 Along this line I regard Harold Cruse's *The Crisis of the Negro Intellectual* (New York: William Morrow, 1967) as required reading.

13 See Cruse, *The Crisis of the Negro Intellectual.*

14 See John Rawls, *A Theory of Justice* (Cambridge: Belnap Press of The Harvard University Press, 1971).

3 African "Philosophy"?: Deconstructive and Reconstructive Challenges

Originally published in *Contemporary Philosophy: Chronicles, Vol. 5: African Philosophy*, Guttorm Fløistad, ed. (Dordrecht, The Netherlands: Martinus Nijhoff, 1987), pp. 9–44; and in H. Odera Oruka, ed., *Sage Philosophy: Indigenous Thinkers and Modern Debate on African Philosophy* (Leiden, New York, København, Köln: E. J. Brill, 1990), pp. 223–248. Revisions have been made for inclusion in this collection.

1 Here I follow a strategy employed to good effect by Richard Rorty in his *Philosophy and the Mirror of Nature* (Princeton, New Jersey: Princeton University Press, 1979).

2 Michael Ryan, *Marxism and Deconstruction: A Critical Articulation* (Baltimore, Maryland: The Johns Hopkins University Press, 1982), pp. 33–34 (emphasis added). Ryan defines "deconstruction" as follows: "In very broad terms, deconstruction consists of a critique of metaphysics, that branch of philosophy . . . which posits first and final causes or grounds, such as transcendental ideality, material substance, subjective identity, conscious intuition, prehistorical nature, and being conceived as presence, from which the multiplicity of existence can be deduced and through which it can be accounted for and given meaning. Standard practice in metaphysics . . . is to understand the world using binary oppositions, one of which is assumed to be prior and superior to the other" (p. 9).

3 Ryan, *Marxism and Deconstruction*, p. 24 (emphasis added).

4 For a discussion of the relation of philosophizing to particular historical circumstancs, see Lucius Outlaw, "African and African-American Philosophy: Deconstruction and the Critical Management of Traditions," *The Journal* (The New York Society for the Study of Black Philosophy), Vol. 1, No. 1 (Winter–Spring 1984), pp. 27–41.

5 Paul de Man, *Blindness and Insight: Essays in the Rhetoric of Contemporary Criticism* (New York: Oxford University Press, 1971). Quoted by Gayatri Spivak in her "Translator's Preface" to Jacques Derrida, *Of Grammatology* (Baltimore, Maryland: The Johns Hopkins University Press, 1976), p. xlix.

6 Jacques Derrida, *L'écriture et la différence* (Paris, 1967). Quoted by Spivak, "Translator's Preface," *Of Grammatology*, p. xviii.

7 For a discussion and critique of representations of knowing via "ocular metaphors" (e.g., regarding knowing as a form of seeing and deciphering) and their consequences in Western philosophy, see Rorty's *Philosophy and the Mirror of Nature*. This book offers an interesting critique of the extent to which this deciphering, characterizing itself most forcefully in the modern period in the form of the *scientization* of Philosophy, has dominated the agenda of Western phi-

losophy, and dominated the self-image of philosophers committed to this agenda such that they have construed the human mind, or human knowing, as the "mirror of nature."

8 A Greek word that, in the classical period, "covered a wide range of meanings expressed by quite different words in most modern languages . . . *word, speech, argument, explanation, doctrine, esteem, numerical computation, measure, proportion, plea, principle*." In Heraclitus's use of the term, three ideas were combined: "human thought about the universe, the rational structure of the universe itself, and the source of that rational structure." The Sophists used the term for arguments and what arguments were about; Plato and Aristotle, on the other hand, used the word *nous*. The greatest extension of the term *logos* as a doctrine came with the Stoics, for whom "Logos was the principle of all rationality in the universe, and as such it was identified with God and with the source of all activity." *The Encyclopedia of Philosophy*, Vols. 5 & 6 (New York: Macmillan, 1972), pp. 83–84.

9 "Homer used the term *nous* to refer to the mind and its functions generally, but in the pre-Socratics it became increasingly identified with knowledge, and with reason as opposed to sense perception. The term subsequently developed in two ways. For Plato it was equated generally with the rational part of the individual soul (*to logistikon*). . . . Aristotle also considered *nous* as intellect distinguished from sense perception. . . . The idea of a cosmic or divine mind represents the other way in which the concept of *nous* developed. . . . The Stoics equated *nous* with the Logos, so that for them it was both cosmic reason and the rational element in man; the two streams of development were thus united." *The Encyclopedia of Philosophy*, p. 525.

10 "This identification of rationality with the philosophical dogmas of the day reflects the fact that, since Kant, philosophy has made it its business to present a permanent neutral framework for culture. This framework is built around a distinction between inquiry into the real—the disciplines which are on 'the secure path of a science'—and the rest of culture. . . . If philosophy is essentially the formulation of the distinction between science and nonscience, then endangering current formulations seems to endanger philosophy itself, and with it rationality (of which philosophy is seen as the vigilant guardian, constantly fending off the forces of darkness)." Rorty, *Philosophy and the Mirror of Nature*, p. 269.

11 Michel Foucault, *The Archaeology of Knowledge and the Discourse on Language*, A. M. Sheridan Smith, translator (New York: Harper & Row, 1972), p. 228. The rules for controlling discourse include the following: *exclusion* (prohibited words; division and rejection, e.g., reason vs. folly, rationality vs. irrationality; "true" vs. "false"); *internal rules* (commentary; the author as unifying principle; disciplines); *qualifications for participants* (verbal rituals; "fellowships of discourse," i.e., writing; doctrinal groups; and social appropriation, or the social distribution of knowledge).

12 For a critical discussion of David Hume's pernicious orientation to the Negro race, see Richard H. Popkin, "Hume's Racism," *The Philosophical Forum*, Special Issue on Philosophy and the Black Experience, Vol. 9, Nos. 2–3 (Winter–Spring 1977–78), pp. 211–226, and "The Philosophical Basis of Modern Racism," in *Philosophy and the Civilizing Arts*, Craig Walton and John P. Anton, eds. (Athens, Ohio: Ohio University Press, 1974).

13 G. W. F. Hegel, "Introduction," *The Philosophy of History*, (New York: Dover Publications, 1956), pp. 91–99. This work is produced from lectures delivered by Hegel in the winter of 1830–31, though there had been two previous deliveries in 1822–23 and 1824–25. See Charles Hegel's "Preface" to *The Philosophy of*

History, pp. xi–xiii. The fact that these ideas were expressed by a person who was to become one of Germany's and Europe's most famous philosophers more than seventy years prior to the European cannibalization of Africa in 1895 should not go unnoticed.

14 See the important discussion of this issue, as it relates to African literature, by Ruth Finnegan, "Literacy versus Non-literacy: The Great Divide? Some Comments on the Significance of "Literature" in Non-literate Cultures," in Robin Horton and Ruth Finnegan, ed., *Modes of Thought: Essays on Thinking in Western and Non-western Societies* (London: Farber and Farber, 1973), pp. 112–144.

15 See V. Y. Mudimbe's very important discussion of the European "inventive" agenda in his *The Invention of Africa: Gnosis, Philosophy, and the Order of Knowledge* (Bloomington: Indiana University Press, 1988).

16 (Lovania, 1945), translated from the Dutch by A. Rubbens; English translation, *Bantu Philosophy*, by Colin King (Paris: Présence Africaine, 1959).

17 In the words of Colin King: "It is my hope that this translation will assist many to find, in the stimulating thought of Fr. Tempels' work, a key to a fuller understanding of African peoples and a deeper grasp of the truth that the true philosophy is that which both accepts and rejects all philosophies; but, in regard to peoples, rejects none: accepting all as they are and as they will become." Colin King, "Note by the English Translator," *Bantu Philosophy*, p. 12.

18 Franz Crahay, "Conceptual Take-off Conditions for a Bantu Philosophy," *Diogenes*, No. 52 (Winter 1965), pp. 55–78.

19 Crahay, "Conceptual Take-off Conditions," p. 57.

20 One might note the following works: V. Brelsford's *Primitive Philosophy* (1935) and *The Philosophy of the Savage* (1938); R. Allier, *The Mind of the Savage*; P. Radin, *Primitive Man as Philosopher* (1927); Marcel Griaule, *Dieu d'Eau: entretiens avec Ogotemmêli* (1948) [English translation, *Conversations with Ogotemmêli* (London: Oxford University Press, 1965)]. More recent works include: M. Fortes and G. Dieterlen, eds., *African Systems of Thought* (London: Oxford University Press, 1965); Ivan Karp and Charles S. Bird, eds., *Explorations in African Systems of Thought* (Bloomington: Indiana University Press, 1980); Daryll Forde, ed., *African Worlds: Studies in the Cosmological Ideas and Social Values of African Peoples* (London: Oxford University Press, 1954).

21 H. Odera Oruka, "Four Trends in Current African Philosophy," in Oruka, *Trends in Contemporary African Philosophy* (Nairobi, Kenya: Shirikon Publishers, 1990), pp. 13–22.

22 A. J. Smet, *Histoire de la Philosphie Africaine Contemporaine: Courants et Problèmes* (Kinshasa, Zaïre: Faculté de Théologie Catholique, Departement de Philosophie et Religions Africaines, 1980).

23 O. Nkombe and A. J. Smet, "Panorama de la Philosophie Africaine contemporaine," *Recherches Philosophiques Africaines,* Vol. 3: *Mélanges de Philosophie Africaine* (Kinshasa, Zaïre: Faculté de Théologie Catholique, 1978), pp. 263–282.

24 This discussion of the classifications of Smet and Nkombe is helped by the insightful discussions of V. Y. Mudimbe, particularly his "African Philosophy as an Ideological Practice: The Case of French-Speaking Africa," in *African Studies Review*, Vol. 26, Nos. 3/4 (September/December 1983), pp. 133–154.

25 The phrase is taken from a complex of arguments, the principal sources of which are the speeches and writings of Edward Wilmot Blyden, who attempted to articulate the difference between Africans and Europeans in terms of Africans' "personality." Blyden's works include: *Africa and Africans* (1903); *Selected Letters of Edward Wilmot Blyden*, Hollis R. Lynch, ed. (New York: KTO Press, 1978);

Liberia's Offering (New York, 1862); *Liberia: Past, Present, and Future* (Washington City: M'Gill & Witherow, 1869); *The Negro in Ancient History* (Washington City: M'Gill & Witherow, 1869); *Christianity, Islam and the Negro Race* (London, 1888; new edition, London: Edinburgh University Press, 1967). For additional readings see Kwame Nkruma, "The African Personality" (pp. 61–66) and Alex Quaison-Sakey, "The African Personality" (pp. 75–82), in Gideon-Cyrus M. Mutiso and S. W. Rohio, eds., *Readings in African Political Thought* (London: Heinemann, 1975).

26 An ideological tradition and political movement that emerged in the late 1800s, at the instigation of Henry Sylvester Williams, a Trinidadian lawyer, and, later, W. E. B. Du Bois, African-American activist scholar and champion *par excellence* of the interests of Africans and people of African descent. A principal manifestation of Pan-Africanism was a series of conferences (1900, London) and congresses (1919, Paris; 1921, London-Brussels; 1923, London-Lisbon; 1927, New York; 1945, Manchester; and 1974, Dar es Salaam, Tanzania, the first Pan-African congress to be held on the continent of Africa) that called upon Africans and peoples of African descent worldwide (hence *Pan*-African) to join together in organized struggle to liberate the continent of Africa from European colonialism and to free African peoples everywhere from domination and the invidious discrimination of racism. See Immanuel Geiss, *The Pan-African Movement* (New York: Africana Publishing Co., 1974).

27 The "Négritude Movement," as it is called, had its name drawn from the central concept that, like Blyden's "African personality," attempts to distinguish Africans from Europeans by defining the African in terms of a set of character traits, dispositions, capabilities, natural endowments, etc., in their relative predominance and overall organizational arrangements, which were thought to form a Negro *essence*, that is, our *Négritude*. Originating in literary circles at the instigation of Aimé Césaire, Léon Damas, and Léopold Sédar Senghor, the Négritude Movement quickly exploded the boundaries of these circles as the powerful political forces contained in its arguments played themselves out and took root in the fertile soil of the discontent of colonized Africa. This movement, as I will later argue, represents one of the major deconstructive challenges to Western Philosophy. See "What is Négritude?" (pp. 83–84) by Léopold Sédar Senghor, and "Remarks on African Personality and Négritude" (pp. 67–70) by Alioune Diop, in *Readings in African Political Thought, op.cit.*

28 "African humanism" is another recurrent theme in discussions of the past quarter-century that have attempted to identify values and life practices indigenous to African peoples which distinguish them, in non-trivial ways, from peoples of European descent. In the words of M. Gatsha Buthelezi: "Long before Europeans settled in South Africa little more than three centuries ago, indigenous African peoples had well-developed philosophical views about the worth of human beings and about desirable community relationships. A spirit of humanism — called *ubuntu* (humanness) in the Zulu language and *botho* in the Sotho language — shaped the thoughts and daily lives of our peoples. Humanism and communal traditions together encouraged harmonious social relations." M. Gatsha Buthelezi, "The Legacy of African Humanism," in *Natural History*, 12 (1984), p. 2.

29 In some cases, discussions of African socialism are quite similar to arguments regarding African "humanism" to the extent that the claim is made that "traditional" Africa (i.e., Africa before its colonization by Europeans) was indigenously "socialist," prior to the discussions of Marx and other Europeans, in view of Africa's "communal traditions" (as Buthelezi puts it). In other discussions, the

objective is to fashion a particularly *African* form of socialism, one more in keeping with the historical and cultural realities of black Africa. See, for example, Léopold Sédar Senghor, *Nationhood and the African Road to Socialism*, Mercer Cook, trans. (Paris: Présence Africaine, 1962).

30 An expressly political/ideological venture that, in service to its conception of the goal of African liberation, involves the importation of the Engels-Lenin scientization of Marxism and its consolidation and institutionalization in highly centralized, authoritarian, revolutionary political parties and movements.

31 The title of a book by Kwame Nkrumah, first president of the post-colonial independent state of Ghana. In this work Nkrumah offers what he terms "philosophy and ideology for decolonization": "consciencism is the map in intellectual terms of the disposition of forces which will enable African society to digest the Western and the Islamic and the Euro-Christian elements in Africa, and develop them in such a way that they fit into the African personality. The African personality is itself defined by the cluster of humanist principles which underlie the traditional African society. Philosophical consciencism is that philosophical standpoint which, taking its start from the present content of the African conscience, indicates the way in which progress is forged out of the conflict in that conscience." Kwame Nkruman, *Consciencism* (New York: Monthly Review Press, 1970), p. 79.

32 This the name for yet another cultural nationalist program that emerged during the period of anti-colonial struggles in Africa. Here again the objective is to argue in behalf of a set of indigenous and/or reconstructed values, practices, and social arrangements which, supposedly, will best serve contemporary Africa. A chief proponent of "authenticity" has been President Mobutu of Zaïre.

33 A prominent example of works in this group is Alexis Kagame's *La Philosophie Bantu-Rwandaise de l'Etre* (Brussels: Académie Royale des Sciences Coloniales, 1956).

34 Mudimbe, "African Philosophy as Ideological Practice," p. 138.

35 See, for example, Theophilus Okere, *African Philosophy: A Historico-Hermeneutical Investigation of the Conditions of its Possibility* (Lanham, Maryland: University Press of America, 1983).

36 Paulin Hountondji has offered one such characterization: "In its popular meaning the word 'philosophy' designates not only the theoretical discipline that goes by the same name, but, more generally, all visions of the world, all systems of virtually stable representation that lie deep beneath the behavior of an individual or a group of people. . . . 'Philosophy,' in that sense, appears as something which is held on to, a minimum system of creeds more deep-rooted in the self than any other systems . . . 'philosophy,' in that sense, is more a matter of assumption than of observation. . . . It matters little whether the individual or society concerned are conscious or not of their own 'philosophy'; in strict terms, spontaneous 'philosophy' is necessarily unconscious . . . all told, it constitutes a testimony to the intellectual identity of the person or the group." Paulin Hountondji, "The Myth of Spontaneous Philosophy," *Consequence* 1 (January–June 1974, pp. 11–37), pp. 11–12.

37 Mudimbe takes care to note that, contrary to other African scholars (notably Paulin Hountondji and Marcian Towa), he does *not* employ "ethno-philosophy" as a perjorative characterization: "I am using the term in its etymological value: ethnos-philosophia or weltanschauung of a community." Mudimbe, "African Philosophy as Ideological Practice," p. 149, note 7.

38 Mudimbe, "African Philosophy as Ideological Practice," p. 142.

39 Mudimbe, "African Philosophy as Ideological Practice," p. 146.

40 Again, Kagame's works are representative. Others include: Kwame Gyekye,

"Philosophical Relevance of Akan Proverbs," in *Second Order*, Vol. 6, No. 2 (July 1975), pp. 45–53; J. Olu Sodipo, "Notes on the Concept of Cause and Chance in Yoruba Traditional Thought," in *Second Order*, Vol. 2, No. 2 (July 1973), pp. 12–20; John A.A. Ayoade, "Time in Yoruba Thought," pp. 71–89, and Helaine K. Minkus, "Causal Theory in Akwapim Akan Philosophy," pp. 91–132, both in Richard A. Wright, ed., *African Philosophy: An Introduction*, 2d ed. (Lanham, Maryland: University Press of America, 1979).

41   The term "ethno-philosophy" is problematic. It is used by some to classify a group of works that, it is argued, mistakenly attribute achievements in Philosophy to "traditional" Africa. Hountondji was at one time a leading proponent of this view. (See, for example, his "The Myth of Spontaneous Philosophy," "An Alienated Literature," "History of a Myth," and "African Philosophy, Myth and Reality" in Paulin Hountondji, *African Philosophy: Myth and Reality* (Bloomington: Indiana University Press/Hutchinson: London, 1983). Tempels's *Bantu Philosophy* and the work of Alexis Kagame (e.g., *La Philosophie Bantu-Rwandaise de l'Etre*) are, in this view, major perpetrators of this error. The argument, overly simplified, is the following: To say of "traditional" Africans that they produced philosophies is to use "philosophy" in a wide and improper sense to cover the taken-for-granted mores, customs, behavior, etc., of a *group* of people. Tempels had said that the Bantu were not conscious of their "philosophy," hence it was left for him (and others like him) to interpret the Bantu's philosophy for them. But, Hountondji, et al. argue, Philosophy (*à la* Crahay) presupposes the critical self-consciousness of an *individual*, requires discussion and writing. Thus Tempels's and Kagame's recapitulations of the life-practices and beliefs of the Bantu and Bantu-Rwanda peoples more closely approximate *ethnology* than philosophy. But, in their critical discussions *of* these matters, they—Tempels and Kagame—*are* doing philosophy; the peoples they wrote about were not. Hence their writings (Tempels's and Kagame's) are termed "ethno-philosophy," a hybrid of ethnology and philosophy. And so the argument goes.

This issue deserves space for its own discussion, more than it is possible to devote to it here. Suffice it to say that I, like Mudimbe, differ with Hountondji and others who use "ethno-philosophy" as a term of derision, or at least as a characterization that denies "traditional" Africans the capacity for and/or achievement of critical self-reflection of a kind that can appropriately be identified as philosophizing. [At the heart of the Hountondji criticism is a privileging of philosophizing as Philosophy, as, in his words, *science*, a privileging of writing as a necessity for the practice of Philosophy, and the equally erroneously privileging of "critical self-reflection" as something not yet achieved by "traditional" Africans.] *No* people who do not involve themselves in and succeed at reflecting on the nature and conditions of their life and, as a result, identifying rules, principles, values, etc., for the conduct of that life, which they then mediate to succeeding generations, will last more than one generation. Obviously, African peoples have been successful in this regard. And a great deal of ethnological literature provides ample evidence of the results of this kind of reflexive praxis among African peoples. Why, then, is it proper to deny of these peoples the recognition that they were participants in activities *we* now call "philosophy"? At the very least, Odera Oruka is on a more correct path with his category of "philosophic sagacity." Finally, *any* attempt to recount (i.e., to construct) a (as opposed to *the*) history of philosophy will be to reconstruct a history of philosophy *as practiced by particular individuals who are part of particular cultural life-worlds*. Such a recounting will necessarily include (or presuppose) an "ethnological" moment, the penetrating and equally deconstructive critiques of European ethnological practices in Africa by

Mudimbe, Hountondji, and others notwithstanding. Furthermore, this recounting will be governed by what *we* (i.e., the person[s] doing the reconstructing) take the word "philosophy" to mean.

42 Abiola Irele, "What is Négritude?" in Abiola Irele, *The African Experience in Literature and Ideology* (London: Heinemann, 1981), pp. 67–88.

43 We must not overlook the contributions to this phase of the debate by European scholars such as Jean-Paul Sartre through his *Black Orpheus* (originally published as an introduction to a collection of Négritude writings) and Janheinz Jahn, author of "NTU — African philosophy," in his *Muntu: The New African Culture* (New York: Grove Press, 1971), a work that discusses the forging of the "unity" of "neo-African culture" during the 1950s, the period of the Négritude movement.

44 L. S. Senghor, "Psychologie du négro-africaine," in *Diogène*, No. 37 (Paris, 1962); English quotation from J. Reed and C. Wake, *L. S. Senghor: Prose and Poetry* (London: Heinemann, 1976), p. 30. Quoted by Irele, "What is Négritude?" p. 75.

45 Irele, "What is Négritude?" p. 67.

46 Jean-Paul Sartre, *Black Orpheus*, S. W. Allen, translator (Paris: Présence Africaine, 1976), pp. 7–11 (originally published as the Preface to *Anthologie de la nouvelle poésie négre et malgache de langue française*, L. S. Senghor, ed. (Paris: Presses Universitaires de France, 1948)).

47 *Stolen Legacy* (New York: Philosophical Library, 1954) reprinted by Julian Richardson Associates: San Francisco, California, 1976.

48 Henry Olela, "The African Foundations of Greek Philosophy," in Wright, ed., *African Philosophy: An Introduction*; and Henry Olela, *From Ancient Africa to Ancient Greece* (Atlanta, Georgia: Select Publishing Co., 1981).

49 For arguments in behalf of this thesis, see, for example, Chancellor Williams, *The Destruction of Black Civilization* (Chicago: Third World Press, 1974); and Cheikh Anta Diop, *The Cultural Unity of Black Africa* (Chicago: Third World Press, 1978).

50 Lancinay Keita, "The African Philosophical Tradition," in Wright, ed., *African Philosophy*, pp. 35–54.

51 (New Brunswick, New Jersey: Rutgers University Press, 1987).

52 Hountondji, "African Philosophy, Myth and Reality," in *African Philosophy: Myth and Reality*, pp. 56, 66.

4 Africana Philosophy

A substantial revision of "African, African American, Africana Philosophy" published in *Philosophical Forum*, Vol. 24, Nos. 1–3 (Fall–Spring 1992–1993), pp. 63–93. This revised version will be published in *The Journal of Ethics*, Vol. 1, No. 1 (1997).

1 Important examples are Placide Tempels's *Bantu Philosophy*, trans. Colin King (Paris: Présence Africaine, 1959); and Marcel Griaule's *Conversations with Ogotemmêli* (New York: Oxford University Press, 1965).

2 An important contribution to efforts to raise to canonical status articulations of traditional African thinkers or sages is H. Odera Oruka's *Sage Philosophy: Indigenous Thinkers and Modern Debate on African Philosophy* (Leiden, The Netherlands: E. J. Brill, 1990).

3 Two very rich collections of such texts, though not presented as "philosophy," are *African-American Social & Political Thought, 1850–1920*, ed. Howard Brotz (New Brunswick, New Jersey: Transaction Publishers, 1992, 2d ed.); and Dorothy Sterling, ed., *We Are Your Sisters: Black Women in the Nineteenth Century* (New York: W. W. Norton, 1984).

4 For examples of these recent endeavors see the collection *Philosophy Born of*

Struggle: Anthology of Afro-American Philosophy from 1917 (Dubuque, Iowa: Kendall/Hunt, 1983), edited by Leonard Harris.

5 *Bantu Philosophy*, Colin King, translator (Paris: Présence Africaine, 1959). One finds in the literature of this discussion references to earlier works, though these were not concerned exclusively with Africa, if at all: V. Brelsford, *Primitive Philosophy* (1935) and *The Philosophy of the Savage* (1938); R. Allier, *The Mind of the Savage* (no date); and Paul Radin, *Primitive Man as Philosopher* (New York and London: Appleton, 1927).

6 See Marcel Griaule's "Introduction" to his *Conversations with Ogotemmêli*.

7 Franz Crahay, "Conceptual Take-off Conditions for a Bantu Philosophy," *Diogenes*, No. 52 (Winter 1965), pp. 55–78.

8 For example: M. Fortes and G. Dieterlen, eds., *African Systems of Thought* (London: Oxford University Press, 1965); Ivan Karp and Charles S. Bird, eds., *Explorations in African Systems of Thought* (Bloomington: Indiana University Press, 1980); Daryll Forde, ed., *African Worlds: Studies in the Cosmological Ideas and Social Values of African Peoples* (London: Oxford University Press, 1954).

9 Certainly one of the most poignant critiques of European encounters involving the "invention" of Africa and one of the most informed discussions of African philosophy is V. Y. Mudimbe's *The Invention of Africa: Gnosis, Philosophy, and the Order of Knowledge* (Bloomington, Indiana: Indiana University Press, 1988). I am deeply indebted to Mudimbe for his sharing of his great learning and for his active participation in the formation of contemporary African philosophy as a discursive venture.

10 Leonard Harris, "Introduction," in Harris, ed., *Philosophy Born of Struggle: Anthology of Afro-American Philosophy from 1917* (Dubuque, Iowa: Kendall/Hunt, 1983).

11 For discussions of these historical periods and their guiding ideas/ideals, see, for example, Robert H. Brisbane, *Black Activism* (Valley Forge, Pennsylvania: Judson Press, 1974); and August Meier, *Negro Thought in America, 1880–1915* (Ann Arbor: University of Michigan Press, 1966).

12 See W. E. B. Du Bois, "Of Mr. Booker T. Washington and Others," in *The Souls of Black Folk* (1903); reprinted in Howard Brotz, ed., *African American Social and Political Thought, 1850–1920*, pp. 509–518.

13 See, in particular, Du Bois's "The Conservation of Races," in Brotz, ed., *African American Social and Political Thought, 1850–1920*, pp. 483–492.

14 For discussions of black nationalism see, among others, John Bracey, August Meier, and Eliott Rudwick, eds., *Black Nationalism in America* (New York: Bobbs-Merrill, 1970); and A. Pinkney, *Red, Black, and Green: Black Nationalism in The United States* (New York: Cambridge University Press, 1976).

15 C.L.R. James, *The Independence of Black Struggle* (Washington, DC: All African Peoples' Revolutionary Party, 1975); James Boggs and Grace Lee Boggs, *Revolution and Evolution in the Twentieth Century* (New York: Monthly Review Press, 1974).

16 See W. E. B. Du Bois, *The Autobiography of W.E.B. Du Bois: A Soliloquy on Viewing My Life from the Last Decade of Its First Century* (New York: International Publishers, 1968).

17 For a survey of African-American philosophy, see Leonard Harris, "Philosophy Born of Struggle: Afro-American Philosophy from 1917," in *Philosophical Perspectives in Black Studies*, Gerald McWorter, ed. (Urbana, Illinois: Afro-American Studies and Research Program, University of Illinois-Urbana, 1982). For representative essays from the period, see the special issue *The Philosophical Forum: Philosophy and Black Experience*, Vol. 9 (Winter-Spring

1977–78), especially William Jones's "The Legitimacy and Necessity of Black Philosophy: Some Preliminary Considerations."

18   (Philadelphia: Temple University Press, 1989).

19   (Montclair, New Jersey: Montclair State College Press, 1970).

20   These three essays were presented during the Africana Philosophy International Research Conference held at Haverford College during the summer of 1982.

21   *The Philosophical Forum: Philosophy and Black Experience*, Vol. 9 (Winter–Spring 1977–78) and Vol. 24, Nos. 1–3 (Fall–Spring 1992–1993).

22   (Lanham, Maryland: University Press of America, 1988); (Lanham, Maryland: University Press of America, 1980), respectively.

23   Johnny Washington, *Alain Locke and Philosophy: A Quest for Cultural Pluralism* (Westport, Connecticut: Greenwood Press, 1986).

24   Laurence Thomas, *Living Morally: A Psychology of Moral Character* (Philadelphia: Temple University Press, 1989), and *Vessels of Evil: American Slavery and the Holocaust* (Philadelphia: Temple University Press, 1993).

25   Howard McGary and Bill E. Lawson, *Between Slavery and Freedom: Philosophy and American Slavery* (Bloomington: Indiana University Press, 1992); Bill E. Lawson, ed., *The Underclass Question* (Philadelphia: Temple University Press, 1992).

26   Bernard Boxill, *Blacks and Social Justice* (Totowa, New Jersey: Rowman & Allanheld, 1984).

27   Anthony Appiah, *In My Father's House: Africa in the Philosophy of Culture* (New York: Oxford University Press, 1992), *Assertion and Conditionals* (New York: Cambridge University Press, c1985), and *For Truth in Semantics* (Oxford & New York: Basil Blackwell, 1986).

28   Seray Serequeberhan, *African Philosophy: The Essential Readings* (New York: Paragon House, 1991), and *The Hermeneutics of African Philosophy: Horizon and Discourse* (New York: Routledge, 1994).

29   In addition to other published works by these persons, see, for example, Anita Allen, "The Role Model Argument and Faculty Diversity"; Adrian Piper, "Xenophobia and Kantian Rationalism"; Michele Moody-Adams, "Race, Class, and the Social Construction of Self-Respect"; Frank M. Kirkland, "Modernity and Intellectual Life in Black"; Tommy Lott, "Du Bois on the Invention of Race" in *The Philosophical Forum*, Special triple issue: African-American Perspectives and Philosophical Traditions, John Pittman, guest ed., Vol. 24, Nos. 1–3 (Fall–Spring 1992–93).

30   "A Returning to the Source: The Philosophy of Alain Locke," *Quest* (December 1990), pp. 103–113; Alienation in the Later Philosophy of Jean-Paul Sartre," *Man and World*, Vol. 19 (1986), pp. 293–309; "An Examination of James Cone's Concept of God and its Role in Black Liberation," *Philosophical Forum*, Vol. 9 (Winter–Spring 1977–78), pp. 339–350.

31   Lewis R. Gordon, *Bad Faith and Antiblack Racism* (New Jersey: Humanities Press, 1995) and *Fanon and the Crisis of European Man: An Essay on Philosophy and the Human Sciences* (New York: Routledge, 1995).

32   Blanche Radford-Curry, "On the Social Construction of a Women's and Gender Studies Major," in *Gender and Academe: Feminist Pedagogy and Politics*, Sara Munson Deats and Lagretta Tallent Lenker, eds. (Lanham, Maryland: Rowman & Littlefield, 1994); "Choosing Change," with Nancy Greeman and Ellen Kimmel, American Philosophical Association's *Newsletter on the Black Experience* (Spring 1992); "Institutional Inertia to Achieving Diversity: Transforming Resistance into

Celebration," with Helen Bannan, Nancy Greeman, and Ellen Kimmel, *Educational Foundations* (Spring 1992).

33 Charles W. Mills, "Marxism, Ideology, and Moral Objectivism," *Canadian Journal of Philosophy*, Vol. 24, No. 3 (September 1994), pp. 373–393; "Non-Cartesian 'Sums': Philosophy and the African-American Experience," *Teaching Philosophy*, Vol. 17, No. 3 (September 1994), pp. 223–243; "Under Class Under Standings," *Ethics*, Vol. 104, No. 4 (July 1994), pp. 855–881; "Do Black Men Have a Moral Duty to Marry Black Women?" *Journal of Social Philosophy*, Vol. 25 (June 1994), pp. 131–153.

34 The notion of a "geographic race" makes use, in the first instance, of geographical references to groups of people who share distinctive biologically based characteristics but who are not thereby regarded as constituting a "pure" biological type. Likewise, I speak of African and African-descended peoples as a geographical (on and from the continent of Africa), biological, and cultural "race" with a number of ethnie or ethnic groups: Akan, Luo, Wolof, African-American, etc. For a discussion of the concept of "geographic race," see Michael Banton and Jonathan Harwood, *The Race Concept* (New York: Praeger, 1975), p. 62.

35 A. J. Mandt, "The Inevitability of Pluralism: Philosophical Practice and Philosophical Excellence," in Avner Cohen and Marcelo Dascal, eds., *The Institution of Philosophy: A Discipline in Crisis* (La Salle, Illinois: Open Court, 1989), p. 100.

36 V. Y. Mudimbe, "African Philosophy as an Ideological Practice: The Case of French-Speaking Africa," in *African Studies Review*, Vol. 26, Nos. 3/4 (September/December 1983), pp. 133–154; A. J. Smet, *Histoire de la Philosphie Africaine Contemporaine: Courants et Problèmes* (Kinshasa-Limete, Zaïre: Departement de Philosophie et Religions Africaines, Faculté de Théologie Catholique, 1980); O. Nkombe and A. J. Smet, "Panorama de la Philosophie Africaine contemporaine," *Recherches Philosophiques Africaines, Vol. 3: Mélanges de Philosophie Africaine* (Kinshasa, Zaïre: Faculté de Théologie Catholique, 1978), pp. 263–282.

37 Kwame Gyekye, "On the idea of African philosophy," in *An Essay on African Philosophical Thought: The Akan Conceptional Scheme* (New York: Cambridge University Press, 1987; revised edition Philadelphia: Temple University Press, 1995, pp. 187–212), p. 191. For arguments in behalf of the "cultural unity" of Africa, see especially Cheikh Anta Diop, *The Cultural Unity of Black Africa* (Chicago: Third World Press, 1978) and Jacques Maquet, *Africanity: The Cultural Unity of Black Africa*, translated by Joan R. Rayfield (New York: Oxford University Press, 1972).

38 Gyekye, "On the idea of African philosophy," in *An Essay on African Philosophical Thought*, p. 191. For reconstructions and discussions of African thought and life along these lines, one might consult the works by Marcel Griaule, Fortes and Dieterlen, Karp and Bird, or Daryll Forde that were listed in note 8.

39 *Stolen Legacy* (New York: Philosophical Library, 1954; reprinted San Francisco: Julian Richardson Associates, 1976).

40 "The African Foundations of Greek Philosophy," in Richard A. Wright, ed., *African Philosophy: An Introduction*, 3d ed. (Lanham, Maryland: University Press of America, 1984), pp. 77–92, and *From Ancient Africa To Ancient Greece* (Atlanta, Georgia: Select Publishing Co., 1981).

41 "The African Philosophical Tradition," in Wright, ed., *African Philosophy*, pp. 57–76.

42 (Los Angeles: University of Sankore Press, 1986). Essays in this text were select-

ed from presentations during two Association for the Study of Classical African Civilizations conferences held in February 1984 (Los Angeles) and March 1985 (Chicago).

43 (Los Angeles: University of Sankore Press, 1984).

44 *Black Athena: The Afroasiatic Roots of Classical Civilization, Vol. 1: The Fabrication of Ancient Greece 1785–1985* (New Brunswick, New Jersey: Rutgers University Press, 1987).

45 *African & Africans as Seen by Classical Writers. African History Notebook, Volume Two*, Joseph Harris, ed. (Washington, DC: Howard University Press, 1981).

46 *Blacks in Antiquity* (Cambridge, Massachusetts: Belknap Press, 1970).

47 See, for example, Molefi Kete Asante, *Kemet, Afrocentricity and Knowledge* (Trenton, New Jersey: Africa World Press, 1990), especially "Part I. Interiors" in which he sets out a revised version of his theory and method for an "Afrocentric" approach to proper knowledge about African peoples that together (i.e., the approach, employed in various disciplines and studies, and the knowledges obtained by doing so) constitute the field of "Africalogy."

48 Asante, *Kemet, Afrocentricity and Knowledge*, p. 9.

49 Stuart Hall, "New Ethnicities," *Black Film/British Cinema* (London: ICA Document 7, 1988 (pp. 27–31), p. 28; emphasis in original.

50 Stuart Hall, "Cultural Identity and Diaspora," in J. Rutherford, ed., *Identity: Community, culture, difference* (London: Lawrence & Wishart, 1990, pp. 222–237), pp. 223, 225.

5   Africology: Normative Theory

A revision of an essay prepared in response to a request to contribute to the Symposium on "Africology" sponsored by the Department of Afro-American Studies, The University of Wisconsin—Milwaukee, April 24–25, 1987.

1 Personal correspondence from Patrick Bellegarde-Smith (Department of Afro-American Studies, The University of Wisconsin-Milwaukee), co-organizer of the Africology Symposium, dated August 5, 1986.

2 See note 1.

3 *The Archaeology of Knowledge and the Discourse on Language*, A. M. Sheridan Smith, translator (New York: Harper & Row, 1972); *The Foucault Reader*, Paul Rabinow, ed. (New York: Pantheon Books, 1984).

4 *Contemporary Schools of Metascience*, 3d ed. (Chicago: Henry Regnery, 1973).

5 Hereafter this complex of endeavors will be referred to as "Black" or "African-American" Studies.

6 Foucault, *The Archaeology of Knowledge*, p. 13.

7 *The Archaeology of Knowledge; Madness and Civilization: A History of Insanity in the Age of Reason*, translated by Richard Howard (New York: Random House, 1965); *The Order of Things: An Archaeology of the Human Sciences*, translated by Alan Sheridan (New York: Random House, 1970); *The Birth of the Clinic: An Archaeology of Medical Perception* (New York: Pantheon Books, 1973); *Discipline and Punish: The Birth of the Prison*, translated by Alan Sheridan (New York: Pantheon Books, 1977); *The History of Sexuality, Volume I*, translated by Robert Hurley (New York: Random House, 1978). For a bibliography of Foucault's writings, see James Bernauer and Thomas Keenan, "The Works of Michel Foucault, 1954–1984," in "The Final Foucault: Studies on Michel Foucault's Last Works," a Special Issue of *Philosophy and Social Criticism*, Vol. 12, No. 2–3 (Summer 1987), pp. 230–269.

8 Foucault, *The Archaeology of Knowledge*, p. 12.

9   *Ibid.*, p. 12.

10 Paul Rabinow, "Introduction," *The Foucault Reader*, pp. 4–5.

11 "It is intended to give a special temporal status to a group of phenomena that are both successive and identical (or at least similar); it makes it possible to rethink the dispersion of history in the form of the same; it allows a reduction of the difference proper to every beginning, in order to pursue without discontinuity the endless search for the origin; [it] enables us to isolate the new against a background of permanence, and to transfer its merit to originality, to genius, to the decisions proper to individuals." Foucault, *The Archaeology of Knowledge*, p. 21.

12 "They make it possible to group a succession of dispersed events, to link them to one and the same organizing principle, to subject them to the exemplary power of life . . . , to discover, already at work in each beginning, a principle of coherence and the outline of a future unity, to master time through a perpetually reversible relation between an origin and a term that are never given, but are always at work." *The Archaeology of Knowledge*, p. 22.

13 "There is the notion of 'spirit,' which enables us to establish between the simultaneous or successive phenomena of a given period a community of meanings, symbolic links, an interplay of resemblance and reflexion, or which allows the sovereignty of collective consciousness to emerge as the principle of unity and explanation." *The Archaeology of Knowledge*, p. 22.

14 *The Archaeology of Knowledge*, p. 22. "But the unities that must be suspended above all are those that emerge in the most immediate way: those of the book and the *œuvre*. . . . The frontiers of a book are never clear-cut: beyond the title, the first lines, and the last full stop, beyond its internal configuration and its autonomous form, it is caught up in a system of references to other books, other texts, other sentences: it is a node within a network." *The Archaeology of Knowledge*, p. 23.

15 Foucault, *The Archaeology of Knowledge*, p. 25.

16 Foucault, *The Archaeology of Knowledge*, pp. 25–26.

17 Foucault, *The Archaeology of Knowledge*, p. 28.

18 Foucault, *The Archaeology of Knowledge*, p. 28.

19 Radnitzsky, *Contemporary Schools of Metascience.*

20 Radnitzsky, *Contemporary Schools of Metascience*, p. xi, emphasis in original.

21 Radnitzsky, *Contemporary Schools of Metascience*, p. 3.

22 Radnitzsky, *Contemporary Schools of Metascience*, p. 2.

23 Radnitzsky, *Contemporary Schools of Metascience*, pp. 386–387.

24 Radnitzsky, *Contemporary Schools of Metascience*, p. 387.

25 Radnitzsky, *Contemporary Schools of Metascience*, p. 388.

26 Radnitzsky, *Contemporary Schools of Metascience*, p. 388.

27 Radnitzsky, *Contemporary Schools of Metascience*, p. 390, emphasis in original.

28 Radnitzsky, *Contemporary Schools of Metascience*, p. 391, emphasis in original.

29 Radnitzsky, *Contemporary Schools of Metascience*, p. 391.

30 Radnitzsky, *Contemporary Schools of Metascience*, p. 393.

31 Radnitzsky, *Contemporary Schools of Metascience*, p. 7.

32 Radnitzsky, *Contemporary Schools of Metascience*, p. 8.

33 Radnitzsky, *Contemporary Schools of Metascience*, p. 230.

34 Radnitzsky, *Contemporary Schools of Metascience*, p. 231.

35 Radnitzsky, *Contemporary Schools of Metascience*, p. 390.

36 When discussing metascience, Radnitzsky uses the term "tradition" to emphasize the *historical dimension* of a research enterprise, while "school" normally implies contemporality. *Contemporary Schools of Metascience*, p. 8.

37 Kai Nielsen, "Ethics, Problems of," in *The Encyclopedia of Philosophy*, Vols. 3&4,

(New York: Macmillan & The Free Press, 1967 [pp. 117–134]), p. 121.

38 Nielsen, "Ethics," p. 126.

39 Nielsen, "Ethics," p. 126.

40 Nielsen, "Ethics," pp. 126–127.

41 "It has been widely accepted that there is a prima facie distinction between establishing the facts on any matter and evaluating them. . . . The view that denies this prima facie distinction between establishing facts about the world as it is and making a word estimate of those facts is called 'ethical naturalism.' According to ethical naturalism, moral judgments just state a special subclass of facts about the natural world . . . not only are ethical statements objective in the sense that covert reference is made to the speaker; they are the kind of objective statement which can be ascertained by some scientific, empirical investigation of the natural world." Jonathan Harrison, "Ethical Naturalism," *The Encyclopedia of Philosophy*, Vols. 3 & 4, pp. 69, 74.

42 ". . . A theory . . . which holds that true ethical judgments are true because they cannot be denied without self-contradiction. . . . If ethical logicism were true, our knowledge of moral distinctions would be the work of reason in the sense that all we would need in order to know the truth of the fundamental principles of morals would be a capacity to reason logically." *The Encyclopedia of Philosophy*, Vols. 3 & 4, p. 71.

43 ". . . The theory that, although ethical generalizations are not true by definition, those of them which are true can be seen to be true by any person with the necessary insight . . . a person who can grasp the truth of true ethical generalizations does not accept them as the result of a process of ratiocination; he just sees without argument that they are and must be true, and true of all possible worlds." *The Encyclopedia of Philosophy*, Vols. 3 & 4, p. 72.

44 *The Encyclopedia of Philosophy*, Vols. 3 & 4, p. 73.

45 Nielsen, "Ethics," p. 127.

46 Maurice Jackson, "Toward a Sociology of Black Studies," *Journal of Black Studies*, Vol. 1, No. 2 (December 1970, pp. 131–140), pp. 132–133.

47 Philip T. K. Daniel, "Theory Building in Black Studies," *The Black Scholar*, Vol. 12, No. 3 (May/June 1981, pp. 29–36), pp. 31–32.

48 Maulana Ron Karenga, *Introduction to Black Studies* (Los Angeles: Kawaida Publications, 1982).

49 (Port Washington, New York: Kennikat Press, 1973).

50 *Ibid.*, pp. 55–63, emphasis in original.

51 Maulana Ron Karenga, "Ideology and Struggle: Some Preliminary Notes," *The Black Scholar*, Vol. 6, No. 5 (January–February 1975, pp. 23–30), p. 23, emphasis in original.

52 Jackson, "Toward a Sociology of Black Studies," pp. 134, 135.

53 Molefi Kete Asante, "Afrocentric Theory," *Critical Social Issues*, Vol. 1, No. 1 (Spring 1987, pp. 46–56), p. 46.

54 Daniel, "Theory Building in Black Studies," p. 34.

55 Richard B. Brandt, "Ethical Relativism," *The Encyclopedia of Philosophy*, Vols. 3 & 4, p. 75.

56 There is a sizable and still growing body of literature on the various forms and history of black nationalism, cultural nationalism included. Two helpful bibliographies include Betty Jenkins and Susan Phillis, *Black Separatism: A Bibliography* (Westport, Connecticut: Greenwood Press, 1976); and William Helmreich, *Afro-Americans and Africa: Black Nationalism at the Crossroads* (Westport, Connecticut: Greenwood Press, 1977). In addition, also see Rodney

Carlisle, *The Roots of Black Nationalism* (Port Washington, New York: Kennikat Press, 1975); Sterling Stuckey, *The Ideological Origins of Black Nationalism* (Boston: Beacon Press, 1972); and, for a critique of black nationalism in the 1960s, see several essays by Harold Cruse ("Negro Nationalism's New Wave," "The Economics of Black Nationalism") in his *Rebellion or Revolution?* (New York: William Morrow, 1968).

57 For other discussions of Black Studies, see, for example, Armstead L. Robinson et al., ed., *Black Studies in the University: A Symposium* (New Haven: Yale University Press, 1969); John W. Blassingame, ed., *New Perspectives on Black Studies* (Urbana: University of Illinois Press, 1971); *Introduction to Afro American Studies* (Chicago: People's College Press, 1978); and James E. Turner, ed., *The Next Decade: Theoretical and Research Issues in Africana Studies* (Ithaca, New York: Africana Studies and Research Center, Cornell University, 1984).

58 Molefi Kete Asante, *Afrocentricity: The Theory of Social Change* (Buffalo, New York: Amulefi Publishing Co., 1980), p. 5.

59 Asante, *Afrocentricity*, p. 26.

60 Asante, *Afrocentricity*, p. 52.

61 Asante, *Afrocentricity*, p. 55.

62 Asante, *Afrocentricity*, pp. 55–56.

63 Asante, *Afrocentricity*, p. 57.

64 Asante, *Afrocentricity*, pp. 65–73.

65 Asante, *Afrocentricity*, pp. 68–71.

66 Asante, *Afrocentricity*, p. 73.

67 (Philadelphia: Temple University Press, 1987).

68 Asante, *The Afrocentric Idea*, pp. 6, 8, 9, 16.

69 Asante, *The Afrocentric Idea*, p. 8. "Most of the so-called universal concepts fail transculturally, and without transcultural validity there is not universality." *The Afrocentric Idea*, p. 56.

70 Asante, *The Afrocentric Idea*, p. 34.

71 Karenga, *Introduction to Black Studies*, pp. 28–31.

72 Karenga, *Introduction to Black Studies*, pp. 33–35.

73 Karenga, *Introduction to Black Studies*, p. 36.

74 Maulana Karenga, *Kwanzaa: Origin, Concepts, Practice* (Los Angeles, California: Kawaida Publications, 1977), p. 9. For a discussion of "Kawaida," see Imamu Amiri Baraka, *Kawaida Studies: The New Nationalism* (Chicago: Third World Press, 1972).

75 Karenga, *Introduction to Black Studies*, pp. 37–38.

76 Karenga, *Introduction to Black Studies*, p. 361.

77 Karenga, *Introduction to Black Studies*, p. 361.

78 Karenga, *Introduction to Black Studies*, p. 362.

79 Karenga, *Introduction to Black Studies*, pp. 364–366.

80 Karenga, *Introduction to Black Studies*, p. 369.

81 Karenga, *Introduction to Black Studies*, p. 369.

82 Karenga, *Introduction to Black Studies*, pp. 369–370.

83 Karenga, *Introduction to Black Studies*, p. 370, emphasis in original.

84 Karenga, *Introduction to Black Studies*, p. 370, emphasis in original.

85 Daniel, "Theory Building in Black Studies," p. 29.

86 James E. Turner, "Africana Studies and Epistemology: A Discourse in the Sociology of Knowledge," *The Next Decade*, p. xviii.

87 Turner, "Africana Studies and Epistemology, " p. xvi.

88 For a discussion of "cognitive style" see Alfred Schutz and Thomas Luckmann,

Structures of the Life-World (Evanston, Illinois.: Northwestern University Press, 1973).

89 Foucault, *The Archaeology of Knowledge*, p. 7.

90 Foucault, *The Archaeology of Knowledge*, pp. 9, 10.

91 Foucault, *The Archaeology of Knowledge*, p. 48.

92 "To say that a disagreement is 'fundamental' means that it would not be removed even if there were perfect agreement about the properties of the thing being evaluated. . . . There is fundamental ethical disagreement only if ethical appraisals or valuations are incompatible, even when there is mutual agreement between the relevant parties concerning the nature of the act that is being appraised." Brandt, "Ethical Relativism, "The *Encyclopedia of Philosophy*, p. 75.

93 For important discussions see Cheikh Anta Diop, *The Cultural Unity of Black Africa* (Chicago: Third World Press, 1978); and Jacques Maquet, *Africanity: The Cultural Unity of Black Africa*, translated by Joan R. Mayfield (New York: Oxford University Press, 1972).

94 For example, see Abdul Hakimu Ibn Alkalimat and Nelson Johnson, "Toward the Ideological Unity of the African Liberation Support Committee: A Response to Criticism of the ALSC [African Liberation Support Committee] Statement of Principles adopted at Frogmore, South Carolina, June–July, 1973," Greensboro, North Carolina, February 1–3, 1974.

95 For a particularly insightful discussion of this process, see Peter Berger and Thomas Luckmann, *The Social Construction of Reality* (Garden City, New York: Doubleday, 1967).

96 (New York: Harcourt Brace Jovanovich, 1981).

97 For an incisive — and controversial — critique of epistemological endeavors in Western "Philosophy," see Richard Rorty, *Philosophy and the Mirror of Nature* (Princeton: Princeton University Press, 1979).

98 See Jürgen Habermas, *The Theory of Communicative Action, Vol. 1: Reason and the Rationalization of Society*, Thomas McCarthy, translator (Boston: Beacon Press, 1984).

6   *Against the Grain of Modernity: The Politics of Difference and the Conservation of "Race"*

Published in *Man and World*, Vol. 25, No. 3/4 (November 1992), pp. 443–468. Minor revisions made for inclusion in this collection.

1   I borrow the notion of "ethnie" from Anthony D. Smith, *The Ethnic Origins of Nations* (Oxford: Basil Blackwell, 1986).

2   For an example of recent discussions of the unreality of "race" by a contemporary philosopher, see Anthony Appiah, "The Uncompleted Argument: Du Bois and the Illusion of Race," in *"Race," Writing, and Difference*, Henry Louis Gates Jr., ed. (Chicago: The University of Chicago Press, 1986), pp. 21–37.

3   For an insightful discussion of many of the issues involved, see Iris Marion Young, *Justice and the Politics of Difference* (Princeton, New Jersey: Princeton University Press, 1990).

4   I regard a certain degree of ethnocentrism — the belief in the superiority of one's own group compared to others — as initially normal, that is, during initial encounters with "strangers." However, I use "perverted ethnocentrism" to refer to the perpetuation of such a view during intergroup competition where that perpetuation involves the accumulation and deployment of power, in various areas of social life, toward the goal of dominating and/or eliminating other groups from the competition.

5   For critical discussion of "Eurocentrism," see Samir Amin, *Eurocentrism* (New

York: Monthly Review Press, 1989). For an example of a counter-construction to the hegemony of Eurocentrism, see Molefi Kete Asante, *Afrocentricity: The Theory of Social Change* (Buffalo, New York: Amulefi Publishing Co., 1980); *The Afrocentric Idea* (Philadelphia: Temple University Press, 1987); "Afrocentric Theory," *Critical Social Issues*, Vol. 1, No. 1 (Spring 1987), pp. 46–56; and *Kemet, Afrocentricity and Knowledge* (Trenton, New Jersey: Africa World Press, 1990).

6   E. D. Hirsch Jr., *Cultural Literacy: What Every American Needs to Know* (Boston: Houghton Mifflin, 1987), p. xiv.

7   Hirsch, *Cultural Literacy*, pp. xv–xvii.

8   Jürgen Habermas, *The Philosophical Discourse of Modernity*, Frederick Lawrence, trans. (Cambridge: MIT Press, 1987), pp. 16–17, 18.

9   Habermas, *Discourse of Modernity*, p. 318.

10 Habermas, *Discourse of Modernity*, p. 365.

11 Habermas, *Discourse of Modernity*, p. 7. For Habermas, Hegel is again key: he "was the first to raise to the level of a philosophical problem the process of detaching modernity from the suggestion of norms lying outside of itself in the past." *Discourse of Modernity*, p. 16.

12 Habermas, *Discourse of Modernity*, p. 2.

13 Immanual Kant, "An Answer to the Question: 'What is Enlightenment?'" in *Kant's Political Writings*, Hans Reiss, ed. (Cambridge: Cambridge University Press, 1970), p. 54.

14 Immanual Kant, "'What is Enlightenment?'," p. 55.

15 John Gray, *Liberalism* (Minneapolis, Minnesota: University of Minnesota Press, 1986), p. 16.

16 Gray, *Liberalism*, p. x.

17 Gray, *Liberalism*, p. 82.

18 W. E. B. Du Bois, "The Conservation of Races," in Howard Brotz, ed., *African-American Social and Political Thought, 1850–1920* (New Brunswick, New Jersey: Transaction Publishers, 1992, pp. 483–492), p. 485.

19 Appiah, "The Uncompleted Argument," p. 29.

20 Appiah, "The Uncompleted Argument," p. 36.

21 Appiah, "The Uncompleted Argument," p. 36.

22 Du Bois, "The Conservation of Races," in Brotz, pp. 485–486, emphasis added.

23 Du Bois, "The Conservation of Races," in Brotz, p. 487.

24 "On March 5, 1987, the one hundred, twenty-seventh anniversary of the Boston Massacre where Crispus Attucks, who was believed to have been a mulatto, was the first to die, eighteen black men assembled in the District of Columbia's Lincoln Memorial Church to formally inaugurate the American Negro Academy. This date was chosen because it recalled 'an event especially sacred to the Negro.' To the men who planned the meeting, Attucks' death in 1770 was a symbol of the patriotic and heroic role black Americans played in the creation of the United States. Consequently, they felt it appropriate that a black society formed to encourage intellectual activity among blacks, and to defend them from 'vicious assaults' should begin its public life on this day." Alfred A. Moss Jr., *The American Negro Academy: Voice of the Talented Tenth* (Baton Rouge and London: Louisiana State University Press, 1981), p. 35. Du Bois was one of the eighteen founding members of the Academy.

25 David L. Hull, "The Effect of Essentialism on Taxonomy—Two Thousand Years of Stasis (I)," *British Journal for Philosophy of Science* 15 (1965, pp. 314–326), p. 322.

26 Du Bois, "The Conservation of Races," in Brotz, p. 487.

27 David L. Hull, "The Effect of Essentialism on Taxonomy," p. 318.
28 David L. Hull, "The Effect of Essentialism on Taxonomy," p. 323.
29 Du Bois, "The Conservation of Races," in Brotz, pp. 484–485.
30 Du Bois, "The Conservation of Races," in Brotz, p. 488.
31 Du Bois, "The Conservation of Races," in Brotz, p. 488.
32 Du Bois, "The Conservation of Races," in Brotz, pp. 488–489.
33 Du Bois, "The Conservation of Races," in Brotz, p. 489.

7 *Life-Worlds, Modernity, and Philosophical Praxis: Race, Ethnicity, and Critical Social Theory*

Prepared for the Sixth East-West Philosophers' Conference, July 30–August 12, 1989, University of Hawaii, Honolulu, Hawaii and published, in revised form, in *Culture and Modernity: East-West Philosophic Perspectives*, Eliot Deutsch, ed. (Honolulu: University of Hawaii Press, 1991), pp. 21–49. Revised for inclusion in this collection.

1 For this discussion, the following works in particular: "Modernity — An Incomplete Project," in *Interpretive Social Science:A Second Look*," Paul Rabinow and William M. Sullivan, eds. (Berkeley and Los Angeles: University of California Press, 1987), pp. 141–156; *The Philosophical Discourse of Modernity*, Frederick Lawrence, translator (Cambridge: MIT Press, 1987); *The Theory of Communicative Action, Vol. 2: Lifeworld and System:A Critique of Functionalist Reason*, Thomas McCarthy, trans. (Boston: Beacon Press, 1987).
2 "Hegel was the first philosopher to develop a clear concept of modernity. We have to go back to him if we want to understand the internal relationship between modernity and rationality, which, until Max Weber, remained self-evident and which today is being called into question." Habermas, *Discourse of Modernity*, p. 4.
3 Habermas, *Discourse of Modernity*, pp. 16–17, 18.
4 Habermas, *Discourse of Modernity*, p. 318.
5 Habermas, *Discourse of Modernity*, p. 7.
6 Habermas, *Discourse of Modernity*, p. 365.
7 Habermas, *Discourse of Modernity*, p. 2.
8 John Gray, *Liberalism* (Minneapolis, Minnesota: University of Minnesota Press, 1986), p. x.
9 The discussion in this section draws on my "Philosophy, Ethnicity, and Race": The Alfred P. Stiernotte Lectures in Philosophy (Hamden, Connecticut: Quinnipiac College, 1989) and my "Toward a Critical Theory of Race," in *Anatomy of Racism*, David Goldberg, ed. (Minneapolis: University of Minnesota Press, 1990), pp. 58–82.
10 Gray, *Liberalism*, p. 24. "It is in the writings of the social philosophers and political economists of the Scottish Enlightenment that we find the first comprehensive statement in systematic form of the principles and foundations of liberalism. Among the French, as among the Americans, liberal thought was bound up at every point with a response to a particular crisis of political order. It is not that the thought of the Scottish philosophers was not conditioned by the historical context in which they found themselves, but rather that they aimed, as perhaps the great French and American liberals did not consistently do, to ground their liberal principles in a comprehensive account of human social development and a theory of social and economic structure whose terms had the status of natural laws and not merely of historical generalizations." *Liberalism*, p. 24.
11 Gray, *Liberalism*, p. 21.
12 Aristotle, *Politics*, Book I, chapter 5, 1252B 30–33.

13 Aristotle, *Politics*, Book I, chapter 5, 1254A 18–24.

14 Aristotle, *Politics*, Book I, chapter 5, 1254A 29–33.

15 G. W. F. Hegel, "Introduction," *The Philosophy of History* (New York: Dover Publications, 1956), pp. 91–99.

16 "The career of the race concept begins in obscurity, for experts dispute whether the word derives from an Arabic, a Latin, or a German source. The first recorded use in English of the word 'race' was in a poem by William Dunbar of 1508. . . . During the next three centuries the word was used with growing frequency in a literary sense as denoting simply a class of persons or even things. . . . In the nineteenth, and increasingly in the twentieth century, this loose usage began to give way and the word came to signify groups that were distinguished biologically." Michael Banton and Jonathan Harwood, *The Race Concept* (New York: Praeger, 1975), p. 13.

17 Banton and Harwood, *The Race Concept*, p. 14.

18 Banton and Harwood, *The Race Concept*, p. 13.

19 "The eighteenth-century Swedish botanist Linnaeus achieved fame by producing a classification of all known plants which extracted order from natural diversity. Scientists of his generation believed that by finding the categories to which animals, plants and objects belonged they were uncovering new sections of God's plan for the universe. Nineteenth-century race theorists inherited much of this way of looking at things." Banton and Harwood, *The Race Concept*, p. 46.

20 Banton and Harwood, *The Race Concept*, pp. 24–25. Both works were closely studied in Europe and the U.S.

21 Banton and Harwood, *The Race Concept*, p. 27.

22 Banton and Harwood, *The Race Concept*, p. 28.

23 Banton and Harwood, *The Race Concept*, pp. 29–30. These authors observe that while Gobineau's volumes were not very influential at the time of their publication, they were later to become so when used by Hitler in support of his claims regarding the supposed superiority of the "Aryan race."

24 "*Homo sapiens* was presented as a species divided into a number of races of different capacity and temperament. Human affairs could be understood only if individuals were seen as representatives of races for it was there that the driving forces of human history resided." Banton and Harwood, *The Race Concept*, p. 30.

25 Banton and Harwood, *The Race Concept*, pp. 47–49.

26 "An article by an anthropologist published in 1962 declared in the sharpest terms that the old racial classifications were worse than useless and that a new approach had established its superiority. This article, entitled 'On the Non-existence of Human Races,' by Frank B. Livingstone, did not advance any new findings or concepts, but it brought out more dramatically than previous writers the sort of change that had occurred in scientific thinking. . . . The kernel of Livingstone's argument is contained in his phrase 'there are no races, there are only clines.' A cline is a gradient of change in a measurable genetic character. Skin colour provides an easily noticed example." Banton and Harwood, *The Race Concept*, pp. 56–57.

27 "When we refer to races we have in mind their geographically defined categories which are sometimes called 'geographical races,' to indicate that while they have some distinctive biological characteristics they are not pure types." Banton and Harwood, *The Race Concept*, p. 62.

28 Banton and Harwood, *The Race Concept*, p. 63. "The main mistake of the early racial theorists was their failure to appreciate the difference between organic and superorganic evolution. They wished to explain all changes in biological terms." Banton and Harwood, *The Race Concept*, p. 66.

29 Banton and Harwood, *The Race Concept*, pp. 72–73, emphasis in the original.

30 Banton and Harwood, *The Race Concept*, p. 77.

31 Banton and Harwood, *The Race Concept*, p. 147.

32 Michael Omi and Howard Winant, *Racial Formation in the United States* (New York: Routledge & Kegan Paul, 1986).

33 William Petersen, "Concepts of Ethnicity," *Harvard Encyclopedia of American Ethnic Groups* (Cambridge: Harvard University Press, 1980, pp. 234–242), p. 234.

34 Petersen, "Concepts of Ethnicity," p. 234.

35 For a fuller discussion of the career of paradigmatic "ethnicity" see Omi and Winant, *Racial Formation in the United States*, pp. 14–16.

36 Michael Novak, *The Rise of the Unmeltable Ethnics: Politics and Culture in the Seventies* (New York: Macmillan, 1972).

37 Michael Novak, "Pluralism: A Humanistic Perspective," *Harvard Encyclopedia of American Ethnic Groups* (pp. 772–781), p. 774.

38 Novak, "Pluralism: A Humanistic Perspective," p. 774.

39 This is one of Harbermas's worries, and, in one of its expressions directed at an African-American political tradition, is of particular concern to me: "After the American civil rights movement — which has since issued in a particularistic self-affirmation of black subcultures — only the feminist movement stands in the tradition of bourgeois-socialist liberation movements. The struggle against patriarchal oppression and for the redemption of a promise that has long been anchored in the acknowledged universalistic foundations of morality and law gives feminism the impetus of an offensive movement, whereas the other movements have a more defensive character." Habermas, *The Theory of Communicative Action*, Vol. 2, p. 393.

40 Jacques Derrida, "White Mythology: Metaphor in the Text of Philosophy," in *Margins of Philosophy*, Alan Bass, translator (Chicago: The University of Chicago Press, 1982, pp. 207–271), p. 213.

41 Novak, "Pluralism: A Humanistic Perspective," p. 775.

42 Novak, "Pluralism: A Humanistic Perspective," p. 775.

43 Novak, "Pluralism: A Humanistic Perspective," p. 776.

44 Habermas, *Discourse of Modernity*, pp. 314–315.

45 Habermas, *Discourse of Modernity*, p. 300.

46 Habermas, *Discourse of Modernity*, pp. 321–322.

47 Habermas, *Discourse of Modernity*, pp. 322, 316.

48 Habermas, *Discourse of Modernity*, pp. 322–23.

49 "One relentlessly elaborates the transcendent power of abstractive reason and the emancipatory unconditionality of the intelligible, whereas the other strives to unmask the imaginary purity of reason in a materialist fashion." Habermas, *Discourse of Modernity*, p. 324.

50 Habermas, *Discourse of Modernity*, p. 326.

51 Habermas, "The Tasks of a Critical Theory," *The Theory of Communicative Action*, Vol. 2, p. 383.

52 "The bourgeoisie which led the development of capitalism were drawn from particular ethnic and cultural groups; the European proletariats and the mercenaries of the leading States from others; its peasants from still other cultures; and its slaves from entirely different worlds. The tendency of European civilization through capitalism was thus not to homogenize but to differentiate — to exaggerate regional, subcultural, dialectical differences into 'racial' ones." Cedric J. Robinson, *Black Marxism: The Making of the Black Radical Tradition* (London: Zed Press, 1983), pp. 26–27.

53 As Robinson noted (*Black Marxism*, p. 83):

There were at least four distinct moments which must be apprehended in European racialism; two whose origins are to be found within the dialectic of European development, and two which are not:

1. the racial ordering of European society from its formative period which extends into the medieval and feudal ages as "blood" and racial beliefs and legends.

2. the Islamic, i.e. Arab, Persian, Turkish and African, domination of Mediterranean civilization and the consequent retarding of European social and cultural life: the Dark Ages.

3. the incorporation of African, Asian and peoples of the New World into the world system emerging from late feudalism and merchant capitalism.

4. the dialectic of colonialism, plantocratic slavery and resistance from the 16th Century forwards, and the formations of industrial labour and labour reserves.

54 "There is a kind of progressive Tower of Babel, where we are engaged in building an edifice for social transformation, but none of us are speaking the same language. None understands where the rest are going." Manning Marable, "Common Program: Transitional Strategies for Black and Progressive Politics in America," in Marable, *Blackwater: Historical Studies in Race, Class Consciousness and Revolution* (Dayton, Ohio: Black Praxis Press, 1981), p. 177.

8   The Future of "Philosophy" in America

A revision of a presentation made as part of the "Philosophy in Transition" Symposium during the Annual Meeting of the Central Division of the American Philosophical Association on April 26, 1991, The Palmer House Hotel, Chicago, and published in the *Journal of Social Philosophy*, Vol. 22, No. 1 (Spring 1991), pp. 162–182. Revised for inclusion in this collection.

1 John Rajchman, "Philosophy in America," in John Rajchman and Cornel West, eds., *Post-Analytic Philosophy* (New York: Columbia University Press, 1985), p. xxvii.

2 Avner Cohen and Marcelo Dascal, eds., "Preface," *The Institution of Philosophy: A Discipline in Crisis* (La Salle, Illinois: Open Court, 1989), p. xi.

3 John Rajchman, "Philosophy in America," p. xii.

4 (Dubuque, Iowa: Kendall/Hunt, 1983).

5 For a discussion of "the project of modernity," see Jürgen Habermas, *The Philosophical Discourse of Modernity*, translated by Frederick Lawrence (Cambridge, Massachusetts: MIT Press, 1987).

6 Dante A. Puzzo, "Racism and the Western Tradition," *Journal of the History of Ideas*, Vol. 25 (pp. 579–586), p. 579.

7 "Racism and the West: From Praxis to Logos," in David Theo Goldberg, ed., *Anatomy of Racism* (Minneapolis: University of Minnesota Press, 1990, pp. 83–88).

8 Vol. 1: *The Fabrication of Ancient Greece 1785–1985* (New Brunswick, New Jersey: Rutgers University Press, 1987).

9 *Stolen Legacy* (1954, publisher not indicated; reprinted San Francisco: Julian Richardson Associates, 1976).

10 *The Negro* (New York: Oxford University Press, 1970 [originally published New York: Henry Holt and Company, 1915]; *Black Folk, Then and Now* (New York: Henry Holt and Company, [c. 1939]).

11 *Anteriorité des civilisations négres: mythe ou verité historique? (The African Origin of Civilization: Myth or Reality)* (Paris: Présence Africaine, 1967).

12 *Black Folk Here and There* (Los Angeles: Center for Afro-American Studies, University of California, Los Angeles, 1987).

13 *Kemet, Afrocentricity and Knowledge* (Trenton, New Jersey: Africa World Press, 1990).

14 *Kemet and the African Worldview: Research, Rescue and Restoration* (Los Angeles: University of Sankore Press, 1986); Jacob H. Carruthers, *Essays in Ancient Egyptian Studies* (Los Angeles: University of Sankore Press, 1984).

15 *From Ancient Africa to Ancient Greece* (Atlanta, Georgia: Select Publishing, 1981).

16 See Herbert W. Schneider, *A History of American Philosophy*, second edition (New York: Columbia University Press, 1963), p. 29, for a discussion of the joining of philosophical thought to social action during the American Enlightenment of the 1700s.

17 Maurice Mandelbaum, "History of Ideas, Intellectual History, and the History of Philosophy," *History and Theory, Beiheft 5: The Historiography of Philosophy*, 1965 (pp. 33–66), pp. 65–66.

18 On "unit-ideas" as the "component elements" in a history of philosophical doctrines or systems, see Arthur O. Lovejoy, "The Study of the History of Ideas," in *The Great Chain of Being: A Study of the History of an Idea* (Cambridge, Massachusetts: Harvard University Press, 1964 [1936]), pp. 3–23.

19 Michel Foucault, *The Order of Things: An Archaeology of the Human Sciences* (New York: Vintage Books, 1973), pp. xi–xii.

20 Foucault, *The Order of Things*, p. xiv; Michael Foucault, *The Archaeology of Knowledge and The Discourse on Language*, A. M. Sheridan Smith, trans. (New York: Harper & Row, 1972), p. 28.

21 Richard Rorty, "Philosophy as Science, as Metaphor, and as Politics," in Avner Cohen and Marcelo Dascal, eds., *The Institution of Philosophy: A Discipline in Crisis* (pp. 13–33), pp. 24, 25.

22 Habermas, *Discourse of Modernity*, pp. 7, 365.

23 See Aristotle, *Politics*, Book I, chapter 5, 1254a 18–24, 29–33.

24 For an insightful discussion of early European encounters of Africans, see Winthrop D. Jordan, "First Impressions: Initial English Confrontations with Africans," in *The White Man's Burden: Historical Origins of Racism in the United States* (New York: Oxford University Press, 1974).

25 See G. W. F. Hegel, "Introduction," *The Philosophy of History* (New York: Dover Publications, 1956), pp. 91–99.

26 Larry E. Tise, *Proslavery: A History of the Defense of Slavery in America, 1701–1840* (Athens, Georgia: University of Georgia Press, 1987), p. 118.

27 "In their use of Scripture to defend slavery, proslavery writers could follow one of several courses. The most positive and racist approach looked upon the curse on Ham as a divine decree that set the Negro race apart as an inferior and servile people. The second most positive approach discovered a divine sanction for slavery (irrespective of the enslaved people) in the Old Testament, a negative approval in the Gospels, and the sanction of the Apostles in the Epistles. And the third least positive approach found no condemnation of slavery in Scripture." Tise, *Proslavery: A History of the Defense of Slavery in America*, p. 118.

28 For Hume's discussion of the "natural inferiority" of Negroes to whites see his footnote on p. 228 of his "Of National Characters" in *The Philosophical Works of David Hume*, Vol. 3 (Boston: Little, Brown, & Co., 1854), pp. 217–236. For a critical discussion see Richard H. Popkin, "Hume's Racism," *The Philosophical Forum*, Vol. 9, Nos. 2–3 (Winter-Spring, 1977–78), pp. 211–226.

29 Immanuel Kant, *Observations on the Feeling of the Beautiful and Sublime*, John

T. Goldthwait, translator (Berkeley and Los Angeles: University of California Press, 1960), pp. 110–111. Kant's reference to "Mr. Hume" is, it seems clear, to Hume's note in his "Of National Characters."

30 Thomas Jefferson, "Query XIV," *Notes on the State of Virginia*, in David A. Hollinger and Charles Capper, eds., *The American Intellectual Tradition, Vol. I, 1620–1865* (New York: Oxford University Press, 1989), p. 152.

31 Lovejoy, *The Great Chain of Being*, pp. 46–50.

32 Lovejoy, *The Great Chain of Being*, p. 52.

33 Lovejoy, *The Great Chain of Being*, p. 56.

34 Lovejoy, *The Great Chain of Being*, p. 59.

35 Lovejoy, *The Great Chain of Being*, p. 64.

36 Lovejoy, *The Great Chain of Being*, pp. 67, 76.

37 Lovejoy, *The Great Chain of Being*, p. 216.

38 Lovejoy, *The Great Chain of Being*, p. 222, emphasis in original.

39 Lovejoy, *The Great Chain of Being*, pp. 292, 289.

40 Lovejoy, *The Great Chain of Being*, pp. 297, 293, 306.

41 Lovejoy, *The Great Chain of Being*, pp. 312–313.

42 "See Michael Banton and Jonathan Harwood, *The Race Concept* (New York: Praeger, 1975), p. 13.

43 Banton and Harwood, *The Race Concept*, p. 14.

44 Dante A. Puzzo, "Racism and the Western Tradition," p. 583.

45 Banton and Harwood, *The Race Concept*, p. 13.

46 Jeanne Hersch, "The Concept of Race," *Diogenes*, Vol. 59 (Fall 1967) [pp. 114–133], p. 116.

47 "*Homo sapiens* was presented as a species divided into a number of races of different capacity and temperament. Human affairs could be understood only if individuals were seen as representatives of races for it was there that the driving forces of human history resided." Banton and Harwood, *The Race Concept*, p. 30.

48 A. J. Mandt, "The Inevitability of Pluralism: Philosophical Practice and Philosophical Excellence," in Cohen and Dascal, eds., *The Institution of Philosophy: A Discipline in Crisis*, p.79.

49 Foucault, *The Order of Things*, pp. xi–xii.

50 Foucault, *The Order of Things*, p. xx.

51 Foucault, *The Order of Things*, p. xx.

52 Foucault, *The Order of Things*, p. xvii.

53 The following discussion is drawn from Peter Berger and Thomas Luckmann, "Language and Knowledge in Everyday Life," in *The Social Construction of Reality: A Treatise in the Sociology of Knowledge* (Garden City, New York: Doubleday, 1966), pp. 33–43.

54 Winthrop D. Jordan, *The White Man's Burden*, p. 4.

55 Winthrop D. Jordan, *The White Man's Burden*, pp. 5–7.

56 Winthrop D. Jordan, *The White Man's Burden*, pp. 10–25.

57 See Calvin Hernton, *Sex and Racism in America* (New York: Grove Press, 1966). More recently race and sexuality are the focus of movie-maker Spike Lee's *Jungle Fever*.

58 Winthrop D. Jordan, *The White Man's Burden*, pp. 15–17.

59 The decades-long debates regarding the very idea and possibility, let alone the forms, of "African philosophy" prompted by the publication in 1945 of Placide Tempels's *La Philosophie Bantoue* [*Bantu Philosophy*, A. Rubbens, translator (Paris, France: Présence Africaine, 1959)], a French translation of the original Dutch text, should not go unnoticed.

60 According to Schneider, this English reformer made "a pathetic attempt . . . to

'regenerate' slaves and make them fit for self-government. To a forest tract in Tennessee she took nine adult slaves, a few negro children, and an 'overseer', who had been a Shaker. This group, 'released from the fear of the lash', succeeded in clearing a few acres and erecting a few cabins. Miss Wright then expounded her more ambitious plans for Southern democracy—a mixed white and black co-operative community, in which there would be social equality, *but the blacks would do all the manual labor.* She was obliged to ship her few slaves to Haiti and to take up her residence in New Harmony." Schneider, *A History of American Philosophy,* p. 142, emphasis added.

61 Elizabeth Flower and Murray Murphey, *A History of Philosophy in America,* 2 volumes (New York: Capricorn Books, 1977), Vol. 2, pp. 463–514.

62 Flower and Murphey, *A History of Philosophy in America,* Vol. 1, pp. 351–352; Schneider, *A History of American Philosophy,* p. 152.

63 Flower and Murphey, while discussing developments in moral philosophy in the "Middle Atlantic and Southern States," note that as one strand of New England tradition "the abolitionist's stand was essentially a moral or religious sentiment in which slavery was seen not as a functioning economic institution, but as a violation of a higher moral law." *A History of Philosophy in America,* Vol. 1, p. 314.

64 Particularly pertinent to such probings, in addition to Berger and Luckmann's *The Social Construction of Reality,* are Alfred Schutz and Thomas Luckmann, *The Structures of the Life-World* (Evanston, Illinois: Northwestern University Press, 1973); and Gerald Radnitzsky, *Contemporary Schools of Metascience* (Chicago: Henry Regnery, 1973).

65 A. J. Mandt, "The Inevitability of Pluralism," pp. 84, 98, 100.

66 Mandt, "The Inevitability of Pluralism..." pp. 79, 81.

67 See the discussions of "institutionalization" and "legitimation" in Berger and Luckmann, *The Social Construction of Reality,* pp. 45–118.

68 Mandt, "The Inevitability of Pluralism" pp. 90–91.

69 Mandt, "The Inevitability of Pluralism" p. 91.

70 Mandt, "The Inevitability of Pluralism" p. 92.

71 Mandt, "The Inevitability of Pluralism" p. 97.

72 Mandt, "The Inevitability of Pluralism" p. 97.

INDEX